"I met Courtney Ross in the spring of 1993 when the Ross School was two conjoined town houses with eight little girls in 5th grade, and one teacher. This was the very first time that I considered the educational implications of globalization, and how the then new digital technologies could be a vehicle for catapulting over all barriers that divide humankind—with special attention to the arts, humanities, and sciences. The Ross School has grown into a shining star in the broad constellation of education in the State of New York."

—Thomas Hogan, New York State Board of Education
Supervisor for Non-Public Schools

"This book is a fascinating read. It analyzes best practices developed and tested in the Ross schools and it brings together cutting-edge interdisciplinary research with the most innovative approaches in education, providing policymakers and practitioners around the world with a blueprint for making schools more relevant to our global era. It is an exemplary case study of creative developments in designing school curricula. . . . It makes a significant contribution to school reform efforts in the twenty-first century."

—Rita Süssmuth, Former President of the German Parliament

"Courtney Ross has devoted her life to holistic education for young people. Educating the Whole Child for the Whole World tells the marvelous story of how one day they will be our future leaders and help create a peaceful, just, sustainable and healthy society."

—Deepak Chopra

"This important new book tells the powerful story of Courtney Sale Ross' indefatigable research in order to create a model for education in this global era."

—Monsignor Marcelo Sánchez Sorondo, Chancellor,
Pontifical Academy of Science

"Courtney Ross deserves admiration for her creativity and determination in building a new model for 21st century learning."

—Georges Charpak, Nobel Laureate in Physics

"Courtney Ross and the City of Stockholm have been collaborating for a decade to develop a school to teach 'the whole child for the whole world.' I am always surprised by Mrs. Ross' deep knowledge, commitment, and generosity in constructing schools aligned to our global world. Her achievements in education are definitely worthy of the honor of this marvelous new book!"

—Thomas Persson, Director of Education,
The City of Stockholm, Sweden

Educating the Whole Child for the Whole World

The Ross School Model and Education for the Global Era

EDITED BY

Marcelo M. Suárez-Orozco and
Carolyn Sattin-Bajaj

NEW YORK UNIVERSITY PRESS
New York and London

NEW YORK UNIVERSITY PRESS
New York and London
www.nyupress.org

© 2010 by New York University

Library of Congress Cataloging-in-Publication Data

Educating the whole child for the whole world :
the Ross School Model and education for the Global Era /
edited by Marcelo M. Suárez-Orozco and Carolyn Sattin-Bajaj.
p. cm.
Includes bibliographical references and index.
ISBN 978-0-8147-4140-5 (cl : alk. paper) — ISBN 978-0-8147-4141-2 (e-book)
1. Holistic education—New York (State)—East Hampton.
2. Ross School (East Hampton, N.Y.) 3. Education and globalization.
I. Sussrez-Orozco, Marcelo M. II. Sattin-Bajaj, Carolyn.
LC996.N7E38   2010
370.11—dc22   2010016521

New York University Press books are printed on acid-free paper,
and their binding materials are chosen for strength and durability.
We strive to use environmentally responsible suppliers and materials
to the greatest extent possible in publishing our books.

Manufactured in the United States of America
10 9 8 7 6 5 4 3 2 1

Contents

Foreword: Reflections of a Ross School Graduate

——— NICK APPELBAUM ———————————————————————

At the landing of the great Daru Staircase in the Louvre, the Winged Victory of Samothrace statue is on grand display. Outside the Ross School in East Hampton, New York, feet away from my former high school classrooms, stands a copy of the original. On a ninth-grade class trip to Paris, our teacher commented that we would likely be more intimately familiar with the statue than the majority of the Louvre's visitors. We had studied Nike not only from books but from the beautiful replica, seeing it each day on our way to classes, and our teachers, representing a mix of academic subjects, had layered our understanding further. Connections were made constantly and consistently across time, culture, geography, and discipline. We soon understood that we were engaged in an educational process that was designed to elicit critical thinking, cure misperceptions and dimness, and lure us into acts of deep personal and scholarly engagement.

The Ross School was established with a commitment to an intellectually sparkling curriculum and matched with a beautifully thought-out and detailed set of campus facilities. Embellished with life-size reproductions of the world's great art, inside and out, it left no view unenriched. The founding leadership wanted to ensure that its graduates would not be left beset and bewildered by fast-paced global change. The school seemed to have a single-minded focus on transcending that vague certitude about preparing students for the twenty-first century—and actually created a tangible educational model dedicated to achieving it. Our teachers eschewed the treatment of knowledge as "motionless, static, compartmentalized, and predictable," as Paulo Freire, in his *Pedagogy of the Oppressed,* once characterized an accepted practice in education. The school and its work, as educator of students and teachers, had a clear sense of how to make learning come alive through interdisciplinary study that was responsive to the latest thinking, brightening each subject to fix our attention. Deliberations on Nike, for example, both at Ross and in the Louvre, aspired to provide the broadest historical and cultural reflections on the statue's role in building the reputation initially of Rhodes and later of nineteenth-century French power. We took pride in being part of this small community of fourteen- and fifteen-year-olds considering such matters.

Dedicated and passionate, our teachers developed in us a healthy skepticism toward received opinion, allowing us an opportunity to learn how to construct well-reasoned arguments backed by evidence and to develop the skills and temperament to debate and defend them. Each of us soon felt comfortable creating intellectual frameworks through which to consider all manner of intellectual topics.

Our natural curiosity flourished through multiple assignments that encouraged group and, ultimately, individualized study, such as our senior projects. By providing each student the resources to actualize these personally imagined projects, the Ross School engendered in us the belief that our own ideas were worth considering and that we each had the capacity for generating intellectually serious, even significant, creative products. Through a parallel and similarly innovative feature called the process portfolios, we catalogued our progression through assignments and analyzed our own work.

In an age where technology allows information to be accessed at breakneck speed, the real talent, the Ross School curriculum suggests, is in developing the strategies necessary to utilize information in inventive ways. We learned not only how to think but how to analyze our thinking. Our visual connection with schools in China and Sweden through groundbreaking technology in real time prepared us well for today's interconnectedness.

Founded at a time of remarkable social, cultural, and technological transformations, the Ross School offered my classmates and me an education consistently aimed toward the future but also customized to our individual learning needs. The Ross School's adept recalibration of educational priorities has, quite propitiously, transcended its founding campus and spread its approach and philosophy to receptive global locations. Its deliverables to the educational community include a model school, a charter school, an innovative K through 12 curriculum, new ideas about how to create supportive and stimulating learning environments, and a constantly evolving set of teaching practices. These contributions and the joy and ease its graduates have experienced in accepting new learning challenges are the lasting legacies of Courtney Ross's work. These are legacies in which the Ross community can justifiably derive great pride.

Acknowledgments

Marcelo and Carola Suárez-Orozco spent the 2003–4 academic year as scholars in residence at the Ross School in East Hampton. Our year at Ross taught us many things—above all, just how engrossing and joyous precollegiate education can be. But we also learned that making it so is hardly preordained, even when it all appears perfectly effortless to the outside world. It is a labor of quotidian love and care, of sustained engagement, and of a radical, visionary leadership. We are grateful to Courtney Sale Ross and the Ross School faculty, staff, and students for making our Ross sojourn a marvelous and productive experience. Since then and during each and every one of our countless subsequent visits to Ross, including the Ross-Tensta School outside Stockholm, we were always greeted with an openness, warmth, and sense of transparency that is uncommon in schools here and abroad.

Marcelo and Carola Suárez-Orozco happily acknowledge the support of two fellowships at the Institute for Advanced Study, Princeton, New Jersey. At the institute's idyllic campus we found the much-needed time and peace of mind to complete our work on this volume. Marcelo Suárez-Orozco specifically acknowledges the generous support of the Richard Fischer Membership Fund at the Institute for Advanced Study, Princeton, New Jersey. Carolyn Sattin-Bajaj acknowledges Sally Booth and the entire Ross Institute Academy staff for facilitating her visits to the East Hampton campuses to learn about and participate in the school community there. Marcelo Suárez-Orozco and Carolyn Sattin-Bajaj are grateful to Jennifer Hammer, our editor at the New York University Press, for the care, enthusiasm, and judiciousness with which she shepherded this manuscript from its inception to its completion.

Introduction:
Architectures of Care

*Educating the Whole Child
for the Whole World*

MARCELO M. SUÁREZ-OROZCO,
CAROLYN SATTIN-BAJAJ, AND
CAROLA SUÁREZ-OROZCO

We live in an era of rapid change, increasing interdependence, and unprecedented complexity. The global integration and disintegration of markets, shared environmental threats, unstable states, the massive migrations of people, and the ubiquity of new technologies represent a new metacontext challenging the institutions of nation-states the world over. The basic problems of the twenty-first century—including economic meltdowns, environmental degradation, deep poverty, and new health threats—are planetary in scope and cannot be contained, much less meaningfully addressed, by individual nation-states, no matter how strong or isolated. National sovereignty and local identities, powerful as they are, now abut with an equally obvious fact: we live in an ever more miniaturized world (see Sexton, this volume) that is whole and interdependent—either we take planetary challenges head on or together we will face the consequences.

At the dawn of this century, the rate and depth of global change are creating opportunities but also new and more difficult challenges for education at all levels (see Gregorian, this volume). Yet schooling systems remain generally reactive and slow to adapt to shifting economic, technological, demographic, and cultural terrains (Gardner 2004). These changing terrains require a new agenda for schooling that is simultaneously mindful of local and global processes. This demand for a new agenda emerges at a time when education has become a normative ideal all over the world: youth and their parents everywhere want more of formal education than ever before (see, *inter alia*, Dugger 2009; Cohen, Bloom, and Martin 2006; UNESCO 2005).

It is also a time when schooling's virtuous cycles—especially with regard to health and well-being—have never been more clearly understood (Sperling 2006). Schooling today needs to deliver new competencies and sensibilities. To thrive in the new era students will need the tools for finding and solving problems, articulating arguments and deploying verifiable facts or artifacts to substantiate them, learning to learn within and across disciplines, thinking about thinking, and working and networking ethically with others who are likely to be from different national, linguistic, religious, and racial backgrounds (Boix Mansilla and Gardner 2007; Hugonnier 2007; Levy and Murnane 2007; Oakes and Saunders 2008; M. Suárez-Orozco and Sattin 2007). To flourish, students must also be fluent in multiple languages and must possess sophisticated intercultural skills as they increasingly live, learn, debate, and communicate with colleagues, peers, friends, and neighbors in different countries and across many time zones (M. Suárez-Orozco and Sattin 2007; Sussmuth 2007). These priorities must be made explicit and then embraced by everyone interested in education in the era of global integration and interdependence. The challenge to educators, policy makers, curriculum developers, and scholars today is to develop models that nurture engaged and ethical citizens. Yet few schools are up to the task of delivering a quality education to all youth. Disparities in school readiness compound the problems plaguing education in too many high-income countries, the United States perhaps more than most, where segregated schools, outdated pedagogy, irrelevant curricula, overcrowded classrooms, and disengaged students and teachers abound (see Oakes and Saunders 2008).

There is a growing urgency to create, assess, and expand new models of education that are better synchronized with the realities of the globally linked economies and societies of today. This book examines one such model: the ethos and practices of the Ross School and its incubation, promotion, and launching of new ideas and practices into public education. Over the last two decades Ross has come to articulate a systematic approach to education consciously tailored for a new era of global interdependence. It is based on educational principles derived and inspired by groundbreaking work in various relevant disciplines, including Howard Gardner's (1983/1993) theory of multiple intelligences, the new science of mind, brain, and education (see Damasio and Damasio, this volume; Koizumi, this volume; Hinton and Fischer, this volume; Battro, this volume); and the collaborative work of the chaos theorist and mathematician Ralph Abraham (this volume) and the historian William Thompson (this volume) on complex dynamical systems. The task of weaving together these disparate scholarly, scientific, and humanistic traditions into a coherent curriculum is itself an exemplary case study of interdisciplinary collaboration. Developing this model involved multiple stakeholders, including international scholars conducting research at major universities all over the world who, at times, worked alongside Ross School teachers and administrators under the generous and expansive direction of the founder, Courtney Ross (see McCall, this volume).

The evolving theory and practice of Ross align with Courtney Ross's ideas of wellness ("educating the whole child") and of the significance of using space, art, cultural facts, and artifacts as a context for teaching and learning. The approaches to teaching and learning practiced and embodied in the Ross model are a result of the organic integration of work in multiple sites—from university research labs, to the Ross Schools at the east end of Long Island (the lower school in Bridgehampton and the middle school and high school in East Hampton), to the Ross Global Academy Charter School in Lower Manhattan and the Ross Tensta Gymnasium in a Swedish working-class immigrant and refugee enclave in Stockholm (see Booth, this volume). The Ross model is a work in progress dedicated to using basic research to inform private and public education across the globe. It represents a singular experiment in twenty-first-century education and epitomizes the concept of a "research school" (see Hinton and Fischer, this volume), akin to the notion of the "teaching hospital" that revolutionized medical education a century ago.

This book offers an introduction to various facets of the Ross ambition to "educate the whole child for the whole world." It will serve, we hope, as an antidote to the current malaise in education, where much of the research and public debate focuses on what is dystopic, irrelevant, and anachronistic in contemporary schools. It also aims to be a counterpoint to the aspiration that ties too much of education to skepticism (often bordering on nihilism) and the cult of the detached (bordering on anomic), disinterested scholar student. Rather, it highlights a model that privileges vibrant engagement, curious wonderment, and reciprocity in the construction of knowledge.[1]

In this volume, we have gathered examples of the scholarly, artistic, and humanistic work that Courtney Ross has nurtured in the context of developing the Ross Schools. International scholars from a variety of disciplines, as well as veteran teachers, administrators, and students, come together to examine how their work and ideals intersect with the values, worldview, and sensibilities embodied in the ever-evolving practices of the Ross Schools. While each author presents from the vantage point of his or her own disciplinary or artistic field, the overarching idea animating this book is to explore how the Ross model of education aligns with broader trends in the arts, humanities, and sciences at the beginning of the twenty-first century.

At a time when globalization is challenging the very notion of what it means to be an educated, engaged, and ethical citizen, schools all over the world are searching for new ways to think about and practice teaching and learning. The task is tall: How are we to educate children to engage and thrive in the global economies, technologies, and demographies of the future? The Ross model serves as an example of what it will take for education to meet a future where higher-order cognitive and metacognitive skills, interpersonal competencies, and cultural sensibilities will define the citizenry of the advanced, just, and humane societies of the current century.

Architectures of Care

It is a well-known problem that too many schools today function as soulless factories of despair where teachers, administrators, and students mechanically enact their assigned scripts and prescribed roles (see C. Suárez-Orozco, Suárez-Orozco, and Todorova 2008). Boredom is the elephant in the (class) room. Engaging, vibrant, and academically rigorous schools seem to be the exception, not the rule. What can we learn about schools like this?

These schools are typically organized around a master narrative and animated by social practices and cultural models that align to the values, ethics, and worldviews encompassed in that narrative. Shared stories and cherished rituals embody a sense of mission: who we are, why we are here, and where we are going serve as the emotional and ideological bedrock of the school. The culture of a school can be defined as the system of shared meanings, distributed knowledge, rituals, facts, and artifacts that organize life and give a sense of origin, common purpose, and direction. Kroeber and Kluckhohn's (1952) synthetic work on the idea of culture is still useful in suggesting how to think about the ways in which a school's culture can construct meanings, pattern interpersonal relationships, and shape institutional life: "Culture consists of patterns, explicit and implicit, of and for behavior, acquired and transmitted by symbols constituting the distinctive achievement of human groups, including their embodiment in artifacts; the essential core of culture consists of traditional (i.e., historically derived and selected) ideas and especially their attached values; culture systems may, on the one hand, be considered as products of action, and on the other as conditioning elements of future action" (1952, 101).

School cultures are organized around foundational narratives that are developed out of common experiences in the here and now but that also account for origins and, above all, a sense of mission in facing the future. In other words, school narratives are built on collective histories, stories, and the microrituals of belonging that communicate to every member of the school community, "This is who we are, these are our core ideas, these are the values we share, and these are the facts and artifacts that embody our ideals." Cultures are bounded but permeable systems; the boundary's selective permeability is critical for innovation, incorporation, and transformation.

School cultures, like all cultures, are never monolithic, univocal, or static (Rosaldo 1989). Master narratives are often contested, challenged, and rewritten. Rituals of belonging and rituals of rebellion coexist and constitute each other (Gluckman 1963). Cultures contain diversity and contradiction—cultural narratives suggest a plasticity where continuity and change contain and necessitate each other. Cultures are organic, systemic, and always adapting either to autochthonous (internal) or allochthonous (external) forces. A school's selective permeability mechanisms—the ability to regulate, incorporate, and metabolize change by synchronizing outside forces and internal needs and values—are critical for managing continuity and transformation. A cultural system that is able to adapt to new realities and fuse the new according to an internal symbolic logic will manage to navigate change in more intelligent and productive ways.

Entering any institution of society, whether a courthouse, a hospital, or a school, requires crossing certain definite, if not entirely obvious, physical and symbolic boundaries. One enters the Ross School flagship campus in East Hampton by crossing multiple borders. The threshold is physical, symbolic, and ideational. At first sight, the sheer beauty of the physical plant overwhelms the senses. A new visitor does a cognitive double take: Is this a school? Am I in the wrong place? The elegant buildings, immaculate landscaping, and ingeniously functional classrooms belie what we know, or what we think we know, about how school buildings are supposed to look, especially those of us who have spent decades working in and visiting schools serving disadvantaged students across the globe. The aesthetic displays of world art and artifacts strategically arranged suggest at once an ethic of care and a global sensibility not commonly associated with schools even in high-income countries. The metaphor of school as warehouse for students is trumped by the Ross vision-turned-reality: a school as living, breathing, organic sanctuary for learning. The ubiquitous state-of-the-art technology may not surprise an informed visitor: the legendary Steven Ross was the school's co-founder, a charismatic genius behind the creation of the world's largest media company. What is striking, however, is the way in which computers, SMART Boards, and other advanced technologies blend seamlessly with replicas of famous statues from ancient Greece, Rome, Egypt, and India. In this way, the school physically embodies the ideas about the compatibility and interconnectedness of time, space, technologies, and cultures on which the model is based. Students, staff, and visitors alike soon cannot imagine the school designed in any other fashion.

The microrituals of belonging begin at the threshold of the school: upon entering the main hall, the school's Center for Well-Being, visitors, students, teachers, and administrators are all asked to remove their shoes and are provided simple silk slippers to wear. The slippers at once highlight the beauty and uniqueness of the place and, paradoxically, bring us closer, in a tactile way, to the physicality of the space. If a visit occurs during lunchtime, guests are invited to join students, faculty, and staff in the school café, where students across grade levels join teachers, visiting scholars, and sometimes parents and other relatives to enjoy organic meals inspired by dietary traditions of the different peoples about whom students are learning. One week the menu may be based on Incan cuisine, the next on Roman.

A second architecture soon reveals itself: it is not physical but rather interpersonal. It is an ethos and a shared sensibility exposing a different tempo in the patterning of relationships within the school. The foundations of this architecture of care are built on multiple microinteractions in which students and teachers co-construct relational bonds of mutuality, reciprocity, and respect. A young girl spontaneously acknowledges a visitor with a warm smile and a sure voice: "Good morning, may I help you?" A teacher shares breakfast with a handful of students in deep discussion about the Obama administration's new overtures to Cuba or about the latest hip-hop rage. A world-renowned scholar, a "mentor," in the language of the natives, serenely responds to pointed questions from a small group of students about the evolution of the human brain. We witnessed countless examples of such exchanges during our multiple visits to the school. What matters about these microexchanges is not their surface meanings—thoughtful, well-mannered youth interacting with well-prepared and conscientious teachers—but, rather the deep structures that they suggest. In the making of this organic culture of care, a commitment to community and learning synergistically emerges from repeated intimate, personal, and engaging exchanges between students, teachers, and mentors. These microexchanges and the shared sense of purpose and common interests they continuously reinforce reveal the DNA of a Ross cultural identity. Ross is the one of the few schools we have visited where the students are as invested in their peers' and teachers' success as their own.

The Ross mission suffuses the school's multiple architectures. It is a complex task to instill in students a broad, yet nuanced way of thinking about the past and present, an appreciation for how the world functions and malfunctions, and a sense of responsibility and ownership of community, in both the local and the global sense. To achieve its mission, Ross strives in numerous ways to equip students with the skills and sensibilities they need to become engaged citizens of the fast-changing world, or, in more theoretical terms, to develop a certain "habitus." Pierre Bourdieu's (1977a, 1977b) idea of habitus offers a useful tool to understand theoretically how and why, through their experiences at Ross, students come to develop particular habits of mind, interpersonal sensibilities, and an appreciation and openness to other cultures and worldviews. Conceptualizing habitus as a "system of dispositions, which acts as a mediation between structures and practice" (Bourdieu 1977a, 487), this notion helps us analyze how individuals or groups make sense of the world and why they engage with social structures, institutions, and other individuals in the ways they do. At Ross, the motto "Educating the Whole Child for the Whole World" has guided the creation of an elaborate web of structures, rituals, traditions, standards, resources, and opportunities that serve to socialize students and imperceptibly nurture their habitus, thereby eventually leading them to embrace what it means to be a child, and then a citizen, of the world.

The contours of Ross's third architecture become visible only after one spends time observing classrooms, talking with teachers, participating in student presentations, and examining student work. Senior projects and M-term (March term) projects are two defining Ross rituals. They foster in-depth, interdisciplinary, autonomous work, and they often include a strong service component. The projects are one of a series of the building blocks in place designed to cultivate cognitive flexibility, creativity, and metacognitive awareness. The "spiral curriculum" is the third architecture and the backbone of academics at Ross. It is omnipresent at the schools, represented in the elegant school symbol seen in brochures and in multiple artifacts displayed throughout the various campuses (see McCall, this volume; Booth, this volume). Functioning as a kind of conceptual DNA, the spiral curriculum contains the units of meaning designed to flower over time as students move across the grades. It is based on the notion that the phylogenic unfolding of (cultural and historical) change, such as the historical development of geometry and algebra, can offer strategic points of entry to stimulate youth as their own maturational development unfolds (see Abraham, this volume; Thompson, this volume). Thus the spiral curriculum is in fact a kind of curricular application of the old and ever controversial idea that ontogeny recapitulates phylogeny—that the history of the species is contained in the various developmental sequences of each individual (see Koizumi, this volume). According to this curricular philosophy, teaching geometry and algebra in the order they first emerged historically is better suited to a child's ability to master material at different developmental moments in his or her own life cycle (see Abraham, this volume; Thomson, this volume; Booth, this volume). Students at Ross relish this approach to learning and speak effusively about how, unlike previous schooling experiences that were often boring and repetitive, the progression of concepts at Ross makes intuitive sense to them. As a Somali youngster dressed in a hijab told us during a visit to the Ross Tensta School in Stockholm, the new spiral curricular unit on riverine Mesopotamian cultures she was studying "makes learning more interesting. Before I did not see the whole picture. It was boring to learn all these separate things. Now it [the unit] makes sense to me." An important lesson can surely be seen here at the metacognitive level—a youth spontaneously reflecting about her own learning.

The Culture of Engagement

The three architectures of Ross house a culture of engagement. Engagement is the high octane for teaching and learning. It is the antidote to the endemic problem of boredom and anomie plaguing many schools. An engaged child is fully present: working at the edges of his or her competence with the careful assistance and scaffolding provided by a caring mentor. In recent years, a considerable body of scholarship suggests the significant role of engagement in learning and academic success. Engagement—often defined as the extent to which students are connected to what they are learning, how they are learning it, and the people with whom they are learning it—appears to play a central role in how well they do in school (Fredricks, Blumenfeld, and Paris 2004; Greenwood, Horton, and Utley 2002; Goslin 2003; Marks 2000; National Research Council 2004; Steinberg, Brown, and Dornbusch 1996).

Engagement occurs along a continuum and through a dynamic interplay of a variety of dimensions—including what we have termed the behavioral, cognitive, and relational (C. Suárez-Orozco, Suárez-Orozco, and Todoi, 2008)—all of which contribute significantly to academic performance (Fredricks, Blumenfeld, and Paris 2004; Goslin 2003; Greenwood, Horton, and Utley 2002). Highly engaged students are actively involved in their education, completing the tasks required to perform well in school. Marginally engaged students may be doing "good enough" academic work, but they are not reaching their full academic potential. Further along this continuum there may be a substantial gap between students' intellectual potential and their academic achievement. In cases of more extreme disengagement, lack of interest in academics, erratic class attendance, and inadequate assignment completion can lead to multiple course failures that often foreshadow dropping out of school (Rumberger 2004). Academic disengagement may not be immediate but may occur over time in response to the accruing difficulties associated with various community, school, and family circumstances and the consequent adjustments and compromises students must make in response to them. Disengagement is often also a symptom of repeated exposure to an alienating and irrelevant curriculum, pedagogy, and school culture, and schools are deeply implicated in this dangerous trend.

In observing and interviewing Ross students and teachers, we identified three dimensions of academic engagement— behavioral, cognitive, and relational. These synergetic and interdependent variables suggest an ideal of what the purpose of education might be.

Behavioral engagement reflects students' participation and effort in academic tasks. This is the dimension of engagement most easily observable as one strolls through a school: Are the students participating in class discussion? Do they spontaneously respond to the teacher without being called on? Does a critical mass of students pose queries of its own? Do students help one another complete class assignments? Are they turning in homework? Do they appear attentive and interested? (Bryk and Schneider 2003; Stanton-Salazar 2004; C. Suárez-Orozco, Suárez-Orozco, and Todorova 2008). Some students may in fact be quite engaged, though they may not appear to be so to an observer: "I am a person who is really quiet in class. I may be doodling while I am listening but I am still really into what is going on," a senior confided to us.[2] Thus, when it comes to engagement, there may be more going on than meets the eye. Though behavioral engagement is critical—without doing the work students will not get the grade (Bang et al. 2009)—students' investment in class often depends largely upon whether a school's curriculum, course content, and teaching are *cognitively engaging* as well as on the students' *relational engagement* with their teachers.

Cognitive engagement is the degree to which students are engrossed and intellectually involved in what they are learning. It is the antithesis of the adolescent lament of being bored in school. Ross students talked about a myriad of ways in which they were engaged with ideas and learning throughout their educational experience. It begins with a point of view that, as one student noted, he does not typically encounter in friends who have not gone to Ross: "It gave me a global perspective I would never have if I had gone to a public school or probably to most any other private school." A graduating student remarked that he appreciated "the philosophy of the school—that it is important to understand the whole as well as the parts." Another student underlined the significance of the multiple perspectives he had been offered and the resulting healthy "skepticism toward received opinion" (see Appelbaum, this volume). This student explained, "I am so glad I went to Ross. I think I would have been a follower if I had gone elsewhere. It taught me to be a critical thinker and to look at things from different points of view."

Some students felt that they were most cognitively engaged when "we would get into these pitched philosophical discussions." Debating ideas in the classroom offered students a chance to stretch their intellectual capacities in a safe space. Other students reported being most intellectually engaged when they were allowed to explore materials on their own: "I was most engaged when I was doing some sort of independent research on science-related research projects," a graduating senior told us. Another said, "I am most engaged when I am given some leeway to choose what to work on. And I think that is definitely one of the strengths of Ross. Teachers know how to guide you through a range of choices."

The senior project is the capstone of the Ross education. Through this project, students delve deeply into a passion under the guidance of a mentor. "My senior project was definitely the height of my Ross experience. I wrote a paper on the evolution of the jazz saxophone solo, and I also performed and recorded three jazz pieces that showed the advancement of the jazz idiom from the 1920s through the 1950s. . . . My mentor was a master musician who played with some of the greats like Charlie Parker and Miles Davis. He really knows his stuff and you could just feel he wanted to pass it on."

Senior projects were dazzling in their sophistication and range—from the use of gene bank data to analyze genes associated with Parkinson's disease, to an examination of U.S. immigration dilemmas, to the design of a modern "green" beach house for four. Students, by virtue of their interdisciplinary education, often used multiple approaches and had an eye toward issues of global relevance. One student used photography to draw attention to the world water crisis. Another examined fair trade in chocolate by first research-ing the topic, then writing a long essay, developing a "signature" truffle rec-ipe, assembling a series of recipes, self-publishing a book, and baking all the delicacies for the senior event. Students almost always described the senior project as their most grueling educational experience but also, universally, their most rewarding. A graduating senior summed up the words of many: "I procrastinated and took forever and thought I never would get it done, but I learned so much, and in the end I had something I really was proud of."

At Ross, we found something we would wish for all students—relation-ships with teachers that acted as a powerful catalyst for learning. Relational engagement is the extent to which students feel connected to their teachers, peers, and others at school. For most students, research has established that successful learning is linked to the quality of relationships they forge in their school settings (Cauce, Felmer, and Primavera 1982; Dubow 1991; Goslin 2003; Levitt, Guacci-Franco, and Levitt 1994; Wentzel 1999). Social relations provide a variety of functions—a sense of belonging, emotional support, tan-gible assistance and information, guidance, role modeling, and positive feed-back (Cobb 1976; Sarason, Sarason, and Pierce 1990; Wills 1985). Research suggests that relationships in school play a particularly crucial role in pro-moting socially competent behavior in the classroom and fostering academic engagement and achievement (Fredricks, Blumenfeld, and Paris 2004). Ross students were exceptionally articulate in describing just what about their relationships with their teachers served to help them stay cognitively and, in turn, behaviorally engaged in their learning.

A first characteristic of many of the Ross teachers is their level of exper-tise and mastery of their subject matter. Many students talked about how important it was to them to respect their teacher's knowledge, expertise, and intelligence. "My English teacher is a very smart guy that helped me with my writing more than anyone. I just liked being really challenged," said one senior. Another remarked, "My science teacher is smart and knowledgeable. She knows a lot, and when you ask a question about something she doesn't know she finds out and reports back to you about it the next day."

A second ingredient that many students reported to us, which emerges in this last quote, was a willingness to return effort with effort—in essence students were prepared to work hard because they saw how much energy their teachers were expending. As one student commented, "Our cultural history teacher pushed us hard—we wrote our longest essays for him—but he made you want to do it. You wanted to do it because you wanted to match his energy." Another said, "My science teacher is determined that all of her students learn. Because she cares so much I never want to disappoint her. She cares so much and works so hard that I just do not want to let her down." This passion and commitment are critical ingredients that do not go unnoticed or unappreciated by students. A graduating senior who was unusually independent reflected on a teacher who had particularly reached him: "I am not one to seek out extra help, but whenever I went to my ninth-grade English teacher he would offer me extra information beyond what we learned in class. He would just go the extra mile and you could see he was really into it, and that made me interested beyond what I thought I was." Another noted, "My science teacher is so willing to help—the more interested you are the more she invests. If you just want to get by she will support you at that level, but if you want to learn deeply about something she will provide you endless amounts of information."

The capacity of teachers to guide thought-provoking yet respectful discussions was something else that students noted and appreciated. An outgoing senior confided: "A great teacher really knows how to get a discussion going. My twelfth-grade English teacher never talked down to us. He would listen really closely. When we debated he would acknowledge if he was wrong, which meant I could do the same. It was like being in a conversation with a smart, knowledgeable friend." Critical in this endeavor is the respectful nature of the exchange. Another student mentioned, "My best teachers really knew how to be open to opinions different than their own."

Ross students also widely referenced teachers' enthusiasm. Teachers who loved their subject, loved their students, and really cared whether the students learned were universally noted to be among the most engaging (among a particularly engaging cohort of teachers). A senior told us, "My twelfth-grade English teacher puts everything into his students. You can tell he loves his students." A graduate sheepishly noted: "My ninth-grade English teacher was incredibly enthusiastic. It may sound kind of silly, but when we would have a breakthrough he would jump on a table and yell 'Eureka!'"

Being flexible was yet another important ingredient revealed by our student interviews. As one student said, "A great teacher has certain flexibility—as long as you accomplish the project they are open to your sculpting it your own way." But a universe of too many possibilities can lead to immobility; another student said, "I am horrible at making decisions. I remember one time I had to do a research project for science class and then make a presentation and I was blocked—there were just too many possible things to choose from. So my science teacher just told me that I should do something on wastewater cleaning. And I remember thinking, 'You must be kidding?'

But she gave me this kit, and I played around with it, and I really got into it." Thus a great teacher is closely attuned to student needs and interests. Some students do best when they are provided with flexibility and leeway from the beginning to end of a project; others need guidance early on and then they are off; and still others need scaffolding all the way through from beginning to end. The art, science, and magic of teaching involve deducing what students need and giving them the support appropriate at each juncture in their educational trajectory.

Ultimately, the quality of the relationship is vital to cultivating relational engagement. Caring relationships, based on mutuality and respect, enhance feelings of belonging and reciprocity. This sense of belonging, in turn, has implications for increasing social involvement, motivation, school attendance, academic engagement, and, ultimately, achievement (Hamre and Pianta 2001; Pianta 1999). One student noted that the class size was important: "The small classes let you really know your teachers as well as all of the kids, so you feel like a part of a community." Another spoke about how the most responsive teachers had the wisdom of knowing how to quietly listen: "My best teachers really knew how to connect with their students. They know how to listen without necessarily giving an opinion." On the other hand, being willing to answer questions when they were posed was equally important. A student told us, "You can just tell that my English teacher never thinks your questions are stupid. He deeply contemplates your questions and then gives you these complete, logical answers that leave you with, I know it sounds kind of weird, but with this feeling of being at peace." And a graduating senior told us, "I could talk to my advisor [who also taught him anthropology and psychology] about anything." When we followed up by asking, "About what you were learning or about life?" he responded, laughing, with "Both!"

A particularly thoughtful student reflected on the alchemy of what it takes to be a truly engaging teacher. "My most engaging teachers really know their field. They impress me with how smart they are and how well they know their material. And if they do not know something, they take the time to find out and tell us. Our most effective teachers also have just the right balance of being authoritative but not being too opinionated and never talking down to us." Thus, to foster relational engagement, teachers have a tough balancing act. They must be not only deeply knowledgeable about their own subject matter but also willing and able to work across disciplines. Students expect them to be informed but never condescending. They appreciate when they are listened to without being given advice but expect that it be provided when asked for. As adolescents in the U.S. context, they want to be provided with ample choices in their assignments, but they want their teachers to be able to step in and provide scaffolding when needed. Knowledge, enthusiasm, humor, a capacity to stimulate good discussion, and clarity in communication are all crucial ingredients in the recipe for engaging teaching. In all cases, mutual respect is fundamental to achieving relational engagement. What is given is clearly returned: students spoke with reverence and love for the teachers that had touched their lives and expanded their minds. At Ross, students reported deep appreciation for having found extraordinary teachers to launch them on their journey of learning.

The relationships that develop organically in the classrooms, hallways, and cafeteria at Ross are natural extensions of the carefully designed educational model on which the schools are built. Delving deeper into the process by which Ross was constructed, understanding its foundational concepts, and situating it within a broader framework of the state of education in the era of global interdependence help to highlight what is at the heart of the Ross model and its collaborative creation. In what follows, we provide a synthetic overview of the chapters that make up this book. We invited scholars in related fields ranging from behavioral neuroscience to cultural and social psychology, as well as other thinkers and practitioners, to reflect upon how their research and ideas relevant to education have aligned with the work developed at Ross over the last few decades. The authors engage with a model of schooling that takes as its point of departure the idea that basic research ought to inform the practice of educating children and youth to better participate in the globally linked economies and societies of today.

This book begins with the brief reflections of Nick Appelbaum, a Ross School alumnus, who brings the theory of Ross to life by sharing a personal narrative of what it means to be a student there and how it has shaped his subsequent educational and life experiences. Through Appelbaum's narrative, we begin to understand how the architectures of care and engagement work in concert to engender students' sustained curiosity and excitement about learning. Creativity and independent learning are not superficial ideas that Ross teachers see as supplementary to their daily practice in the classroom. Rather, they understand them to be a central part of students' growth and development. Relationships were essential to Appelbaum's successful educational experiences: at an early age, teachers encouraged Appelbaum to explore his own interests, talents, and skills by introducing him and his peers to a diverse range of concepts, media, and materials. He felt part of a unique community of learners, and he explains, "We understood that we were engaged in an educational process that was designed to elicit critical thinking, cure misperceptions and dimness, and lure us into acts of deep personal and scholarly engagement." By the time Appelbaum reached his final year at Ross and was faced with the daunting task of completing his senior project, he was prepared for the challenge. He graduated emboldened by the experience and fortified by the belief that "our own ideas were worth considering and that we each had the capacity for generating intellectually curious, even significant creative products."

Vartan Gregorian is one of the leading voices in the field of education today. He provides a broad overview of the changing dynamics of education in his chapter, "Education in an Era of Specialized Knowledge." Gregorian begins by asking the central questions that societies and schools are currently facing: What does it mean to be an "educated" person in the age of information, and how can educational institutions help students get there? He discusses the challenges associated with education in a time of unbridled information and communication, and he calls on schools, particularly institutions of higher education, "to develop and enunciate a clear philosophy of education" and to work with primary and secondary education systems to implement it. Gregorian understands the integration of knowledge and the promotion of lifelong learning as critical to the goals of cultivating engaged citizens in an educated society. He points to Ross as a flourishing example of these core principles and as a template for how to convert philosophy and vision into an educational reality.

John Sexton, president of New York University, has indeed "developed and enunciated a clear philosophy of education." He is well known for being the architect of the "global network university," one of the most intriguing ideas in education today. Sexton argues that education must prepare students "to become engaged and contributing citizens." But, he explains, "In the 21st century, this task takes on new meaning. The great compression of our world—a consequence of the spread of technology and information, the interdependence of economies, the transnational nature of major human challenges, and an increasing embrace of diversity—will only accelerate" (see Sexton n.d.). In his chapter, "The Case for Global Education," Sexton sheds light on the challenges and opportunities of education in the twenty-first century. He shares with readers his vision of an education for global citizenship that nurtures curious students who approach new situations and unfamiliar people by asking the question, "What can I learn from you?" For Sexton, educational institutions will continue to be the engines of societal transformation and progress; he calls on schools, colleges, and research universities to adapt to the demands and possibilities of globalization. He finds strong parallels between New York University's global vision and Ross's, and he names a shared "ardent commitment to foster responsible and responsive citizens" as a factor critical to their students' success. Ultimately, Sexton defines a rigorous global education as one that "encourages—urges—students to test existing knowledge and to uncover new knowledge through a constant, often vigorous encounter with a range of perspectives." He sees this definition embodied by the mission and practices at Ross.

In his chapter about the consequences of confounding policy and science, Howard Gardner argues that policy derived directly from theory frequently fails to address the concrete issues that dominate the public sphere. He focuses specifically on the rapid expansion of assessment and evaluation in education as an example of this unsuitable marriage of fields. Gardner illustrates this point by referring to personal experiences of repeatedly being called on to develop measures of "multiple intelligences" based on his groundbreaking theory. Gardner juxtaposes these issues with a lucid description of how the Ross Schools, driven by a well-articulated set of educational priorities and values, serve as a different and welcome model for the interplay of research and practice.

Science will henceforth shape education in ways previously unimaginable to scientists and educators alike. Renowned neuroscientists Antonio and Hanna Damasio introduce us to the nascent field of mind-brain education and highlight some of the impressive early advances that have been made in the area of brain research related to education. The authors provide a basic overview of how the brain processes information, how it learns, and how the mind relates to the brain and body. Furthermore, they highlight the possibilities for neuroscience to contribute to the world of education. Citing their own collaboration with the Ross Schools as a promising example, the Damasios explicate the power of mind-brain research to help us understand students' learning experiences in new and different ways and to improve current approaches to student engagement and pedagogy.

Christina Hinton and Kurt Fischer's chapter, "Research Schools: Connecting Research and Practice at the Ross School," builds on the Damasios' introduction to the field of mind-brain education. In it, the authors foreground the imperative to create avenues through which biologists, neuroscientists, and other research scientists have opportunities to work directly with educators. Students and practitioners are too often left out of the important conversations about education. Using their experiences conducting research at Ross Schools and serving as mentors, the authors offer a vision of how the concept of a "research school" can be brought to bear in current educational debates. Hinton and Fischer refer to the "culture of openness" at Ross as part of what makes it an ideal place to develop a partnership between scholars and practitioners. In describing the collaborative structures being created between Ross and the Harvard Graduate School of Education, Hinton and Fischer illuminate aspects of the Ross model that are pioneering in the field of education generally.

Hideaki Koizumi engages with the Ross model, and specifically with the spiral curriculum, from the perspective of a scientist and inventor who has revolutionized the way in which neuroscientists can measure activity in the human brain. Koizumi, one of Japan's leading scientists, begins his chapter, "Toward a New Educational Philosophy," with an exploration of the quintessential role that the concepts of the spiral and vortex have played in physics, and he describes their historical relevance across many scientific fields. Next, he addresses the idea of using phylogeny to guide an educational curriculum. Koizumi argues that an "education that follows such a natural flow is a more natural fit for humanity." Finally, he embarks on a thorough discussion of the vastly underexplored territory of neuroscientific research related to education and learning. In this discussion, Koizumi advances an ambitious agenda for improving current conceptions of the artistic mind and the scientific mind and preparing students to be globally and environmentally conscious members of society. Woven throughout this chapter are repeated references to the Ross model, and with these careful tributes Koizumi makes clear how powerfully both the Ross School and its founder have influenced his thinking.

Nurturing student engagement and creativity takes center stage at the Ross Schools. The technological advances of the past few decades have opened up new and exciting realms in which human creativity can now be fostered and expressed. With these innovations, however, come additional challenges. The contribution to this volume of Elizabeth Daley (with Holly Willis) explores some of the new media technology currently being used by educational institutions to support student creativity. The authors describe how institutions—in this case, the University of Southern California (USC) and the Ross Schools—have engaged with the opportunities and struggles that accompany the proliferation of such new media. Specifically, Daley and Willis highlight the ways in which both the USC School of Cinematic Arts and the Ross Schools have integrated technology across all areas of learning and have made multimedia literacy a cornerstone of their educational missions. They also explore the importance of developing educational standards for technology skills and competence. Building on the comprehensive media curricula that Daley helped to develop for students as dean of the School of Cinematic Arts at USC, Daley and Willis lay out a clear vision for these standards.

The creative mind can be nourished in many different ways. In Sherry Turkle's chapter, we learn about the importance of objects—artistic and mundane—in igniting the passions of children who eventually became some of the most important inventors and scientists of our time. Turkle, a world-renowned scholar at MIT, engages with the current debate over the plummeting number of U.S.-born scientists and engineers. She asserts that a renewed focus on "the philosophy and practice of education" is needed to begin to address the roots of the issue. Turkle holds up the Ross Schools and their philosophy that "respects the importance of the tactile, the sensuous, and the aesthetic in all aspects of the curriculum, with no exemption for science and technology" as the consummate example of how schools might approach the teaching and learning of science today. The powerful, interwoven architectures of Ross are recognized again. In this case the physical campus, replete with art, artifacts, and architecturally impressive and intelligent spaces, complements a philosophical approach to learning that privileges students' active participation and ownership over the passive transmission of information.

Turkle also rejects the false dichotomy between science and art and instead offers rich descriptions of how art materials can become "objects-to-think-with." Her years working intimately with MIT students interested in science and her experiences as a mentor at the Ross School serve as a starting point for this chapter. In it, Turkle shows us firsthand the centrality of objects in stimulating in young people an organic and persistent interest in scientific exploration. Only when the ludic, the kinesthetic, and the sensual are brought back to education, Turkle argues, will engagement and passion beat back the boredom and mediocrity now pervasive in schools.

Like Turkle, Ralph Abraham is interested in addressing the widespread disengagement with science and, especially, mathematics currently seen in classrooms across the United States and elsewhere. According to Abraham, one of the foremost mathematicians and scholars of the chaos theory, something does not add up in the way we are teaching math today. He has used insights gleaned over the course of his distinguished career to understand the development of a now pervasive "math anxiety" and to devise an approach to teaching math that seeks to avoid it. In his chapter, "The Trouble with Math," Abraham recounts his collaboration with Courtney Ross in the early years of the first Ross School, and he describes how, working with teams of teachers and the cultural historian William Irwin Thompson, he contributed to the creation of the spiral curriculum (see also Thompson, this volume). Introducing mathematical concepts according to their actual historical sequencing, Abraham argues, eliminates some of the main factors that contribute to math anxiety. This chapter provides a rough blueprint of Abraham's pioneering ideas about how to teach math—ideas that have undoubtedly changed hundreds of Ross School students' perceptions of and experiences with math.

Visiting a Ross school and living the exciting, multisensory experience of what it means to be a student there is the ideal way to learn about Ross. Short of an actual visit, however, Debra McCall's chapter gives readers access to the Ross model in an immediate and personal way by transporting us to its hallways and classrooms and sharing the evolution of the model and philosophy of education. In "Choreographing the Curriculum: The Founder's Influence as Artist, Visionary, and Humanitarian," McCall traces the flagship school's development—from its delicate birth to its role in the global expansion of Ross. She conveys to readers what Ross aims to achieve and how its founder, Courtney Ross, has led the way in realizing an ambitious educational mission. The chapter unfolds in careful, deliberate steps mirroring the modus operandi of the spiral curriculum. McCall's elaborate descriptions of the theory and practice of Ross shed light on the impressive collaborative process through which the unique educational model was developed.

William Irwin Thompson, one of the chief architects of the spiral curriculum, takes us back even further in the history of Ross in his chapter, "Mathematics and Culture." Thompson shares the story of his own early educational experiences, and through this narrative we learn how his biography helped to shape his understanding of and ideas about teaching and learning history. Thompson argues, using numerous historical references, that significant historical events, works of art, literature, and scientific discoveries are in fact profoundly interconnected and that barriers between disciplines and areas of knowledge are in fact artificial. Thompson's philosophy informs both pedagogy and curriculum at Ross, and this chapter serves to illuminate the deep roots of the spiral curriculum, its intricate logic, and, ultimately, its contribution to education today.

The intrinsic relationships among disciplines that Thompson painstakingly describes are brought to life for Ross students on a daily basis both inside and outside the classrooms. The celebrated Argentine neuroscientist Antonio Battro, who served as a mentor at the Ross School in East Hampton, narrates his experiences working with students to develop a neuroscience project informed by literature and art. Battro's point of departure is a metaphor borrowed from the father of modern neuroscience, Santiago

Ramón y Cajal. The project at Ross was, in Battro's words, an exploration of "how a metaphor can serve as a trigger for interdisciplinary work in a school." Students started with Ramón y Cajal's scientific metaphor equating neurons to butterflies. This served as a launching pad for a host of scholarly investigations ranging from a linguistic analysis of the word *butterfly* in different contexts, to a review of scientific and other texts about butterflies, to time in the laboratory viewing neurons under the microscope. In the end, Battro explains, students combined their skills and knowledge about technology and art, neurobiology and literature to create a remarkable digital video that converted the original metaphor into a living, visual form. With this chapter we begin to understand the beauty of interdisciplinary learning in a new light. We see how the spiral curriculum and its corollary projects can fundamentally transform students' engagement in learning and how, in the context of these projects, deeply supportive relationships among students, teachers, and mentors can organically develop and flourish at Ross.

Many of the chapters in this volume discuss the original Ross School in East Hampton, Long Island, and the educational innovations that have emerged from Courtney Ross's early experiment. But the Long Island school represents only one in an expanding network of schools inspired by the Ross model. In her chapter on the collaboration between Ross and Tensta, a school in Stockholm, Sweden, where over 80 percent of the students come from immigrant and refugee homes, Sally Booth (with Michele Claeys) describes a singular initiative in transnational education. Europe's task of educating large numbers of children of non-European descent—now largely Muslim refugees, asylum seekers, and migrants from Africa, the Middle East, and Asia—requires a new vision and practice of education. Sweden is once again taking the lead in Europe on an issue that will be critical to its future, as immigrant- and refugee-origin youth are a fast-growing population in many countries. Adapting the Ross model to fit a Swedish public high school in a deeply segregated neighborhood proved to be an enormous challenge. This chapter traces the multiple-year effort of a team of principals, teachers, and staff from Ross and Tensta working transnationally to adapt the ideas and philosophy of Ross to a new context. The collaboration has included work to consolidate the Ross curriculum and pedagogy, synthesize the ethos and spirit of Ross, and establish a school environment conducive to the model. This international partnership epitomizes Courtney Ross's commitment to transporting the educational model she has nurtured to various educational contexts across the globe.

In the epilogue, Pedro Noguera, a prominent sociologist of urban education, shares his thoughts and wisdom, based on an address he presented to a Ross School graduating class. The themes he develops strongly resonate with the need to rethink education in troubled times. His is a message of hope in the face of anxiety and fear. Noguera reminds us that an education devoid of play, wonder, optimism, and curiosity will cultivate dry skepticism at best and nihilism and despair at worst. Today's youth face an uncertain future: not only a global economic crisis but a world with multiple and no longer deniable threats to the environment, new and highly contagious infectious diseases, multiple war fronts, and intractable ethnic conflicts within countries and across regions. These are difficult times for youth struggling to forge a sense of identity and purpose. Helplessness and anomie can easily corrode the life-affirming agency of youth to engage the world, transform it, and make it their own. Noguera offers a "third option" beyond Dionysian self-indulgence and nihilistic despair. His words are a powerful reminder that human agency is a liberating, life-enhancing force and must be at the core of any socially conscious, responsible educational project in our global era. Noguera's reflections are a fitting coda to a book dedicated to new visions of education in troubled times. Finally, in the Conclusion, we return to the idea of the "architectures of care" and make the case for rethinking education in the era of global interdependence.

NOTES

1. During the 2009–10 academic year, 490 students were enrolled at the Ross School on Long Island: 52 students in the early childhood program; 89 students in the lower school (grades K–4); 128 students in the middle school (grades 5–8); and 221 students in the high school (grades 9–12). Classes were capped at sixteen, with two to three sections per grade in the lower and middle school and four sections per grade in high school. During the 2009–10 school year approximately 50 percent of the student body received some level of financial assistance based on need, tuition remission, or sibling discounts. Approximately 20 percent of students are members of ethnic minority groups, with Latino and African American students constituting the largest share. In addition to a sizable number of immigrant students, primarily from Central and South America and Europe, the Ross School has a boarding program that hosts approximately forty-five students from Korea, China, Germany, Taiwan, Italy, Brazil, Colombia, and Hong Kong. At the Ross Global Academy (RGA), a public charter school in New York City, 317 students were enrolled in the 2009–10 school year. As is the case for all charter schools in New York, students were accepted into RGA by lottery, and students come from all five of New York City's boroughs. The average class size at Ross Global Academy is twenty-four students, and there are two sections per grade. In 2009–10, over 90 percent of the students at RGA were members of ethnic minorities, predominantly African American, Latino, and Asian,

and approximately 37 percent of the students at RGA qualified for free or reduced-price lunch—a traditional measure of poverty. The Ross Global Academy received an "A" on its 2008-9 progress report from the New York City Department of Education, a report based on students' academic progress. At Ross Tensta Gymnasium in Stockholm, 640 students were enrolled in the 2009-10 academic year. Students at Tensta Gymnasium choose one of five different programs—"social sciences," "natural sciences," "introductory," "trade and administration," and "caretaking"—and the average class size in all the programs is twenty students. While racial origins and ethnic data are confidential in Sweden, we can report that the vast majority of the students at Ross Tensta Gymnasium are new immigrants and refugees from nearly every troubled spot in the world (see Booth, this volume).

2. All student quotations are from Ross students or recently graduated seniors. Students were promised confidentiality during the interviews in order to obtain the most genuine, unbiased reflections. Thus no names are provided in the body of the introduction. Following the principle of full disclosure, the authors wish to share with readers that Carola and Marcelo Suárez-Orozco's son, Lucas, graduated from the Ross School in June of 2009. After spending their sabbatical year from Harvard at the Ross School campus (2003-4) working on a book, the Suárez-Orozcos decided to move permanently to New York so that Lucas could continue his studies at Ross. (Prior to moving to the Ross School, Lucas was enrolled in a private school in the outskirts of Boston.) It was during the year spent at the Ross main campus in East Hampton that Carola and Marcelo Suárez-Orozco formed many of the ideas that went into the making of this chapter. In 2004, Nicole Ross, Steven and Courtney's daughter, endowed the Courtney Sale Ross Chair at New York University, which Marcelo currently occupies. Prior to this appointment Marcelo was the Victor S. Thomas Professor of Education and Culture at Harvard and Carola was the executive director of the David Rockefeller Center for Latin American Studies at Harvard. Marcelo was also a member of the board of directors of the Ross Institute. They have no financial or other material interests in the Ross School.

REFERENCES

Bang, H. J., C. Suárez-Orozco, J. Pakes, and E. O'Connor. 2009. The importance of homework in determining newcomer immigrant students' grades in the USA context. *Educational Research* 1:1-25.
Boix Mansilla, V., and H. Gardner. 2007. From teaching globalization to nurturing global consciousness. In *Learning in the global era: International perspectives on globalization and education,* ed. M. M. Suárez-Orozco. Berkeley: University of California Press.
Bourdieu, P. 1977a. Cultural reproduction and social reproduction. In *Power and ideology in education,* ed. J. Karabel and A. H. Halsey. New York: Oxford University Press.
———. 1977b. *Outline of a theory of practice.* London: Cambridge University Press.
Bryk, A., and B. Schneider. 2003. Trust in schools: A core resource for school reform. *Educational Leadership* 60 (6): 40-44.
Cauce, A. M., R. D. Felmer, and J. Primavera. 1982. Social support in high-risk adolescents: Structural components and adaptive impact. *American Journal of Community Psychology* 104:417-28.
Cobb, S. 1976. Social support as a moderator of life stress. *Psychosomatic Medicine* 385:300-314.

Cohen, J., D. E. Bloom, and M. B. Malin, eds. 2006. *Educating all children: A global agenda.* Cambridge, MA: MIT Press and American Academy of Arts and Sciences.

Dubow, E. F. 1991. A two-year longitudinal study of stressful life events, social support, and social problem-solving skills: Contributions to children's behavioral and academic adjustment. *Child Development* 62 (3): 583–99.

Dugger, C. 2009. South African children push for better schools. *New York Times,* September 24. www.nytimes.com/2009/09/25/world/africa/25safrica.html.

Fredricks, J. A., P. C. Blumenfeld, and A. H. Paris. 2004. School engagement: Potential of the concept, state of the evidence. *Review of Educational Research* 74 (1): 54–109.

Gardner, H. 1983/1993. *Frames of mind: The theory of multiple intelligences.* New York: Basic Books.

———. 2004. *Changing minds: The art and science of changing our own and other people's minds.* Boston: Harvard Business School Press.

Gluckman, M. 1963. *Order and rebellion in tribal Africa.* London: Cohen and West.

Goslin, D. A. 2003. *Engaging minds: Motivation and learning in America's schools.* Lanham, MD: Scarecrow Education.

Greenwood, C. R., B. T. Horton, and C. A. Utley. 2002. Academic engagement: Current perspectives in research and practice. *School Psychology Review* 31 (3): 1–31.

Hamre, B. K., and R. C. Pianta. 2001. Early teacher-child relationships and the trajectory of children's school outcomes through eighth grade. *Child Development* 72 (2): 625–38.

Hugonnier, B. 2007. Globalization and education: Can the world meet the challenge? In *Learning in the global era: International perspectives on globalization and education,* ed. M. M. Suárez-Orozco. Berkeley: University of California Press.

Kroeber, A., and C. Kluckhohn. 1952. *Culture.* New York: Meridian Books.

Levitt, M. J., N. Guacci-Franco, and J. L. Levitt. 1994. Social support and achievement in childhood and early adolescence: A multicultural study. *Journal of Applied Developmental Psychology* 15:207–22.

Levy, F., and R. Murnane. 2007. How computerized work and globalization shape human skill demand. In *Learning in the global era: International perspectives on globalization and education,* ed. M. M. Suárez-Orozco. Berkeley: University of California Press.

Marks, H. M. 2000. Student engagement in instructional activity: Patterns in the elementary, middle, and high school years. *America Educational Research Journal* 37 (1): 153–84.

National Research Council. 2004. *Engaging schools: Fostering high school students' motivation to learn.* Washington, DC: National Academies Press.

Oakes, J. L., and M. Saunders. 2008. *Beyond tracking: Multiple pathways to college, career, and civic participation.* Cambridge, MA: Harvard University Press.

Pianta, R. C. 1999. *Enhancing relationships between children and teachers.* Washington, DC: American Psychological Association.

Rosaldo, R. 1989. *Culture and truth: The remaking of social analysis.* Boston: Beacon Press.

Rumberger, R. 2004. Why students drop out of school. In *Dropouts in America: Confronting the graduation rate crisis,* ed. G. Orfield. Cambridge, MA: Harvard Education Press.

Sarason, I. G., B. R. Sarason, and G. R. Pierce. 1990. Social support: The search for theory. *Journal of Social and Clinical Psychology* 9:133–47.

Sexton, J. n.d. Message from the president. New York University Global Network University. Accessed July 15, 2009. www.nyu.edu/global.network/message/.

Sperling, G.. 2006. The way forward for universal education. In *Educating all children: A global agenda*, ed. J. E. Cohen, D. E. Bloom, and M. B. Malin. Cambridge, MA: MIT Press and American Academy of Arts and Sciences.

Stanton-Salazar, R. 2004. Social capital among working-class minority students. In *School connections: U.S. Mexican youth, peers, and school achievement*, ed. M. A. Gibson, P. Gándara, and J. P. Koyma. New York: Teachers College Press.

Steinberg, L., B. B. Brown, and S. M. Dornbusch. 1996. *Beyond the classroom*. New York: Simon and Schuster.

Suárez-Orozco, C., M. M. Suárez-Orozco, and I. Todorova. 2008. *Learning a new land: Immigrant students in American society*. Cambridge, MA: Harvard University Press.

Suárez-Orozco, M. M., and C. Sattin. 2007. Learning in the global era. In *Learning in the global era: International perspectives on globalization and education*, ed. M. M. Suárez-Orozco. Berkeley: University of California Press.

Sussmuth, R. 2007. On the need for teaching intercultural skills: Challenges and impacts of a globalizing world on education. In *Learning in the global era: International perspectives on globalization and education*, ed. M. M. Suárez-Orozco. Berkeley: University of California Press.

UNESCO. 2005. *Education for all: Literacy for life*. Paris: UNESCO.

Wentzel, K. R. 1999. Social influences and school adjustment: Commentary. *Educational Psychologist* 34 (1): 59–69.

Wills, T. A. 1985. Supportive functions of interpersonal relationships. In *Social support and health*, ed. S. Cohen and S. L. Syme. Orlando, FL: Academic Press.

Part I ——

Rethinking Education
in the Global Era

1

Education in an Era of Specialized Knowledge

VARTAN GREGORIAN

This book offers an occasion for both reflecting on and celebrating the immeasurable contributions that Courtney Ross has made to the field of education. The Ross Schools, which embody her efforts to realize an educational vision enriched by an integration of scholarship, culture, science, and the arts, present a model that is vital for today's students both here and abroad.

How does an individual become educated, cultured, and cultivated in an era of specialization? This is a particularly critical question today because we are in the midst of an information revolution that may well surpass the Industrial Revolution in its impact and far-reaching consequences. For example, according to an IBM study (2006),

It is projected that [by the year 2010] the world's information base will be doubling in size every 11 hours. So rapid is the growth in the global stock of digital data that the very vocabulary used to indicate quantities has had to expand to keep pace. A decade or two ago, professional computer users and managers worked in kilobytes and megabytes. Now schoolchildren have access to laptops with tens of gigabytes of storage, and network managers have to think in terms of the terabyte (1,000 gigabytes) and the petabyte (1,000 terabytes). Beyond those lie the exabyte, zettabyte and yottabyte, each a thousand times bigger than the last. (2)

Nowhere is this flood of information more apparent than in the university. Never mind that much of it is irrelevant to us and unusable. No matter, it still just keeps arriving in the form of books, monographs, periodicals, Web pages, instant messages, social networking sites, films, DVDs, blogs, e-mails, satellite and cable television shows and news programs, and the constant chirping of our Blackberries.

While it is true that attention to detail is the hallmark of professional excellence, it is equally true that an overload of undigested facts is a sure recipe for mental gridlock. Not only do undigested facts not constitute structured knowledge, but unfortunately the current explosion of information is also accompanied by its corollary pitfalls, such as obsolescence and counterfeit knowledge.

Another phenomenon we are confronting is the "Wikipedia-zation" of knowledge and education. At least in part this is a result of the fact that we are all both givers and takers when it comes to running the machinery of the information age, particularly the virtual machinery. I am referring, of course, to the Internet. A notorious event involving Wikipedia has come to represent how easily false information can virally infect factual knowledge. What has come to be known as the Seigenthaler incident (Seigenthaler 2005) began in 2005 when a false biography of the noted journalist John Seigenthaler Sr., who was also an assistant to Robert Kennedy when he was attorney general in the 1960s, was posted on Wikipedia. Among the scurrilous "facts" in the biography were that "for a short time, [Seigenthaler] was thought to have been directly involved in the Kennedy assassinations of both John, and his brother, Bobby. Nothing was ever proven."

This horrendous misinformation—represented as truth—existed on Wikipedia for 132 days before Seigenthaler's son, also a journalist, happened upon it and called his father. Seigenthaler Sr. then had Wikipedia remove the hoax biography, but not before the same false facts had migrated to other sites such as Reference.com, Answers.com, and who knows where else. Probably, somewhere in the estimated twenty-two billion online pages, it still exists. Wikipedia has taken steps to address this problem, but there are an estimated 518 million Web sites on the Internet, with more being created all the time, and there is no central authority, no group, individual, or organization, to oversee the accuracy of the information they purvey.[1]

Clearly, therefore, one of the greatest challenges facing our society and contemporary civilization is how to distinguish between information—which may be true, false, or some tangled combination of both—and real knowledge and further, how to transform knowledge into the indispensable nourishment of the human mind: genuine wisdom. As T. S. Eliot said, "Where is the wisdom we have lost in knowledge? Where is the knowledge we have lost in information?" (1963, 147).

Today's universities—along with our high schools, colleges, libraries, learned societies, and scholars—have a great responsibility to help provide an answer to Eliot's questions. More than ever, these institutions and individuals have a fundamental historical and social role to play in ensuring that as a society we provide not just training but education, and not just education but culture. We need to teach students how to distill, from the bottomless cornucopia of information that is spilled out before them twenty-four hours a day, seven days a week, knowledge that is relevant, useful, and reliable and that will enrich both their personal and professional lives.

This is not an easy task, especially in a nation where, as Susan Jacoby (2008) writes in her book *The Age of American Unreason,*

> the scales of American history have shifted heavily against the vibrant and varied intellectual life so essential to functional democracy. During the past four decades, America's endemic anti-intellectual tendencies have been grievously exacerbated by a new species of semiconscious anti-rationalism, feeding on and fed by an ignorant popular culture of video images and unremitting noise that leaves no room for contemplation or logic. This new form of anti-rationalism, at odds not only with the nation's heritage of eighteenth-century Enlightenment reason but with modern scientific knowledge, has propelled a surge of anti-intellectualism capable of inflicting vastly greater damage than its historical predecessors inflected on American culture and politics. (xi–xii)

What Jacoby so forcefully points out is that ignorance is absolutely not bliss when both the strength of our democracy and the future of our society are at stake. And they may well be, for not only are we distracted and overwhelmed by the explosion of images, news, rumor, gossip, data, and bits of information that bombard us every day, but we also face dangerous levels of fragmentation of knowledge because of the advances of science and the accumulation of several millennia of scholarship. Not so long ago, Max Weber, writing about the fragmentation of knowledge and the advent of specialization, criticized the desiccated narrowness and the absence of spirit of the modern specialist. This same phenomenon prompted Dostoevsky to lament in *The Brothers Karamazov* (1879) about the scholars who "have only analyzed the parts and overlooked the whole and, indeed, their blindness is marvelous!" In the same vein, as early as the 1930s José Ortega y Gasset, in his *Revolt of the Masses* (1930/1932, ch. 12), decried the "barbarism of specialization." Today, he wrote, we have more scientists, scholars, and professionals than ever before, but fewer cultivated ones. To put the dilemma in twenty-first-century terms, I might describe this as everybody doing their own thing, but nobody really understanding what anybody else's thing really is.

Unfortunately, the university, which was conceived of as embodying the unity of knowledge, has become an intellectual multiversity. The process of both growth and fragmentation of knowledge under way since the seventeenth century has accelerated in our time and only continues to intensify. The modern university consists of a tangle of specialties and subspecialties, disciplines and subdisciplines, within which specialization continues apace. The unity of knowledge has collapsed. The scope and the intensity of specialization are such that scholars and scientists have great difficulty in keeping up with the important yet overwhelming amount of scholarly literature of their own subspecialties, not to mention their general disciplines. Even the traditional historical humanistic disciplines have become less and less viable as communities of discourse. As the late professor Wayne C. Booth (1987/1988, 311) put it wistfully in a Ryerson lecture he gave twenty years ago that still, sadly, sounds like breaking news from the education front: "Centuries have passed since the fabled moment . . . when the last of the Leonardo da Vincis could hope to cover the cognitive map. [Now], everyone has been reduced to knowing only one or two countries on the intellectual globe. . . . [In our universities] we continue to discover just what a pitifully small corner of the cognitive world we live in."[2]

In that connection, T. S. Eliot, whom I quoted earlier, could have been describing the disconnected aspects of modern higher education when he wrote in a commentary on *Dante's Inferno* that "the definition of hell is a place where nothing connects with nothing." If you think that is overreaching for a correlation to our universities, you may have to think again: the fragmentation of knowledge and the continuing proliferation of specialties are unquestionably reflected in the undergraduate and graduate curricula of our universities. Today, many major research universities make available over eighteen hundred undergraduate courses. Although college catalogs may euphemistically describe this as a "curriculum," a 2002 report from a national panel of educators and business leaders under the auspices of the Association of American Colleges and Universities (AACU) instead characterized these offerings as rarely more than a collection of courses, devoid of direction, context, and coherence. The AACU panel noted, moreover, that nothing had changed since 1985, when another association study (AACU 1985, 2) concluded: "As for what passes as a college curriculum, almost anything goes."

The strength of teaching and learning at today's universities is further diluted by an overreliance on part-time faculty. If the faculty is the core of the university, as I firmly believe it is, then the university is as strong, or as weak, as its faculty. Anything that fragments or diminishes the faculty also fragments and diminishes the university. But we are moving toward the point where most teachers are part-timers, adjuncts, and graduate students. The growth of part-time faculty has been phenomenal, doubling between 1970 and 2003, from 22 percent of the faculty to 44 percent (Forrest Cataldi, Fahimi, and Bradburn 2005). These individuals have no job security and lack the protective mantle of academic freedom, since the things that tenure-track scholars do with impunity—such as teaching controversial material, fighting grade changes, or organizing unions—can get them severed from their positions with no questions asked. P. D. Lesko, the head of the National Adjunct Faculty Guild, has said that part-timers "are terrified of being rigorous graders, terrified to deal with complaints about the course materials, terrified to deal with plagiarists. A lot of them are working as robots. They go in, they teach, they leave. No muss, no fuss." But Ms. Lesko adds: "If you're afraid to give an honest grade or an honest opinion, you're not teaching" (quoted in Schneider 1999, A18).

With all the pressures they are subject to, university faculty are the people we must rely on to help students learn how to balance analysis and synthesis and to guide them through the confusing maze of course content. They face a Herculean task, however, because the trend toward breaking our expanding knowledge base into smaller and smaller unconnected fragments of academic specialization continues unabated—even as the world looks to higher education for integration and synthesis. The result is that students find it exceedingly difficult to integrate knowledge in multidisciplinary, interdisciplinary, cross-disciplinary, or transdisciplinary study.

Personally, I am concerned that if we continue to accept this as a valid approach to education, there will be an ever-increasing blur between consumption and digestion, between information and learning, and often no guidance—or even questioning—about what it means to be an educated and cultured person. This is unmapped territory when it comes to education—one without a focused curriculum to integrate knowledge and train students in synthesis and systemic thinking. I do not believe the nation can afford this trend in the long run. It would lead to higher education becoming an academic superstore: a vast collection of courses stacked up like sinks and lumber for do-it-yourselfers to figure out and try to assemble into something meaningful.

In other words, the commonwealth of learning we have valued over many centuries has fractured. Our commitment to the grand end of synthesis, general understanding, and integration of knowledge continues to evaporate as we wander the aisles of the new university, which all too often resembles an academic Home Depot. The late William Bouwsma, a preeminent historian, lamented the movement away from integration and toward specialization, noting that specialization, "instead of uniting human beings into a general community of values and discourse, by necessity has divided them into small and exclusive categories/coteries, narrow in outlook and interest. This, in turn, tends to isolate and alienate human beings. Social relations are reduced to political relations, to the interplay of competitive and often antagonistic groups. Specialized education makes our students into instruments to serve the specialized needs of a society of specialists." Bouwsma described "a broad decline in the idea of a general education, which for all practical purposes has become little more than a nostalgic memory. Indeed, the body of requisite knowledge has become so vast that no one can hope to master more than a small segment of it. So in the popular mind, an educated man [or woman] is now some kind of specialist; and in a sense, we no longer have a single conception of the educated [individual] but as many conceptions as there are learned specialists" (Bouwsma 1975, 207).

Nowhere is this better reflected than in the concept of literacy. It, too, has lost its unity. It, too, has been fragmented. According to the *Oxford Unabridged Dictionary,* literacy is the quality or state of being literate; it means being possessed of education, especially the ability to write and read. Today, however, we are using the term *literate* to mean knowledgeable about a specific subject: we have proponents of technological literacy, civic literacy, mathematical literacy, geographic literacy, scientific literacy, ethical literacy, artistic literacy, cultural literacy, analytical literacy, and so on. My favorite one is "managerial literacy." According to the *New York Times Magazine's* (1989) assessment of the book *Managerial Literacy: What Today's Managers Must Know to Succeed* (Shaw and Weber 1990, 68), this particular "literacy" includes 1,200 terms and concepts. We are told that if you are conversant with at least 80 percent of them you can confidently engage in "meaningful conversations with other experienced managers."

Erik Erikson once remarked that human beings are the "teaching species" (2000, 203), and if that is so, then we are certainly also the learning species. And it is clear from the literacy boom that we have never before had so much to learn. Learning to learn, then, has become one of the most important lifelong skills that education, especially higher education, can give students. Yet paradoxically higher education continues to provide an antiquated model for acquiring fragments of knowledge rather than modeling a lifelong process for integrated learning and systemic thinking. On this point, we should recall B. F. Skinner's (1968, 89) wise observation that "education is what survives when a man has forgotten all he has been taught."

What must survive a student's higher education today is a facility for lifelong learning. Consider how steep the learning curve has become in the professional workplace. Knowledge has become so ephemeral that management experts have tried to get a handle on the educational challenge by using a yardstick they call the "half-life of knowledge." This is the amount of time it takes for half of one's professional knowledge to become obsolete. I've seen estimates that, overall, the half-life of knowledge is dwindling down to something like just a few years. For technical fields, it is even less; half of what software developers know now, for example, will likely be irrelevant in just eighteen months (for estimates of the half-life of knowledge, see Kapp and McKeague 2002, 9; Chee Hean 2001). In fact, computer science professors David Lorge Parnas and Michael Soltys (2006, 2) warn that "much of what students learn about [software] products will be irrelevant before they *graduate*." As Maryanne Rouse (n.d.) has written, "We used to think of the long run as ten to fifteen years; in many technology-dependent industries the long run may now be six months or less. And while the pace of knowledge-creation is accelerating, the half-life of knowledge becomes shorter each year. What this means for us is that concepts are far more important than facts and the ability to analyze and synthesize has much greater value than the ability to memorize. In short, school may be multiple choice but real life is all essay." Put another way, there are no boundaries between learning and life, and educators simply cannot emphasize that enough to their students.

Paradoxically, the same information technologies that have been the driving force behind the explosion of information, growth of knowledge and its fragmentation, also present us with the best opportunity and tools for meeting the challenge of that fragmentation. If the new information technologies themselves seem fragmenting, they are also profoundly integrative.

Technology is radically modifying the space/time constraints of communications channels—and it is offering great opportunities for making connections among disciplines and across disciplines. Online communications and even our ubiquitous hand-held electronic devices have provided new tools and opportunities for the scholarly community to share resources, though we must not forget that while the Internet, satellites, and fiber optics have advanced communication, the raw input is still human speech and human ideas. The university remains at the nexus of these developments—the public commons where ideas and technology meet and interact. Thus the process of assimilating new information technologies can help us think hard and deeply about the nature of knowledge and even about higher education's mission. But progress in using technology to integrate disciplines on campus has often been disappointingly slow. Unless higher education does a better job teaching students how to synthesize and systematize information, our society faces many serious problems. In his book *1984*, George Orwell (1949) describes a world in which information is denied, true knowledge is rejiggered to suit those in power, and propaganda is substituted for both. Arthur Koestler's novel *Darkness at Noon* (1941/2006) draws a similar picture of a society in which reality is manipulated so that fiction easily replaces fact. Ironically, in the twenty-first century citizens could be denied knowledge by being inundated with mountains of raw and unconnected data. Advances in technology may also deceive us into thinking that whatever is not in the computer or data bank does not exist. But God did not create life with two computers.

In the presence of the above-mentioned developments, higher education must create and enunciate a clear philosophy of education: one that deals with the process and nature of learning; one that deals with continuities rather than discontinuities, synthesis rather than separation; and one that treats the elementary, secondary, and higher education levels as a sixteen-year-long learning continuum in which the issues of general education, unnecessary, wasteful duplication, and the coherence and integrity of our curricula are dealt with. We must also confront the reality that, at present, becoming an expert in any field or subfield requires an increasingly narrow focus to allow subject mastery, while the generalist's knowledge often tends to become increasingly superficial in order to allow broad coverage. Thus the need for breadth of coverage invariably conflicts with the need for coverage in depth. Often our own training, narrow and focused in an earlier age, keeps many in the academy from participating in the discoveries that are creating newer disciplines. That is not merely a problem for the present but a crisis for the future as well. Thus we need to reexamine the fundamentals of our liberal arts curricula in order to see whether they are enabling liberal learning in which the issues of criteria, process, values, standards, norms, logic, aesthetics, taste and discernment, and organization of knowledge have a central focus and role.

Perhaps one way to approach this problem would be through a reassessment of the introductory courses that are offered at most universities. Instead of focusing on one or two aspects of a subject, why not create introductory courses that are a true overview of a field? For example, taking an introductory course on biology is not the same as being taught about the depth, breadth, and scope of science or about the scientific method. And introductory courses on economics hardly provide students with an in-depth understanding of the intertwined complexities of global economic systems. I think we can actually see an example of that, now, as we watch the economic dominoes fall across the globe, spurred on by the subprime mortgage crisis in the United States. If all you had to base your understanding of what is happening to the world economy today—why oil and food prices are soaring, why the U.S. dollar is weak, why the unemployment rate in the United States is up and the middle class in Europe has to tighten its belt—was an introductory course in economics, you would probably be as befuddled as many of us are when we listen to the nightly business report!

The economics professor Gary Wolfram (2007) explains some of the concepts he would like to see included in an introductory economics course this way:

> On my first day of class I refer to the Sherlock Holmes story, *A Scandal in Bohemia* (Doyle, 1892). In the story, Watson finds himself near the apartment that he used to share with Holmes and decides to stop by for a visit. Holmes, in the course of conversation, asks Watson how many steps there are leading up from the hall to his room. Watson replies that although he treaded them hundreds of times he does not know how many there are. Sherlock says, "You have not observed. And yet you have seen. That is just my point. Now I know that there are seventeen steps, because I have both seen and observed." What we should be teaching students in introductory classes is to both see and observe. They should, for example, be able to see that a military draft will allow the government to obtain soldiers at low cost to the federal budget, but observe that the opportunity cost of a draft is the lost private sector production that results from conscripting people.

Nicholas Lemann, dean of the Columbia School of Journalism, has also commented on the need for integration in introductory coursework. In a summit entitled "Journalism in the Service of Democracy," according to the summit report,

> Lemann noted that there are two required courses at the Columbia School of Journalism: "A History of Journalism for Journalists" and "Evidence and Inference," which focuses on hypothesis testing. For these courses, said Lemann, they bring in social scientists, direct students to Karl Popper's work on falsification, etc., with the intent of trying to "map the academic material very powerfully onto journalism." Lemann also noted that although students

take some courses outside, the main construct they teach is the substance inside the journalism school—not sending students outside to get it. "This," he said, is because of the "mapping to practice" we're trying to do—have students make web sites, make the faculty associated with this program think through who they might need to bring in to help teach this course, what's the body of essential knowledge, etc. Said Lemann, "I want that kind of rich thought and knowledge to exist inside our school." (Connell 2008, 53–54)

These are wonderful ideas for how universities might help students bring some structure to the vast amount of information they are constantly exposed to and will continue to be later in life. Other suggestions in this same vein include offering thematic seminars and interdisciplinary team teaching that might focus on subjects such as the origin of the cosmos, which would involve discussions with a geologist, an astrophysicist, a mathematician, a philosopher, a religious expert, and so forth. Another course might introduce students to the Ptolemaic, Copernican, and Einsteinian worldviews, which would involve becoming acquainted with critical elements of science, philosophy, history, and religion. Another example might be exploring the concept of agape and eros in three literary traditions, Western, Islamic, and Buddhist, which would mean learning about three different cultures. To develop a nuanced and multifaceted sense of how recent events have affected regions around the globe, one could bring together several historians to explore the origins and conclusion of the cold war from the Russian, European, Asian, and American points of view.

The above are suggestions about how to develop a deeper understanding of certain ideas and fields, but whether we like it or not, colleges and universities, and increasingly high schools, must teach students not only what we should know but also what we don't know—and what the limitations of knowledge are. This is not a new challenge—it goes way back to the Socratic notion that true knowledge is knowing what you know *and* what you don't know. So while the computer allows us to access more information—faster and in a more usable form—we must keep in mind another caution from Neil Postman (1990, 7): "The computer cannot provide an organizing moral framework. It cannot tell us what questions are worth asking," or even why they should be asked.

Computers—as much as we have all come to depend on them—also cannot help us answer a question I have often asked myself: How would the last man or woman on earth respond to even a friendly interrogation by the Martians? Let's say that our friends on the Red Planet have heard through the extraterrestrial grapevine that for one reason or another our entire civilization has been destroyed, so they get in their spaceships and fly to Earth just to see what's left of their cousins in the solar system. When they come upon this last person, they treat him or her with great sympathy and say, "We are going to have you meet with our greatest scribe who will record the entire history of your civilization so it will be preserved for others throughout the universe to study and learn from in the future."

Now, let's say that this last person is you. They bring you the scribe, who sits poised before the Martian's intergalactic version of a computer and begins to eagerly ask you questions so he can record your answers. He begins with geography: we know what the land masses on your planet look like, he says, but can you tell me the names of all the nations and states they were divided into? What were the names of the great rivers, the mountain ranges, and the seas, and what were the different languages that people spoke in these different areas? And how did you travel from one place to another? We know you had conveyances you called trains and cars and airplanes, but can you tell me how they worked? And what about radios and televisions and satellites and those fiber optic cables you were all busy stringing all over the place? How did your communications travel over those things?

Once the scribe has exhausted your store of information on those subjects, he goes on to ask about the religions and philosophies of human beings. "We're very confused," he says. "We have a long list of the names of the religions that people on Earth followed, but we don't quite understand the differences between them and why you argued about them century after century." Then he begins to read the list to you: Hinduism, Islam, Judaism, Jainism, Sikhism, Shintoism, Confucianism, Baha'i, and then the different forms of Christianity: Catholics, Protestants, Baptists, Southern Baptists, Lutherans, Pentecostals, Evangelicals, Amish, Mormons, Jehovah's Witnesses, Seventh Day Adventists, Greek Orthodox, Eastern Orthodox, Russian Orthodox . . . well, the list might go on for a while longer. Then the scribe asks, "Can you contrast and compare the tenets of each of these faiths for me?"

"What about your political and governmental systems?" asks the Martian scholar. "Democracy, fascism, communism, socialism, monarchies, commonwealths, duchies, emirates, kingdoms, principalities, republics, socialist republics: how do these work and how did each system evolve?"

By now you might have racked your brains for every last bit of information you think you have about life on Earth, but gently, the Martian continues to ask questions: "Tell me," he says, "about your art and culture: we know that primitive humans began painting pictures on caves, for example, and that later they began making images for worship. Later, we understand, they painted pictures to commemorate important events or to be used as social commentary, but in the last few centuries, ideas in the art world seemed to explode: there was Impressionism, Postimpressionism, Cubism, Surrealism, Expressionism, Op Art, Pop Art, abstract art, Modernism, Postmodernism—can you help us understand the connections between these movements and how they influenced each other?"

Well, of course, this is just a story, but I am doing so to make a point about how difficult it is in our increasingly complex world to have an *individual* sense of how everything we see, read, hear, or learn about fits together—or does not—so imagine the task of the university in trying to provide such integration to its educational offerings!

Perhaps to some degree we must accept that we live in an age of extraordinary specialization and fragmentation of knowledge and that this is not going to change. Hence, it is clear that neither society nor higher education can abandon specializations or subspecializations or sub-subspecializations. After all, the division of labor has greatly advanced the cause of civilization. Specialization is an instrument of progress. Complexity, by necessity, requires specialization. We will always need disciplines and specialists—and without strong disciplines there cannot be effective interdisciplinary or multidisciplinary scholarship or teaching.

But for greater understanding we also need generalists, trained in the humanities, sciences, and social sciences. The challenge is to provide synthesis and systemic perspectives. We need to create a common discourse with a common vocabulary among the various disciplines. Unfortunately, generalists are not held in high regard on campus or in our society—unless, of course, they are famous or became generalists after first earning credibility as specialists.

And since our society *respects* specialists and sometimes *suspects* generalists, perhaps the way to solve the shortage of generalists is by creating a new specialty in the general area of synthesis and systems. Ortega y Gasset proposed as much in his 1944 book, *The Mission of the University*. He wrote: "The need to create sound synthesis and systemization of knowledge . . . will call out a kind of scientific genius which hitherto has existed only as an aberration: the genius of integration. Of necessity this means specialization, as all creative effort does, but this time, the [person] will be specializing in the construction of the whole" (70).

I believe that the concept of *wholeness* must also include an understanding of *context*. Neither specialized nor integrated knowledge can be of deep or lasting value unless, like a valuable jewel, it is in an appropriate setting. For the jewel that is knowledge, history and historical context provide the most important setting. After all, even knowledge, just for the sake of accumulating it, means nothing, just as culture for culture's sake is shallow and ultimately without significance. Perhaps one useful way to express the idea of context is through an analogy to the game of chess. Everybody understands how chess works: you have to concentrate on the techniques of the game, the different theories and moves, and try to anticipate what your opponent is thinking as well. But mastering those abilities only makes you a person who is adept at games. To be steeped in context, to thoughtfully apply the rules of the game, to build on them and develop knowledge and wisdom over time, you also have to think about the table on which the game is being played. Why? The answer is clear: because, although you may be a champion at chess, as the different pieces move around the table, the context changes, even the game itself changes. So my advice is, always know the table on which you are going to play chess. And what is that table? It is history. It is context. It is facts. It is the accumulated knowledge and experience of humankind.

Without integrating historical context into knowledge and into the way we use and draw upon knowledge in our lives we may be subject to what some have called "self-inflicted amnesia." The Nobel laureate Czeslaw Milosz (1980) has commented eloquently on this state of affairs, writing: "Certainly, the illiterates of past centuries, then an enormous majority of mankind, knew little of the history of their respective countries and of their civilization. In the minds of modern illiterates, however, who know how to read and write and even teach in schools and at universities, history is present but blurred, in a state of strange confusion; Molière becomes a contemporary of Napoleon, Voltaire, a contemporary of Lenin. Also, events of the last decades, of such primary importance that knowledge or ignorance of them will be decisive for the future of mankind, move away, grow pale, lose all consistency."

Moreover, the consequences of such historical amnesia are destructive. As the philosopher Theodor Adorno (1968, 35) warns, "Forgetting is inhuman because man's accumulated suffering is forgotten. The historical trace of things, words, colors and sounds is always the trace of past suffering. As soon as all tradition is extinguished, inhumanity begins."

Let me also suggest that inhumanity begins when education is denied— or when it is provided, but without concern for the future and how teaching and learning will serve the next generation of students and those who follow after them. Hence, I've outlined a daunting challenge for higher education, one that calls on our institutions to develop and enunciate a clear philosophy of education. Colleges and universities must address the reintegration of knowledge, the process and nature of lifelong learning in our fast-paced times, and, most ambitiously, must join other institutions in addressing the continuities and discontinuities of knowledge within our entire pre-K to university educational system.

While we must reexamine and restructure higher education, we must also treat it with the respect that is due to a national treasure. After all, for more than two centuries American colleges and universities have been the backbone of our nation's progress, helping make it an economic, cultural, scientific, technological, and political power. Not coincidentally, America also became an educational power. The excellence of the American university is reflected in the fact that the largest share of foreign students who choose to study abroad come here (Bowman 2007). Henry Rosovsky (1987), the economist and educator, estimates that between two-thirds and three-quarters of the world's best universities are located in the United States. He asks, "What other sector of the economy can make a similar statement? . . . In higher education, 'made in America' is still the finest label." Referring to that label, Rosovsky cautions: "My only advice is to add 'handle with care'" (13–14).

NOTES

1. These estimates were taken from the World Wide Web Size Web site, worldwidewebsize.com, on July 17, 2009.

2. The Ryerson lectures, held annually at the University of Chicago since 1974, feature scholars whose work is deemed by the university's faculty to have lasting significance. Wayne C. Booth delivered his Ryerson lecture in 1987.

REFERENCES

Adorno, Theodor W. 1968. Thesen uber Tradition. In *Ohne Leitbild: Parva aesthetica,* ed. T. W. Adorno. Frankfurt: Suhrkamp.
Association of American Colleges and Universities. 1985. *Integrity in the college curriculum.* Washington, DC: Association of American Colleges and Universities.
———. 2002. *Greater expectations: A new vision for learning as a nation goes to college.* Washington, DC: Association of American Colleges and Universities.
Booth, Wayne C. 1987/1988. The idea of a university—as seen by a rhetorician [1987 Ryerson lecture]. In *The vocation of a teacher: Rhetorical occasions, 1967–1988,* 309–34. Chicago: University of Chicago Press.
Bouwsma, William. 1975. Models of the educated man. *American Scholar* 44 (2): 195–212.
Bowman, Michael. 2007. U.S. remains top destination for foreign students. *Voice of America News,* November 13.
Chee Hean, R. T. 2001. Speech presented at the National Institute of Education Teachers Investiture Ceremony, Singapore, July 4.

Connell, Christopher. 2008. *Journalism in the service of democracy: A summit of deans, faculty, students and journalists.* New York: Carnegie Corporation of New York. www. carnegie.org/pdf/carn_journ_review_2008.pdf.

Dostoevsky, Fyodor. 1879. *The brothers Karamazov.* Trans. Constance Garnett. http://fyodordostoevsky.com/etexts/the_brothers_karamazov.txt.

Doyle, Arthur Conan. 1892. *The adventures of Sherlock Holmes.* London: George Newnes.

Eliot, T. S. 1963. *Collected poems, 1909–1962.* New York: Harcourt, Brace.

Erikson, Erik. 2000. *The Erik Erikson reader.* Ed. Robert Coles. New York: Norton.

Forrest Cataldi, E., M. Fahimi, and E. M. Bradburn. 2005. *2004 National Study of Postsecondary Faculty (NSOPF:04) Report on Faculty and Instructional Staff in Fall 2003.* NCES 2005-172. U.S. Department of Education, National Center for Education Statistics, nces. ed.gov/Pubsearch/pubsinfo.asp?pubid=2005172.

IBM Global Technology Services. 2006. *The toxic terabyte: How data dumping threatens business efficiency.* July. London: IBM United Kingdom. www-03.ibm.com/systems/ resources/systems_storage_solutions_pdf_toxic_tb.pdf.

Jacoby, Susan. 2008. *The age of American unreason.* New York: Pantheon Books.

Kapp, Karl M., and Carrie McKeague. 2002. *Blended learning for compliance training success.* Princeton, NJ: EduNeering, Inc. www.astd.org/NR/rdonlyres/456DB5F7-D0FE-49B8-AE38-78167D308C7B/0/blendedlearning.pdf.

Koestler, Alfred. 1941/2006. *Darkness at noon.* New York: Scribner.

Lorge Parnas, David, and Michael Soltys. 2006. Basic science for software developers. July 18. www.cas.mcmaster.ca/~soltys/papers/parnas_soltys_basic_2.pdf.

Milosz, Czeslaw. 1980. Nobel Lecture, Oslo, December 8, http://nobelprize.org/nobel_ prizes/literature/laureates/1980/milosz-lecture-en.html.

New York Times Magazine. 1989. To start with . . . ; defining some words to work by. December 3, 1.

Ortega y Gasset, Jose. 1930/1932. *Revolt of the masses: Authorized translation from the Spanish.* New York: Norton.

———. 1944. *The mission of the university.* New York: Norton.

Orwell, George. 1949. *1984.* New York: Harcourt, Brace.

Postman, Neil. 1990. Informing ourselves to death. Paper presented at the annual meeting of the German Informatics Society, Stuttgart, October 11. www.midlandchristianschool-mi.org/informing_ourselves_to_death.pdf.

Rosovsky, H. 1987. Highest education [2 parts]. *New Republic,* July 13 and 20.

Rouse, Maryanne. n.d. Teaching philosophy. Faculty page for Maryanne Rouse, University of South Florida, College of Business Administration, Department of Management and Organization, www.coba.usf.edu/departments/management/faculty/rouse/teach.htm.

Schneider, A. 1999. To many adjunct professors, academic freedom is a myth. *Chronicle of Higher Education,* December 10.

Seigenthaler, J. 2005. A false Wikipedia biography. *USA Today,* November 29.

Shaw, Gary, and Jack Weber. 1990. *Managerial literacy: What today's managers must know to succeed.* Homewood, IL: Dow Jones-Irwin.

Skinner, B. F. 1968. *The technology of teaching.* New York: Appleton-Century-Crofts.

Wikipedia biography controversy. n.d. http://en.wikipedia.org/wiki/Wikipedia_biography_controversy. Accessed April 6, 2010.

Wolfram, Gary. 2007. Teaching introductory economic concepts. Paper presented at Free Market Forum, Hillsdale College, September 27–29.

2

The Case for Global Education

JOHN SEXTON

We live in a world without boundaries, a global community we enter with only a keypad stroke. What does it mean to educate citizens who are instantly linked to people on every continent, who share a fluency in the technologies of communication that erase borders and enliven languages, who take for granted a transparent, permeable world? Those of us who are passionate about the possibilities of education are summoned to design a mode of learning for a world in hyperchange. We are asked to prepare tomorrow's citizens not for a single, predefined career until retirement but for a life of accelerating, unpredictable velocity. At the same time, we are responsible for transmitting the cumulative wisdom of the past, the fruit of the finest minds and hearts that preceded us, and for imparting the qualities of rigor and compassion that must be cultivated in order to flourish.

Our students are growing up in an America whose strength will lie in the flexibility of its intelligence for innovation, not in the durability of its manufactured goods. What narrative can we offer to illuminate their world, to help them negotiate the precarious balance between what is worth conserving and the speed of change that the twenty-first century demands?

In the ethos in which I was raised, the American ideal was the melting pot, as if the wondrous differences among students would be best blended into a single, homogeneous entity. Fortunately, in countermeasure, I was also raised in New York, a city whose essence is the cacophony of accents, music, customs, and cultures that encompass the globe. There are other great cities, but no other is the world in miniature. New York City is the first experiment in what turns out to be this century's challenge—to create a community of communities, savoring our distinctiveness while reaching out to each other to invent a future enriched by difference and expansive with possibility.

In his wonderful book *The Rhetoric of Reaction*, the Princeton economist Albert O. Hirschman, while analyzing political discourse in advanced democratic societies, expresses "a concern over the massive, stubborn and exasperating otherness of others." He writes of the unsettling experience of being shut off not just from the opinions but from the entire life experience of large numbers of one's contemporaries. Citizens array themselves within democracies in a few clearly defined groups holding different opinions, and so it can easily happen that these groups become walled off from each other. "As the process feeds on itself, each group will at some point ask about the other in utter puzzlement and often with mutual revulsion, How did they get to be that way?" Hirschman published these words in 1991. Today, the world is wired; it has grown small. What happens in distant places is known and, more important, experienced almost everywhere—by almost everybody—immediately and unavoidably. The faith assumption of education for global citizenship is that students will ask, not "How did they get to be that way?" but, with voracious curiosity, "What can I learn from you?" How can I translate your world into mine and mine into yours—without diluting our distinctiveness?

The world that I see emerging will have six or eight idea capitals. These cities will bring together people of the imagination and inventiveness conferred by the kind of education I am describing. The twenty-first century is the urban century, because great cities—in their juxtapositions of difference, their celebration of complexity, and their encouragement of diversity—are natural magnets for global citizens. How will idea capitals be renewed and revitalized in a world of hyperchange? They will be anchored by educating institutions—schools, colleges, and research universities that recognize the necessary vector from data and information to knowledge and wisdom. They will develop students who can ask profound questions of the past and skillfully apply its lessons to our pressing dilemmas. Their graduates will have incisive minds and receptive hearts, the results of an education that invites them to be active listeners and nimble interpreters of our dizzying, dazzling world.

We are devoted to encouraging those kinds of students—and we will need them. We need them now. For the issues confronting us must be viewed from multiple perspectives; they do not have one definition, let alone a single resolution.

- How do we provide quality health care at low cost to all citizens?
- What does it take to reduce the achievement gap in education?
- What needs to be done to overcome racism, sexism, and homophobia?
- How should we treat new immigrants?

One response to the perplexing, persistent problems we face is fear and the reductive simplification that results. It is human to long for an effortless answer—and to resist the intricacy of difficulties that do not lend themselves to solution by a keystroke. In our era, we are witnessing a palpable decline in the public's appetite for nuance, complexity, and critical thinking. We celebrate our time for its unprecedented access to information; the Internet provides the newest basis for such a belief. But the Internet, for all its gifts, is unedited. We click from link to link among its offerings, increasingly addicted to its pace. Along with a world that is always on the express track, however, has come a proliferation of unfiltered information. And information alone cannot address our complex problems, which demand the ability to think well and wisely, to discern the valuable and distinguish it from the trifling.

Unmediated, the Internet cannot educate. It works not only for but also against the ideal of an informed and intellectually curious public. It does enable those who were previously passive and powerless to become actors and interlocutors in the unfolding drama of public discourse and politics. And yet, even as it empowers vast numbers of citizens, it is also a vehicle for the proliferation of rumor and misinformation. The absence of accountability combines with a vacuum of formal checks to allow pseudofacts to spread exponentially.

One unsurprising response to this barrage of undifferentiated information is a kind of nihilism about knowledge, which leads almost inexorably to an equation of fact and opinion and the reduction of argument to assertion. Paradoxically, this trend breeds and feeds a version of unreflective dogmatism. Dogmatism and fundamentalism render the newly transparent world opaque with intolerance. Their adherents and promulgators cannot allow the paradox of global education—that the more our students can interpret their own unique histories in the context of the world's diversity, the more readily they can understand the very different histories and viewpoints of those they meet.

The education to which we are dedicated is one that sees the learning environment as a microcosm of the world. In that environment our students discover affinities with those who are seemingly unlike them. At the same time, they are not afraid of articulating their divergence from those who appear to be identical to them. Like their music, they will be able to mix it up; they will have the capacity to compose, theme by theme, in their own harmonies and dissonance, a worldview of their own.

Urban universities draw their life force from their surroundings—the glorious cities that house and nurture them, cities that are rich reservoirs of intellectual and cultural talent. All of us who lead those universities share a common institutional DNA, one that reflects what I call our "locational endowment" in global cities: a concentration of mind and matter, an entrepreneurial spirit, an embrace of complexity alongside openness, a connection to the world beyond our walls. Indeed, our campuses are literally without walls.

Courtney Ross has translated her vision of education for the children of the twenty-first century into pioneering educational models from which we continue to learn. My institution, New York University, shares the Ross vision of schools as laboratories of learning that nurture the gifts students will need to thrive in the global community of the twenty-first century. And we share as well the humility of recognizing that the students we send forth will have to be far better than we have been in vanquishing the darker forces that dominate the headlines and undermine the global world I have just described.

In the most familiar usage of the word, *globalization* describes a transformation in the world economy. Commerce and communication increasingly transcend boundaries, and transactions once merely local now routinely touch multiple continents and implicate several different legal regimes. In this sense, globalization is ubiquitous, unavoidable, and undeniable—affecting for good and ill the relationships of governments, markets, and the daily lives of institutions and citizens everywhere. This understanding of globalization is the simplest, the most conventional. Understood in this widely accepted sense, globalization is profoundly consequential and often controversial. Moreover, it is beyond dispute that the economic consequences for contemporary education of interdependence and world competition will be enormous. We will be forced to adjust to marketplace competition from commercial providers, to the advent and pervasiveness of online education, and to the explosion of technologies and the information they deliver.

Beyond its most common meaning, *globalization* also refers to a deeper and even more fundamentally transformative force—embodying cultural and societal developments that touch the whole range of human experiences. Globalization does not merely require us to coordinate with those beyond our borders in ways we never imagined; it changes the nature of our borders and the structure and content of the cultures nourished and developed within them. The penetration of American culture is but one example. There are streets and storefronts in once remote parts of the world that could be transplanted from any American suburb. Undeniably, on many of those same streets, treasured traditions are threatened by an accelerating process of homogenization. Ironically, even as globalization makes us ever more aware of the diversity of our cultural and social histories, it threatens the diversity it spotlights and celebrates.

Globalization in this broader sense is just as much a revolutionary force as is its economic counterpart; it has as catalytic potential, both positive and negative. But connection and mutual enrichment need not destroy diversity: they can elevate and celebrate it. Neither synthesis nor synchronization requires sameness. It is for us to find a way to harness globalization, maximizing its benefits and minimizing its costs. I believe that our ability to do so will vary directly with our aptitude for reflection and our capacity to listen. We will need modesty, not certitude. We will need to generate in ourselves and in our students a desire to discover new insights equal to our eagerness to exchange our insights with others.

At New York University, we share with Courtney Ross an ardent commitment to foster responsible and responsive citizens. Education, as we understand it, encourages—urges—students to test existing knowledge and to uncover new knowledge through a constant, often vigorous encounter with a range of perspectives. It requires not a surrender of conviction but conviction tempered by discovery in pursuit of the advancement of knowledge wherever it leads.

The central test for coming generations will be to develop ways to manage, in this miniaturized world of immediacy, a vast richness of race, faith, culture, and thought. If those we educate are to avoid the devastating balkanization we continue to witness, they will need to create pathways of comprehension across traditional divisions. They will seek educating institutions that offer them opportunities for active, interdisciplinary thinking and innovative leadership; full engagement in the global community; and a passion for lifelong learning—attributes essential for global citizenship.

REFERENCES

Hirschman, Albert O. 1991. *The rhetoric of reaction: Perversity, futility, jeopardy.* Cambridge, MA: Belknap Press.

3

A Tangled Web

Reflections on the Roles of Science,
Policy, and Assessment in Education

HOWARD GARDNER

In no area of human endeavor are science and policy more regularly confounded than in the sphere of education. Two spheres that should be kept at arm's length are almost routinely collapsed with one another. Today policy makers in the United States go even further—bridging three spheres! The findings of science and the pronouncements of policy are automatically linked to questions of assessment and evaluation. Almost as soon as a finding is reported or a policy is proposed, pressures mount for an objective measurement of it. A climate results in which the overly broad claim and the quick fix are the rule—and in which careful planning and continual reflection, over a long period of time, are lamentably rare.

Render unto Caesar

While reflective individuals have always tried to explain happenings in the world, science as we know it is a relatively recent phenomenon. Only since the time of Copernicus, Galileo, and Newton have researchers put forth testable claims about the workings of the universe; carried out experiments and observations to test these claims; revised their claims in terms of the findings; and described both models and results in a way that other scientists can replicate or refute. While no sphere of human life is free of considerations of value, science stands out in its attempts to be objective. At least in the ideal, the scientist lays out his expectations and methods as scrupulously as possible, reports his data reliably, carries out replications in order to strengthen his findings, and stands ready to admit error and to alter models in light of the work carried out by himself or by other scientists.

In sharp contrast, the world of policy propounds what *should* be the case and marshals tools that can help to achieve that desired goal. From the time that communities first existed, leaders have promulgated goals and sought to realize them through policy/political means. In a complex modern society, of course, most policies are contested; many people—elected, appointed, or self-appointed—promote their favored policies in the marketplace of ideas and practices.

The realm of education is inextricably bound with human values. There is no such thing as an education that is objectively the best—judgments of quality are inherently bound to one's stated goals. And these goals are almost always up for negotiation. In the United States, I have quipped, one can never devise a system that would equally please the three Jesses: civil rights activist Jesse Jackson, ardent right-wing politician Jesse Helms, and wrestler-turned-governor Jesse Ventura of Minnesota.

Nonetheless, the temptations to elide the realms of science and policy are overwhelming. Like Odysseus, who was powerfully attracted to the song of the sirens, educational policy makers are seduced by the aura of scientific legitimacy. Consider the confirmation, a half century ago, that the right and left hemispheres of the brain carry out different cognitive functions, with the left hemisphere being dedicated primarily to linguistic and logical process-ing and the right hemisphere having dominance for spatial and emotional processing. Though it is not clear what they might have expected to be the case, individuals all over found this a fascinating finding. And before long, educators and even businesspeople were speaking about the importance of utilizing right-hemisphere capacities. Entire industries sprung up in the name of right-brain education, left-brain education, whole-brain education, brain gymnastics, and the like.

Step back for a minute, however, and the superficiality, even foolish-ness, of succumbing to the song of sirens becomes apparent. If one believes that spatial or emotional or artistic or nonrational thinking is impor-tant, then one should promote that way of thinking. If, on the other hand, one does not value that way of thinking, then the fact that it is housed in one or another hemisphere is irrelevant. Would anyone have a legiti-mate reason to recommend a different policy just because of the man-ner in which processing happens to occur, or to not occur, in the brain? Another example: in 1994, Richard Herrnstein and Charles Murray published *The Bell Curve*, a book that was to become famous (or, some would say, infa-mous). In this book, the authors argue that psychometric intelligence is very difficult to change. They go on to suggest that, in view of this finding, it might be well to counsel less intelligent individuals to pursue less cerebral careers and perhaps even live in a community where they would feel less intimidated by the cognitive elite. Before his death I had the opportunity to discuss this putative scientific finding with Herrnstein. While we disagreed about the supposed intransigence of measured intelligence, we agreed that one could draw diametrically opposite conclusions. Either, with Herrnstein and Murray, one could say that it is difficult to change IQ and so one should not devote efforts to doing so. Or one could take a more melioristic stance and attempt to change it. One might find, to Herrnstein and Murray's surprise, that psychometric intelligence could indeed be changed; in fact, one might even find an easy way to change it, through change in diet, powerful early experiences, innovative modes of teaching, new technologies, and the like.

Multiple Intelligences as Science and Policy

I use the example of intelligence because it is an area in which I myself have propounded a theory. On the basis of evidence drawn from several scientific disciplines, I proposed, in the early 1980s, that the psychometric notion of a single intelligence was flawed (Gardner 1983/1993). I argued that human beings, rather than differing only in their position in a single bell curve, are better thought of as having several relatively autonomous intellectual faculties, which I called the multiple intelligences. All of us have the several intelligences (linguistic, musical, spatial, etc.), but we differ—for both genetic and experiential reasons—on our particular configurations of intelligences.

Now, "MI theory," as it has come to be called, is quite controversial in psychology. The controversy stems from different quarters and for different reasons (Schaler 2006). Important among them is the fact that most tests of human capacities correlate with one another, and this correlation supports the claim of a single underlying test/task factor, often called "general intelligence" or "g." Even those who are sympathetic to my theory lament the fact that I have not developed a set of sleek tests probing the several intelligences. In their view, only the administration of a battery of such tests will indicate whether there is a rationale for positing several intelligences or whether we are better off reverting to the notion of a single intelligence, arrayed on a single bell curve.

MI theory is put forth as a scientific theory. To be sure, it relies on the synthesis of findings from several disciplines rather than from an examination of statistical correlations (or lack of correlations) among measures of different intellectual capacities. I would defend this way of doing science. Otherwise, the theory is best described as empirical rather than as experimental. But I introduce this example here because, in the case of MI theory, the bridge from science to policy was frequently and deliberately crossed. Indeed, within a few years of the publication of *Frames of Mind*, educators in many parts of the world cited the theory as a rationale for what they were doing. Some organized curricula around the MI; some said that materials should be so presented as to address each of the intelligences; some said that there should be classes to develop each intelligence; some said that individuals with the same intellectual profile should be grouped, while others argued that grouping should be heterogeneous, with individuals displaying different profiles of intelligence complementing one another within the same four walls.

Of course, as I was soon to realize, this example was no different in principle from the ones cited earlier. From the fact of two halves of the brain, from the hypothesis that it is difficult to enhance psychometric intelligence, one cannot reliably adduce any policy implications. Unbeknownst to me, MI theory was turning out to be a Rorschach test, an inkblot projective instrument. Educators read about the theory and simply used it to justify what they wanted to do anyway—whether heterogeneous grouping, new ways of selecting children for gifted programs, or equal classroom time for the arts and the sciences.

I don't want to leave the impression that no educational implications follow from MI theory. After decades of pondering the issue, I have reached two strong conclusions: (1) in view of vast differences in learning profiles, one should individualize education; and (2) because people learn in different ways, important concepts should be presented in a multitude of complementary ways. Yet even these modest recommendations harbor value judgments. One could decide that individual differences are divisive and thus deliberately treat individuals in the same way in an attempt to make them more similar to one another. Or one could argue—on the basis of research or of analysis—that there is one best way to teach each topic and that therefore that optimal mode of teaching should be used with everyone, irrespective of particular profiles of intelligences.

The Policy Perspective

While there may be certain constants in education across time and space, there is little question that education needs to change as conditions in the world change. Once literacy had become widespread, for example, the ways in which written materials were deployed necessarily affected what went on in schools and classrooms. With little question, the widespread use of the new digital media is already bringing about comparable changes in educational practices and will bring about more dramatic ones in the future.

In a recent book, *Five Minds for the Future* (Gardner 2007a), I substituted the hat of the policy maker for the expected test-and-task paraphernalia of the psychologist. I called for the development—in school and in the workplace—of five distinct human faculties: the disciplined mind; the synthesizing mind; the creating mind; the respectful mind; and the ethical mind. I described each kind of mind, why it was important, how it could be cultivated, and ways in which it could be misunderstood or misapplied.

Writing as a policy maker is quite different from writing as a psychologist. When giving an exposition of multiple intelligences, I was making a statement about how the world—or, more precisely, how the mind/the mental world—can best be described. I adduced whatever evidence was available to support the pluralistic view that I was advocating. And I laid open the possibility that future research might uncover other kinds of intelligence, configure the boundaries among intelligences in new ways, or reveal confusions or misstatements that needed to be corrected. And indeed, over a twenty-year period, each of these possibilities has been realized.

In writing about five minds for the future, on the other hand, I began with my own analysis of what the world is like today and the epochal ways in which it is changing. I chose to focus on the factors of globalization, though I could have written as well with respect to technological or economic or epistemological changes. In this focus, I was clearly influenced by my experiences in working with Courtney Ross and in observing how the three Ross Schools have evolved in the first decade of this century.

Given my concern with the forces of globalization, I nominated five minds as being especially precious going forward. I would defend these five minds as reasonably important ones, minds that clearly merit cultivation. But I would not in any way assert that they are uniquely privileged. I could as well have written about the consumer mind, the technological mind, the digital mind, the empathic mind, the global mind, or any of a large number of possibilities. No empirical evidence could prove that my list was better or worse than others or that my predictions were more or less accurate than others. All I could say was this: I hope that, at the end of the day, the picture I've drawn about possible minds seems reasonable and that my educational suggestions prove helpful to persons who consider them in good faith.

Of course, when one writes as a policy maker, one entertains at least a faint hope that one's examples and arguments will be appealing to policy makers. In truth, it is too soon to know whether a significant number of persons involved in policy, either in the United States or abroad, will take these recommendations to heart. But already, from both business audiences and educational audiences, I have encountered what might be termed the quintessential American question—How does one assess these various minds?

The Issue of Assessment: Multiple Intelligences

As a psychologist, I certainly understand and have some sympathy with the impulse to create measures of the multiple intelligences. And indeed, shortly after MI theory was announced, I myself succumbed to the temptation to do so. In Project Spectrum (Gardner et al. 1998), working with several colleagues, I developed measures of task performances that were, by argument, related to each of the intelligences. The measures probed how preschool children create music, build with blocks, tell stories, play board games, examine specimens from nature, role-play, recreate the large classroom through block play, and various other skills. Rather than bringing the children to the measures, we created a child-friendly environment—one resembling a children's museum—and observed the children carefully over the course of a year. We believe that through such observations it is possible to identify the intelligences that the child favors as well as the ones in which the child's skills develop most rapidly and most deeply.

From the experience with Project Spectrum, I drew a number of conclusions. First of all, measures of intelligences should be as "user friendly" as possible. Optimally one watches the intelligences at work, or at play, in a comfortable and natural environment. Second, the measures should tap the child's developing cognitive capacities with the materials in question and not simply chronicle what the child likes to do. Third, any measure of intelligences is necessarily partial and tentative; the profile of intelligences clearly changes over time. Relatedly, and optimally, one should assess the child's intelligences through a number of complementary measures, rather than putting all of one's measurement eggs in one basket. Indeed, I came to the conclusion that the development of reliable and valid measures of the multiple intelligences for any age group would be a multi-million-dollar enterprise taking place over a number of years. While I hoped that someone would undertake this task, I did not myself wish to do so.

Of course, Project Spectrum is not the only entry in the MI assessment derby. If you travel to the Web, you will find any number of putative measures of the multiple intelligences. One psychologist, Branton Shearer, has devoted the better part of two decades toward perfecting a measure that he calls the Multiple Intelligences Developmental Assessment Scales (MIDAS).

In examining these measures I always make two points. First of all, the measures should be "intelligence fair"—that is, they should look directly at the intelligence, rather than examining it through linguistic or other lenses. Personal testimony is fine, but it is not a substitute for a measure of the ability in question. Second, a portrait of a person's intelligence is probably most reliable if it includes testimony from those who know the person best.

In this context, the best measures of MI that I've seen come from an unexpected source and were developed without input from me. The Explorama at Danfoss Universe, a theme park in southwestern Denmark, includes several dozen games and tasks that can be engaged by individuals ranging in age from five to eighty. These tasks actually do call on a full range of intelligences. Any person who spends a day or so at the Explorama will learn a great deal about his or her absolute and relative strengths and weaknesses. An especially ingenious aspect of the Explorama is the provision of a digital "personal assistant" that asks one to predict one's own performances on the diverse tasks. A comparison of predictions with actual accomplishments turns out to be an unobtrusive yet elegant measure of intrapersonal intelligence (Gardner 2006).

The Issue of Assessment: Minds for the Future

Once the five minds for the future had been delineated, I was asked about how one could measure these intelligences and how one could enhance them. My friend and colleague Charles Handy suggested to me that one could train disciplinary, synthesizing, and respectful minds. In contrast, he suggested, one must "select" for creativity and ethics—by the time that one fashions measurements for these capacities, it is too late to do much with an individual who is uncreative or unethical.

To proceed in order, the disciplined mind is the easiest to assess. That is because we already have reasonable measures of how individuals fare with the various scholarly disciplines and with the areas (professions, arts, crafts) in which individuals can achieve expertise. It is important that these measures be kept up to date and that they focus on actual disciplinary thinking, rather than on facts and figures, which are, strictly speaking, nondisciplinary.

Because we (as educators and as psychometricians) have not thought much about the skill of synthesizing, effective measures do not yet exist. But I do not think that they would be unduly difficult to devise. The important factor is a delineation of what makes for a good synthesis for the purpose at hand. And so, for example, a synthesis should not be too far-reaching or too narrow; it should meet the standards of experts but be understandable by motivated laypersons. It should draw on the most reliable and comprehensive sources and arrange them in a way that makes sense both to the synthesizer and to his or her chosen audience. As we develop effective ways of teaching synthesis, I fully expect that we will have adequate ways of assessing this increasingly indispensable skill.

While disciplinary and synthesizing skills can be taught, I am skeptical that creativity can be taught in a didactic way. Indeed, I've often remarked that it is easier to thwart creativity—for example, by punishing risk taking or by insisting that there is always a single right answer—than to teach it. That said, without question, certain educational and work situations are more likely than others to allow for or even foster creativity. Open-ended questions, encouragement of brainstorming, sanctioning of risk taking, and permission to fail are all the marks of a creativity-engendering environment.

To be sure, it is possible to identify "little C" creativity—those small changes that occur regularly in a domain. However, history teaches us that major instances of creativity are often rejected out of hand when first propounded. In the end, we can decide on legitimate creative advances only after they have exerted recognizable effects on the domain in question—and this process can take decades. Hence, while assessment of modest degrees of creativity may be possible, assessment of middle or capital C creativity may be elusive.

I think that respect in an environment is readily assessed, even if not subject to quantitative measurement. The assessor observes how individuals treat one another, especially how those in power treat those with less authority, how peers treat one another, and how a stranger is treated (I am always suspicious when too much of a fuss is made over a visitor, such as myself; a truly respectful environment does not make sharp distinctions among people on the basis of their presumed status.) This is not to say, however, that an environment of respect is easy to set up. The temptations to evince disrespect, intolerance, respect tied to too many conditions, and the lamentable tendency to "kiss up and kick down" are ubiquitous.

No mind is more important in our era than the ethical mind. It is vital that, as workers and citizens, we strive to do the responsible, right thing, even when it goes against our self-interest. (Of course, it is not hard to do the right thing when it happens to coincide with our own selfish desires.) As we have had ample opportunities to observe in recent years, a society cannot function well if workers do not honor the norms of their profession or if citizens do not take their responsibilities seriously and serve only themselves.

When it comes to ethics, some quantitative measures exist—how many suspensions for cheating, how many censures or losses of license as a result of unethical conduct, proportion of people voting and how informed these voters are. However, the ethical fiber of a group, institution, or community transcends these numerical indices. In the last analysis, informed and sympathetic observers, using all of the tools at their disposal, are best placed to render judgments of ethical fiber. Our studies of "responsibility at work" suggest some of the dimensions to which an ethical inspectorate ought to be sensitive (Gardner 2007b).

From the discussion of multiple intelligences and minds of the future, my perspective on assessment emerges. In no way am I an opponent of assessment. Indeed, in my own work, and in the work of my associates, students, and children, I consider regular, deeply critical assessment to be essential. Yet at the same time I have little admiration for much of what passes as assessment in our schools or at the workplace. All too often, even routinely, we bring the person to the assessment rather than having the assessment built into the environment of work, study, play, and citizenship. We may gain some leverage in terms of reliability but often lose even more in terms of validity.

And so I tend to prefer assessment made by knowledgeable observers, with much experience under their belts, rather than via the administration of short-answer, easy-to-score examinations. Professionals make complex judgments under conditions of uncertainty, and those educational inspectors who are professionals should proceed in similar fashion. To be sure, such qualitative assessments will be more expensive, and inspectors may sometimes have sharply different views (which, in their own way, can prove quite instructive). Under these circumstances at least the assessment is focused on the right dimensions, and, equally important, the assessment itself stands as an example of what is, or should be, valued in the relevant institution.

In the end, there is no escaping questions of value, once one leaves the pristine cloud chamber of the physicist or the petri dish of the biologist. Even if the nature of intelligences themselves can be probed in a disinterested way, once one decides what to assess and how to assess it one has stepped ineluctably into the realm of values. The situation is even more blatant when it comes to positing the minds that will be at a premium in the future. The choice of minds will inevitably entail a value judgment; and the decision whether to evaluate, and how to do so, is inevitably and ineluctably intermeshed with questions of value. For these reasons we should be especially vigilant when individuals—whether scientists, policy makers, or politicians—state educational goals and invoke educational measures as if they were self-evident or beyond question. Whether or not they are deluding themselves, they are certainly deluding those who read or hear their words.

In the schools that she has conceived and developed, Courtney Ross draws on significant educational research; she is a careful consumer of that research and she makes judicious use of it. At the same time, she has no hesitation in laying out her own vision of the kinds of minds that are needed in the future; and she has been able to put forth, with enthusiasm, her conception of how best to achieve these goals. It will take years to determine whether her schools will exert significant impact on education in the United States and abroad. But it is already clear that those enrolled in the schools have had a rare and invaluable opportunity to stimulate their intelligences and prepare their minds for life in an ever more connected and global society.

REFERENCES

Gardner, Howard. 1983/1993. *Frames of mind: The theory of multiple intelligences.* New York: Basic Books.
———. 2006. *Multiple intelligences: New horizons.* New York: Basic Books.
———. 2007a. *Five minds for the future.* Boston: Harvard Business School Press.
———. 2007b. *Responsibility at work.* San Francisco: Jossey-Bass.
Gardner, H., D. H. Feldman, M. Krechevsky, and J. Chen, eds. 1998. *Project Spectrum* [series of curriculum materials]. New York: Teachers College Press.
Herrnstein, Richard, and Charles Murray. 1994. *The bell curve: Intelligence and class structure in American life.* New York: Free Press.
Schaler, Jeffrey A. 2006. *Howard Gardner under fire: The rebel psychologist faces his critics.* Chicago: Open Court.

Part II

The New Science of Engagement

Mind, Brain, and Education in a School Context

4

Mind, Brain, and Education

ANTONIO DAMASIO AND HANNA DAMASIO

From the very beginning of her career as a professional educator, Courtney Ross was alert to the possibility that brain science could make a contribution to how teachers teach and students learn. Education is about enriching and shaping human minds, and it stands to reason that the more we know about the workings of the human mind the better prepared we shall be to understand the complex task of educating. It is just as clear that our knowledge of the human mind has gained substantially from what neuroscience tells us about the workings of the *mind-making brain.*

In this chapter, we review theoretical and factual advances in neuroscience that we regard as capable of changing our current views of humanity. We suspect that such advances are of considerable interest to educators, and it is our hope that, in time, the new knowledge will be of use to those who, like Courtney Ross, wish to have education deliver all of its promises.

Minds and Brains: Some Unconventional Answers to Traditional Questions

In the simplest of descriptions, minds are sequences of images of different sensory types such as visual, auditory, tactile, somatic, gustatory, and olfactory. Images represent objects, actions, and relationships among objects. Images are the currency of our minds.

Images

It is accurate to say that, at any one time, there are nothing but images in our minds. All of our perceptions—of any object we confront or of any event that is actually happening—are made of images; all of the recollections of objects and events that we retrieve from memory are images as well. The words and sentences one hears are, to begin with, auditory images, and those that we see on a written page are, to begin with, visual images. The feelings of whatever emotion we have—from joy to compassion to admiration—are images too, the only difference being that, in the case of feelings, the images are based on the body itself, as changed by an emotional state, as opposed to being based on an external object or event.

Images are not around merely for the sake of perceiving and recollecting. In order to reason we must play with images in a process appropriately known as imagination. We can let our imagination roam free, undirected by a specific goal, or we can guide our imagination toward the solution of a problem, in the thinking mode that is normally designated as reasoning. Thus all aspects of creativity—whether in the arts, the sciences, technology, or plain human relations—turn out to be a matter of image manipulation. When we are deprived of abundant imagination our creativity dries up.

The Self

Most definitions of mind, including the one offered above, assume that there is an owner and perceiver for that mind, in other words, a subject. Without a subject, which we like to call *self*, there is no way for a mind to know that it exists. Curiously, in our view, selves are also made of images, meaning that selves are composed of the same cloth of which the rest of mind is made. Selves are an *add-on* to the rest of the mind. Whenever we are awake our brains generate not only a plain mind process but also a self, the knower/perceiver/protagonist. That is why a breakdown in the ability to generate images also compromises one of the main ingredients of consciousness. A conscious mind is a plain mind with a self inside.

Brain Maps

The human brain is the indispensable substrate for the human mind. The brain's ability to generate a mind depends on its ability to process sensory stimuli in a chain of events that culminates in making perceptual *maps* of those stimuli. Without the possibility of making maps—for example, of visual patterns, or body patterns, or auditory patterns—it is not possible to generate images. Without mapmaking, minds such as ours would just not occur. In the long history of biological evolution, brains of numerous species have been able to respond adequately to stimuli but have not succeeded in making maps and thus have not generated minds.

We now have a clear sense that the critical anatomical feature required for mapmaking is the cerebral cortex. The brains of species that have only nuclei of neurons but not cerebral cortices do not have minds—we can eat snails, or frog meat, to our heart's content without thinking twice about the creature's mind. Regrettably, most every other animal that we eat did have a mind, however simple, and often even some budding sense of self.

Mind Does Not Mean Consciousness

Curiously, it appears that only a small part of the contents of our minds ever comes to the light of consciousness. In other words, the self process is not powerful enough to illuminate the entire mind. The nonconscious component of our minds is thus far larger than previously conceived and includes not only the classical Freudian unconscious but also a vast cognitive unconscious. A substantial part of our creativity operates nonconsciously, although it requires conscious guidance to achieve its goals. Intriguingly, even some of those guidance systems can become unconscious and steer us in automatic highly skilled behaviors.

What Are Brains and Minds For?

Brains developed in evolution for one particular purpose: *regulating life* in the organism to which they belong, specifically the organism's body-proper that they inhabit. Long before there were organisms with brains, organisms were able to cope with life, but they could not be adventurous outside their small ecological niche. Brains gradually increased the ability of organisms to cope with more and more varied kinds of environments and to adapt more and more efficiently to novel situations. Eventually, humans with the largest and best-equipped brains could roam the earth and adapt successfully to any place on it, even the North Pole.

The history of the evolutionary development of the brain is the history of the appearance of new components capable of the following feat: representing more and more adequately the organism's body-proper and the external world, along with creating more and more detailed and specific memories of the events in which an organism participates. At a very high point in development brains have the ability to make maps with amazingly detailed descriptions of stimuli.

Minds, as we have seen, are the side effect of maps, while consciousness is tied to the emergence of the self and brings on a measure of individual control over the mental proceedings. In turn, the self is responsible for the development of individually and socially oriented reasoning and planning. The ability to navigate our individual future while considering the future of others is a consequence of consciousness. In other words, consciousness is not just about more refined representations of one's self and of one's surroundings; it is also about recording what one represents so that one can make sense of the experience.

In brief, brains exist for optimizing life regulation, and because brains that are optimal life regulators are capable of making maps, brains have given us minds. Consequently, minds are also very much a part of life regulation, all the more so after they are enriched by a self and acquire new capabilities.

How Does the Mind Relate to the Body?

The answer to this question depends on one's perspective. In practical terms, because minds are generated in the brain's cortical maps and because the brain is a part of the body, it is reasonable to say that the mind *is* in the body, that it is a part of the body. But to our subjectivities there appear to be two parallel processes, a mind process and a body process, and it is thus reasonable to accept that illusory intuition and say that mind and body interact continuously, the mind modifying the state of the body and, vice versa, the state of the body modifying that of the mind. Considered in this perspective, the physiology of mind-body relationships is now known in great detail. For example, when a certain object causes us to emote, our endocrine systems and our viscera change their operation and thus change the configuration of the body. But the inverse is equally true: physical fatigue or disease in the body-proper has a powerful influence on the operations of the mind.

Opting to acknowledge two perspectives, that of the mind and that of the body, has a curious cost: one is often labeled "dualistic," for obvious reasons. Nonetheless, the position has nothing whatsoever to do with Descartes' famous (and infamous) dualism. Descartes' actual dualism was about *substance*. He thought that the body, as well as the brain as part of the body, was obviously physical. Both had the property of "extension." But Descartes also thought that the mind did *not* have extension and therefore was not physical at all. For Descartes, body and mind were connected—via a bizarre sort of bridge in the pineal gland—but still separate. The kind of "dualism" we propose here denies Descartes', of course, and is known, for those who care, as *aspect* dualism. It consists simply of a reasonable position that acknowledges our natural habit of imagining minds and bodies as different kinds of phenomena, a position that is more or less acceptable depending on the lens with which one studies the problem. And speaking of lenses, the most famous maker of lenses, Spinoza, was an aspect dualist much as we are but was also a critic of Descartes' substance dualism. Spinoza believed that body and mind were one—he was a *monist* in that sense—but that different perspectives would allow one or the other to be seen. One last comment on this issue: it is quite likely that Descartes did not really believe in the version of dualism he defended and that his was a strategic intellectual position meant to silence or at least placate those who, in time, would crucify Spinoza for his views.

How Do Brains Learn?

On the surface, learning is really simple. Brains and their owners/users learn by changing with experience. But where and how the changes take place is not so easy to explain. Let us try: brains are made of billions of neurons, organized in circuits. The essence of a circuit is the contact that two neurons make with each other via a synapse, a contact that is the result of an electrochemical process. Specifically, the passage of a natural electric current down the neuron's axon causes the release of molecules of certain neurotransmitters.

There are literally trillions of synapses in the human brain, and everything we associate with the mind—learning, memory, emotions and feelings, perceptions, reasoning, communication, and so forth—is a result of circuit activity that consists of certain patterns of neurons firing along certain sequences across certain synapses. The change on which learning is based is achieved by making certain neuron "pathways" easier to travel: in other words, by facilitating the synaptic firing along the pathway. It does not matter what we learn—a new face, a new place, a new name, a new melody, or a new skill. Learning always consists of specific synaptic facilitations induced by our individual experiences—what we sense or hear, what we feel. The brain's inclination for change is usually referred to as *plasticity*, a good descriptor of the ability to remodel circuitry as our life unfolds.

Certain regions of the brain contain systems dedicated to learning. The hippocampal system, located in the temporal lobe, is dedicated to the learning of *facts*. The cerebellum and the basal ganglia, both of which are located under the cerebral cortex, form a system that is dedicated to the learning of skills.

It is reasonable to say that education could not take place if brains were not plastic and thus were not receptive to the modifications experience induces. But it is just as important to note that brains are as plastic and receptive to good lessons as to bad. We must make certain that brains are physically healthy so that they can maintain plasticity, since the brain's plasticity is easily affected by physical conditions—learning is compromised by changes in nutrition as well as physical diseases. We should realize, however, that physical health is only part of the challenge for an effective educational environment. Learning is also compromised by anxiety and distraction and by a host of psychiatric conditions.

Curiously, plasticity continues unabated throughout individual existence and is diminished only late in life when certain diseases that affect learning systems wreak havoc on the brain. Alzheimer's disease is the best-known example. When we leave aside such tragic exceptions, however, all we can do is marvel at the brain's eagerness to receive, change, and continue to learn. Talk about lifelong education is not empty talk at all.

What Is the Role of Emotion in Human Behavior?

Long before brains could support overt reasoning based on conscious deliberation, emotions provided intelligent life-saving decisions for many living species. They still do, not only in those simpler species but in ours too. Just because we can and should make conscious decisions based on knowledge and logic does not mean that our brains have left behind the intricate machinery of emotions that carried us so successfully along the path of biological and cultural evolution. We use emotions and the devices that underpin them every day of our lives, frequently as a helping hand in the conscious decision-making process and just as often to orient our behaviors and enrich our humanity. Creativity is not conceivable without emotion. Neither is moral behavior. As for education, it is difficult to imagine how it could proceed without two of the leading consequences of emotion: *engagement* and *attention*.

The brain uses emotional processes to identify salient features of the environment that are especially relevant to the management of life. Over the long history of evolution some of these features have had to do with the basics of survival of the individual and of the species—identification of energy products, threats, and opportunities. But as cultures developed, many of the objects and events in our day-to-day lives have become associated with salient survival features and have become salient themselves. One of the consequences of our robust cultural life is the growing list of such features, from those that have to do with particular human behaviors to those that deal with human depictions in the arts and entertainment. The upshot of this situation is that the setting and manner in which teaching occurs will determine whether the student will be engaged and will attend to the material being presented in a way that can result in learning (see Suárez-Orozco, Sattin-Bajaj, and Suárez-Orozco, this volume).

Overlooking the role that emotion and the related salient features play in engagement and attention is a serious problem for the culture in general and for education in particular. Neuroscience is now providing us with a detailed view of how such processes operate, and we hope that soon many of the new findings will find their way into practical applications in education.

The importance of emotion in education is not confined to its role in engagement and attention. The role that emotions play in the construction of moral behavior and, by extension, building a citizen is just as important. The conventions and rules that constitute ethical codes and that are used by justice systems are the products of the most refined human reason. They are not spontaneous; rather, they are the result of the concerted efforts of civilizations. Those conventions and rules become the ultimate controllers of the less than optimal aspects of our brain's spontaneous behavioral repertoires. Curiously, however, those same brains contain abundant evolutionary knowledge that expresses itself in certain kinds of emotion without which the edifices of ethics and law could not have been built. In other words, efforts to cultivate civilizations do not evolve in a vacuum; they are grounded in powerful precursor processes. These particular emotions are forerunners of behavioral strategies that eventually become moral programs in the true sense of the word. David Hume was well aware of the existence of these precursors in human nature, as was Adam Smith when he talked about "moral sentiments." The Scottish Enlightenment could not have been more prescient.

Today, neuroscience is revealing with welcome detail the brain correlates of moral situations. For example, we have just been able to show how the individual brain works when it is experiencing compassion for the predicaments of others, or when it experiences admiration for the virtues and virtuosity of others. Such emotions and feelings, which are so often conceived as recent additions to the mind repertoire brought about by education within a culture, reveal instead an astounding depth of recruitment of brain function that in no way suggests a recent or superficial addition to humanity. Feeling admiration or compassion recruits the depths of the life-regulating brain and creates an upheaval in the body not different in scale from the physiological disturbance caused by fear, sadness, or joy.

The great news, then, is that our brains come to life equipped with the potential to respond to moral challenges, capable of reacting not just with reproachable behaviors but also with behaviors that are best described as good and beautiful and capable, in brief, of seeding goodness and beauty in the world. And that is precisely the point at which education, informed by all of these potentialities, must take over. Education can guarantee that the morally positive emotional impulses are focused and strengthened and thus make certain that they do become commendable moral behaviors guided by a conscious mind.

Some Future Challenges

In the years ahead neuroscience will tackle an important question that educators already face: What is the effect of modern technology in the formative mind?

Children are now growing up in a digital age, one in which information is just as frequently presented in virtual form as it is via traditional "real" objects. News and events, history and biology, mathematics and physics all arrive in the growing brain, in no small part, via the agency of screens. What is the effect of such abundant *virtuality* in the human brain and its mind? We simply do not know.

The advantages of virtuality are obvious, from the wealth of available educational materials to, for example, the ease of standardization of presentations across an educational system. But whether the advantages of the glacial screen interface will be accompanied by problematic elements that undermine some of the benefits remains to be established.

Two other traits of the digital age—speed of delivery of contents and the multiplexing of contents within the same time windows—usually receive notice and praise, for obvious reasons. But once again we have no clue about the full range of effects of these features. The ability to multitask appears most welcome and might translate into faster problem-solving skills. But does it? And does the speed of processing and divided attention result in better or worse retention of the contents to be learned? Does it stifle creativity or does it enhance it? Also, what does a sheer increase in processing speed do to processes that, given their biological constraints, are slower, as in the case of certain emotions—relative to freer and faster cognitive processes?

Much-needed research will answer these and related questions and assist educators with the expertise required to enhance the educational value of the new technologies while minimizing the possible disadvantages. But let us make no mistake: we should be grateful for the new opportunities afforded by technical progress and be ready to take judicious advantage of the new possibilities.

5

Research Schools

*Connecting Research and
Practice at the Ross School*

CHRISTINA HINTON AND KURT W. FISCHER

At a typical research conference, Sophie would be tucked neatly into a PowerPoint presentation: underachiever. This description is cold, calm, wrapped in tidy numbers and politically correct phrases. An underachiever is a negative outcome from an equation of risk factors. She does not have a scar on her left knee from the time she fell off the monkey bars. She does not twirl her coffee-colored hair with her pencil when she is lost in a thought. She does not find a friend with tears in her eyes and make silly faces until they both break into an uncontrollable gale of giggles. Most education research treats students, like Sophie, as objects to be manipulated. As Kohn (1999) notes, "Some social scientists specializing in education may as well be crunching numbers about *E. coli* or the electromagnetic spectrum" (25). Education is not about *E. coli*, or outcomes and risk factors: it is about people. Where is the voice of the people in schools in education research? The education system currently relies on a top-down structure whereby researchers write recommendations for policy makers, who impose them on administrators, practitioners, and students. We need to reform this system to involve teachers, students, and administrators as partners in shaping education research and policy.

In most successful sectors of American industry and government, researchers collaborate with practitioners to test theory in practice and adjust research-based developments accordingly. In medicine, researchers work with doctors to refine newly developed medications and procedures through hospital testing. In agriculture, researchers partner with farmers to improve new seeds, equipment, and farming methods through field tests. In traffic safety, meteorology, cosmetics, in field after field, practitioners provide practical results that inform research-based developments. In education, however, there is little sustained interaction between researchers and practitioners, leaving many researchers trapped in an ivory tower of statistical significance, PowerPoint presentations, and academic jargon that is far removed from the smaller, more intimate world of pencils, monkey bars, and giggles.

Researchers should partner with practitioners, students, and administrators to test educational theory in practice. Theory becomes more sophisticated and differentiated when refracted through the complex and dynamic classroom. A method of reading instruction, for example, takes a very different shape in the pristine abstractions of a researcher's mind than when tangled in a classroom of tiny quarrels, waving hands, and two little boys who are taking turns wiggling their ears. Putting theory into practice in the messy classroom provides invaluable feedback for fine-tuning theoretical models and shaping practice. For example, classroom results have revealed that phonologically based interventions are effective for some children with dyslexia but not others. This result has guided researchers to a more nuanced understanding of dyslexia and more effective intervention techniques (Fischer, Bernstein, and Immordino-Yang 2007; Wolf and Bowers 1999). Researchers and practitioners should use formative assessment to continually shape theory and practice throughout the learning process (Lesser 1974; Organization for Economic Cooperation and Development [OECD] 2005).

Recent changes in the landscape of research on learning augment the need for sustained collaboration between researchers and practitioners (Hinton and Fischer 2008). Powerful new brain-imaging tools, breakthroughs in genetics, and innovative cognitive methods have brought biology and cognitive science to the center of research on learning (Fischer, Immordino-Yang, and Waber 2007; Hinton, Miyamoto, and della-Chiesa 2008; OECD 2007; Stern 2005). There is tremendous potential for this new research to improve education, but working across disciplines brings new challenges as well as new opportunities. Biology and cognitive science have deeply rooted disciplinary cultures with field-specific language and methods, which makes integrating this new research on learning with pedagogy especially challenging. A reciprocal interaction between research and practice is needed now more than ever to ensure that research from this emerging field of mind, brain, and education will actualize as improved learning in classrooms.

Research schools support sustainable collaboration between researchers and practitioners. Research schools are living laboratories where researchers work alongside practitioners to train educators, carry out research, and disseminate findings. Research schools partner with a university to field-test theory in vivo and disseminate practical results to other schools, universities, and policy agencies. In this way, they bring the voice of the people in schools into the world of education research and policy. The Harvard Graduate School of Education and the Ross School are building one of the first research school partnerships.

Mind, Brain, and Education

The emerging field of mind, brain, and education is poised to make seminal advances in human development and learning (Fischer, Immordino-Yang, and Waber 2007; Fischer, Daniel, et al. 2007; Hinton, Miyamoto, and della-Chiesa 2008; Stern 2005).[1] Education research traditionally correlates policies and practices with learning outcomes, leaving underlying processes in a "black box" (OECD 2007). Biology and cognitive science enable researchers to peer into the "black box," uncovering underlying learning processes and providing fuller causal explanations. For example, education research has established that most dyslexic students have difficulty analyzing the sounds of words (Fischer, Bernstein, and Immordino-Yang 2007; Wolf 2007). Many of these students can learn to read through different learning pathways that recruit distinctive processes but still demonstrate lower-level sound analysis difficulties (Fink 2006). Biological and cognitive research has helped explain how this pattern of strengths and weaknesses emerges through differences in genetics and corresponding brain processes (Haworth et al. 2007).

By mapping out underlying learning processes and causal relationships, mind, brain, and education research supports more effective and inclusive instruction. With a scientific understanding of underlying learning processes, educators can target instruction more effectively. Understanding causal mechanisms also helps researchers delineate many possible developmental pathways for learning, which enables educators to differentiate instruction to accommodate a wider range of individual differences. For example, as researchers identify biological and cognitive underpinnings of dyslexia and devise targeted interventions, educators become able to guide children with dyslexia along alternative developmental pathways for learning to read (Fischer, Bernstein, and Immordino-Yang 2007).

To ensure that mind, brain, and education research are integrated into practice, we need to overcome challenges of working in a transdisciplinary field (Hinton and Fischer 2008). Biology, cognitive science, and education each have deeply rooted disciplinary cultures, language, and methods that make it difficult for experts in different fields to collaborate. There is a lack of consensus about the meaning of even fundamental terms, such as learning, and methodological tools of measurement are not yet aligned across fields. Scientists working in laboratories are unplugged from the world of educational policies, school cultures, and student differences. As a result, they often carry out research with limited practical relevance (OECD 2007).

On the other side, educators are often unable to understand implications of scientific results and are susceptible to false ideas allegedly based on science (Goswami 2006; OECD 2007; Pickering and Howard-Jones 2007). It is difficult for nonexperts to understand the subtleties of a study's findings, conclusions, and implications. Moreover, grounding ideas in neuroscience and using brain images or explanations make educators more likely to believe the ideas, which has led many commercial and political organizations to promote their ideas about learning as brain-based even when there is no neuroscience research to support their claims (McCabe and Castel 2008; Weisberg et al. 2008). Without a background understanding of biology and cognitive science, educators are unable to distinguish these neuromyths from sound neuroscience. Collaboration between researchers and practitioners is needed to help educators understand scientific findings and steer researchers toward questions that are relevant to educational practice. Continued transdisciplinary progress therefore requires a reciprocal relationship between research on learning and education practice (Fischer, Daniel, et al. 2007; Hinton and Fischer 2008; Schwartz and Gerlach, forthcoming; Shonkoff and Phillips 2000). In this dynamic relationship, research informs practice, and classroom results shape research directions.

To support these kinds of interactions and ensure a strong research base, education needs to build an infrastructure that supports sustainable collaboration between researchers and practitioners. The nucleus of the lasting collaboration between researchers and practitioners in medicine is the teaching hospital. Teaching hospitals partner with a medical school to carry out research and train young professionals. Many of the advances that begin in laboratories of medical schools or biology departments are incorporated into patient care through clinical research programs at teaching hospitals. These hospitals also provide a hands-on classroom for physicians, nurses, and other health professionals. Education needs analogous institutions— research schools—that partner with a university to train educators, carry out research, and disseminate findings (Chen 2010; Dewey 1938; Hinton and Fischer 2008; Hinton 2008; Schwartz and Gerlach, forthcoming).

The Laboratory School

Research schools are rooted in the tradition of Dewey's (1896) laboratory school. Dewey (1939) was discontent with "pure theorizing" (27), detached from practical experience. He believed that educational theory must be tested by its consequences in a living school (Dewey 1938; Mayhew and Edwards 1965; Tanner 1997). Theory is incomplete until it is enacted in the lives of people in schools. Constructivism, for example, is lifeless, locked in an academic journal on the third floor of a graduate school library. This principle comes alive when a child's bewilderment that a wooden block floats in water leads him to run eagerly about the classroom collecting other objects to test, and he begins to build a theory of density. Dewey understood that practical application brings theory to life and provides crucial feedback for developing theoretical models and shaping practice.

In Dewey's time, researchers faced challenges of working across the fields of developmental psychology and education comparable to those that researchers in mind, brain, and education face today. Psychology and child development were blossoming as new fields, providing important insights into how children learn. However, integrating these new findings into pedagogy proved difficult, and many practices in schools were at odds with this new research. As head of the Department of Philosophy, Psychology, and Pedagogy at the University of Chicago, Dewey had both a rich understanding of developmental psychology and close ties with schools. With this dual perspective, he saw firsthand the discrepancies between research and practice (Dykhuizen 1973).

In reaction, Dewey founded the laboratory school at the University of Chicago to align research and practice. The laboratory school was both a school for children and a laboratory for practical testing of theoretical models. As a laboratory, the school had the same relationship to developmental psychology as a teaching hospital has to biology or chemistry—it was a place for putting theory into practice in an experimental setting to deepen understanding. Dewey (1899) wrote: "It is a laboratory of applied psychology. That is, it is a place for the study of mind as manifested and developed in the child, and for the search after materials and agencies that seem most likely to fulfill and further the condition of normal growth" (96). Inquiry was at the heart of the school's culture. Researchers worked with practitioners to test and modify methods and to adjust theory and practice on the basis of experience. In this way, the school grounded research in practice and vice versa.

The laboratory school made important contributions to education. Many of Dewey's theories were generated from his work at the school. Two of his most important works on education, *Democracy and Education* (1916) and *How We Think* (1910), came out of his work with administrators, teachers, and students at the school. Perhaps the most important contribution of the school was the principle that research should be intimately connected to practice, with researchers working side by side with practitioners. As Dewey (1899) expressed, the school "stood for the necessity of considering education both theoretically and practically" (97).

Unfortunately, the laboratory school concept did not persist as Dewey envisioned. Many universities and colleges have schools on campus for the children of faculty and students, but most of those schools are not involved in research and play virtually no role in connecting research and practice. As Tyler (1991) explains: "Most schools and colleges of education that have elementary or secondary schools have continued to employ their schools as the sites for practice teaching, or superior schools for faculty children and the children of other families nearby, but not as laboratories for the serious study of children's learning" (1–2). Educators need to reconnect with Dewey's laboratory school concept and extend it to create research schools that support sustainable connections among research, practice, and policy in education.

The Research School Model

We are still confronted with the same problem that Dewey faced over a century ago—much new research on learning is not embodied in the practices of people in schools. Mind, brain, and education research is generating powerful new insights into how we learn, but without a reciprocal relationship between research and practice, much of this research remains detached from learning in schools. Research schools join researchers and practitioners in living, community-based schools to integrate theory and practice. The research school model has three main components: training, research, and dissemination.

The research school model builds on Dewey's laboratory school concept and extends it to create an infrastructure that supports sustainable connections among research, practice, and policy. Like the laboratory school, research schools are based on the premise that educational theory is incomplete until it takes shape in the daily lives of people in schools. Dewey's laboratory school succeeded for a short time in creating a reciprocal interaction

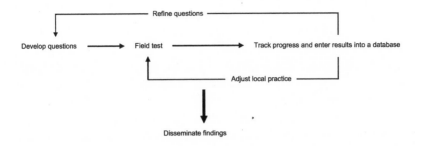

Figure 5.1. Research process at a research school.

between research and practice at the school. Research schools aim to support sustainable integration of research, practice, and policy at the level of the education system. Research schools partner with a university and build a community that views training, research, and dissemination as fundamental aspects of the school's activity. The school provides hands-on training for researchers, teachers, students, and administrators. Researchers learn to work in schools as scholars-in-residence who train practitioners in action research methods, connect them with recent research on learning, and collaborate with them to develop research methods and questions that are both feasible and useful in practice. Practitioners hone their teaching skills, gain experience shaping research, learn how to integrate formative assessment into their practice, and acquire strategies for collecting classroom data, such as journaling and descriptive reviews (Cochran-Smith and Lytle 1993). Students learn to work with researchers and teachers to track their own learning, develop their metacognitive skills (OECD 2005; Schoenfeld 1987), and participate in shaping research questions (Kuriloff et al., forthcoming). Administrators learn a variety of dissemination techniques.

Researchers work with administrators, teachers, and students to carry out research that is relevant to practice. The research process involves developing questions, field-testing innovative techniques, entering results into a database, using classroom results to refine research directions and adjust local practice, and disseminating findings (figure 5.1). Researchers and practitioners collaborate in a cyclic process to integrate theory and practice. They develop theoretical models, implement practices based on these models, work with students to systematically track progress, adjust models to reflect classroom results, implement practices based on revised models, and so forth. Researchers, teachers, and students continue this cyclic process for each theoretical model until it is aligned with classroom results. Researchers then work with administrators to disseminate findings to other schools, universities, or policy agencies.

Dissemination is a key aspect of the research school model. Researchers communicate results with the research community through traditional academic routes, such as journals, books, and conferences. Select research schools also use these techniques to disseminate findings to policy agencies. Researchers work with administrators to build usable knowledge and share information with other schools through professional development workshops, Web sites, magazines, or other means.

Partnership of the Harvard Graduate School of Education and the Ross School

Everyone who has worked with children is familiar with the charm of run-on sentences: "I saw a giraffe, and his neck was so long that it reached the tippy-top of the trees, and I tried really, really hard to get his attention by waving my hands like this, and then he looked *right* at me and . . ." and the child continues to tack on the "ands" and "and thens" in a breathless stream of excitement. Run-on sentences capture the energy of the Ross School. Like run-on sentences, the Ross School seems to gain momentum as it continuously evolves. With vibrancy and flexibility, the school continually adapts to reflect new research on learning.

This culture of openness makes the Ross School an ideal place to build a research school. The research school model cannot be implemented in a school that is shackled by tradition. As Dewey (1899) expressed, an experimental school requires "conditions that will enable the educational practice indicated by the inquiry to be sincerely acted upon, without the distortion and suppression arising from undue dependence upon tradition and preconceived notions" (98). Researchers at Harvard Graduate School of Education found these conditions at the Ross School and quickly joined with Courtney Ross and the Ross School faculty and students to form a partnership.

The Harvard Graduate School of Education is working with the Ross School to build a model research school. The Ross Institute, the research and training arm of the Ross School, is forming a community of scholars-in-residence, administrators, and teachers that collaborate in training, research, and dissemination. The Harvard Graduate School of Education and the Ross School are building a training partnership. Faculty and graduate students from the Harvard Graduate School of Education come to the Ross School as scholars-in-residence and hold professional development workshops that connect Ross School faculty with recent research in mind, brain and education. Simultaneously, Ross School faculty and students teach researchers about learning and pedagogy at the school.

The Harvard Graduate School of Education and the Ross School are conducting research at the school. Researchers are working with the school to systematize existing assessments and develop new assessments for analyzing learning pathways in the schools' innovative spiral cultural history curriculum. For example, they have mapped out learning pathways for the development of global consciousness in Ross School students and alumni. They are also developing and assessing a curricular thread on the brain that integrates psychology, self, and culture. Data from these assessments will be entered into a database to document progress and identify best practices. Researchers are working with administrators, teachers, and students to frame new research questions. Recently, Harvard Graduate School of Education researchers and Ross School faculty have partnered to create a new Ross School course that involves students in action research at the school.

Researchers and Ross School faculty are beginning to coordinate dissemination efforts as well. The Harvard Graduate School of Education has worked with the International Mind, Brain and Education Society (IMBES) to create several mechanisms for disseminating new research in mind, brain and education to other researchers, schools, and policy agencies, including the *Mind, Brain, and Education* journal, the IMBES biannual conference, and the Usable Knowledge Web site (www.uknow.gse.harvard.edu). Multiple means of dissemination are used to span research, practice, and policy. The Harvard Graduate School of Education and the Ross School aim to bring the voice of people in schools into education research and policy, transforming students like Sophie from bundles of stale academic jargon to dynamic, creative partners in education research.

Education needs an infrastructure that connects research, practice, and policy to ensure that new research on learning is integrated into the work of people in schools. As living laboratories that join researchers and practitioners in training, research, and dissemination, research schools will provide a hub to connect research, practice, and policy. Research schools involve practitioners as partners in education research, which provides invaluable feedback for refining theoretical models and educational practices and gives the people in schools a voice in shaping education. In this way, research schools can transform education from a system that is too often ideological and hierarchical to one that is evidence-based and fundamentally democratic.

NOTE

1. This section draws on Hinton and Fischer (2008).

REFERENCES

Chen, D. 2010. Schooling as a knowledge system: Lessons from Cramim Experimental School. *Mind, Brain, and Education* 4:1–12.

Cochran-Smith, Marilyn, and Susan L. Lytle. 1993. *Inside/outside: Teacher research and knowledge.* New York: Teachers College Press.

Dewey, John. 1896. The university school. *University Record (University of Chicago)* 1:417–19.

———. 1899. *The school and society.* Chicago: University of Chicago Press.

———. 1910. *How we think.* Boston: D. C. Heath.

———. 1916. *Democracy and education.* New York: Macmillan.

———. 1938. *Experience and education.* New York: Kappa Delta Pi.

———. 1939. Biography of John Dewey. In *The philosophy of John Dewey,* ed. P. A. Schilpp. New York: Tudor.

Dykhuizen, George. 1973. *The life and mind of John Dewey.* Carbondale: Southern Illinois University Press.

Fink, Rosalie P. 2006. *Why Jane and Johnny couldn't read—and how they learned.* Newark, DE: International Reading Association.

Fischer, K. W., J. H. Bernstein, and M. H. Immordino Yang, eds. 2007. *Mind, brain, and education in reading disorders.* Cambridge: Cambridge University Press.

Fischer, K. W., D. Daniel, M. H. Immordino-Yang, E. Stern, A. Battro, and H. Koizumi. 2007. Why mind, brain and education? Why now? *Mind, Brain, and Education* 1:1–2.

Fischer, K. W., M. H. Immordino-Yang, and D. P. Waber. 2007. Toward a grounded synthesis of mind, brain, and education for reading disorders: An introduction to the field and this book. In *Mind, brain, and education in reading disorders,* ed. K. W. Fischer, J. H. Bernstein, and M. H. Immordino-Yang. Cambridge: Cambridge University Press.

Goswami, U. 2006. Neuroscience and education: From research to practice. *Nature Reviews Neuroscience* 7:2–7.

Haworth, C. M. A., E. L. Meaburn, N. Harlaar, and R. Plomin. 2007. Reading and generalist genes. *Mind, Brain, and Education* 1:173–80.

Hinton, Christina. 2008. From lipstick to learning: Research goes to school. Harvard Graduate School of Education, "Usable Knowledge." Retrieved June 3, 2008, from www.uknow.gse.harvard.edu/decisions/DD308-408.html.

Hinton, Christina, and Kurt W. Fischer. 2008. Research schools: Grounding research in educational practice. *Mind, Brain and Education* 2:157–60.

Hinton, Christina, K. Miyamoto, and B. della-Chiesa. 2008. Brain research, learning and emotions: Implications for education research, policy and practice. *European Journal of Education* 43 (1): 87–103.

Kohn, Alfie. 1999. *The schools our children deserve: Moving beyond traditional classrooms and "tougher standards."* Boston: Houghton Mifflin.

Kuriloff, P., M. Richert, B. Stoudt, and S. Ravitch. Forthcoming. Building research collaboratives among schools and universities: Lessons from the field. *Mind, Brain, and Education.*

Lesser, Gerald S. 1974. *Children and television: Lessons from Sesame Street*. New York: Random House.

Mayhew, Katherine C., and Anna C. Edwards. 1965. *The Dewey School: The laboratory school of the University of Chicago, 1896–1903*. New Brunswick, NJ: Aldine Transaction.

McCabe, D. P., and A. D. Castel. 2008. Seeing is believing: The effect of brain images on judgments of scientific reasoning. *Cognition* 107:343–52.

Organization for Economic Cooperation and Development. 2005. *Formative assessment: Improving learning in secondary classrooms*. Paris: OECD Publishing.

———. 2007. *Understanding the brain: The birth of a learning science*. Paris: OECD Publishing.

Pickering, S. J., and P. Howard-Jones. 2007. Educators' views on the role of neuroscience in education: Findings from a study of UK and international perspectives. *Mind, Brain and Education* 1 (3): 109–13.

Schoenfeld, A. H. 1987. What's all the fuss about metacognition? In *Cognitive science and mathematics education*, ed. A. H. Schoenfeld. Hillsdale, NJ: Lawrence Erlbaum.

Schwartz, M., and J. Gerlach. Forthcoming. The birth of a discipline and the rebirth of the laboratory school for educational philosophy and theory. *Educational Philosophy and Theory*.

Shonkoff, Jack P., and Deborah A. Phillips, eds. 2000. *From neurons to neighborhoods: The science of early childhood development*. Washington, DC: National Academy Press.

Stern, E. 2005. Pedagogy meets neuroscience. *Science* 310:745.

Tanner, Laurel N. 1997. *Dewey's laboratory school: Lessons for today*. New York: Teachers College Press.

Tyler, R. W. 1991. The long-term impact of the Dewey School. Paper presented at the meeting of the John Dewey Society, San Francisco.

Weisberg, D. S., F. C. Keil, J. Goodstein, E. Rawson, and J. R. Gray. 2008. The seductive allure of neuroscience explanations. *Journal of Cognitive Neuroscience* 20:470–77.

Wolf, Maryanne. 2007. *Proust and the squid: The story and science of the reading brain*. New York: Harper.

Wolf, Maryanne, and P. J. Bowers. 1999. The double-deficit hypothesis for the developmental dyslexias. *Journal of Educational Psychology* 91 (3): 415–38.

6

Toward a New Educational Philosophy

HIDEAKI KOIZUMI

Twice, first in 2004 and then in 2006, I spent several days at the Ross School in East Hampton, New York. During my visits, I had the opportunity to observe various classes (from kindergarten through high school), speak with many students, engage in discussions with enthusiastic teachers, and even attend some lectures. A consistent, comprehensive educational vision was evident in each visit. An impressive set of basic principles guides the Ross School vision: the spiral curriculum, which combines the developmental processes of culture and civilization while bridging and fusing art and science to nurture enthusiasm and aspiration. This is a school that instills respect for cultural diversity with the aim of nurturing global-scale understanding and engagement.

This chapter discusses the educational principles of the Ross School from the perspective of brain science, with a focus on the similarities to my research program in Japan.[1] My specialty is physics, and my work is focused on developing various practical applications for the fields of environmental science and mind-brain science through the measurement of atoms and molecules. My work is on the imaging of the human body and the creation of new methodologies to measure the human mind. Specifically, in the field of mind-brain science, I have promoted the development of principles for and practical applications of functional magnetic resonance imaging (fMRI) and near-infrared spectroscopic optical topography (NIRS-OT). In January 1995, the "Trans-disciplinary Symposium on Mind-Brain Science and Its Practical Applications" was held at the Odaira Memorial Hall of Hitachi, Ltd., where we attempted to apply mind-brain science through noninvasive brain-function imaging methods to the fields of education, medical care, information technology (IT), and robotics—fields beyond the framework of industry, government, and academia (Koizumi 1995).

Furthermore, in 1996 I coordinated a four-day international symposium, "Trans-disciplinary Symposium on Global Environment" (see Koizumi 1996a, 1996b), which included a session on the interaction between the brain and the environment (see Koizumi 1996a, 1996b). In 2000, I coordinated the "Trans-disciplinary Symposium: Developing the Brain: The Science of Learning and Education," hosted by the Japan Science and Technology Agency (See Koizumi 1998, 2000). The aforementioned symposia addressed mind-brain science through the previous Science and Technology Agency and addressed education through the previous Ministry of Education, Science and Culture, thereby creating and launching the "Brain Science and Education" research initiative as a symbol of the newly combined entity. In addition, in 2001, Japan's Ministry of Education, Science and Culture and the Japan Science and Technology Agency were combined to create the Ministry of Education, Culture, Sports, Science and Technology.

Since then, under the guidance of Dr. Masao Ito (who was the president of the Science Council of Japan in 2001 and a founding director of the RIKEN Brain Science Institute), my colleagues and I have promoted research in brain science and education and the development of the "Brain Science and Education" initiative as a Japanese government program (Koizumi 2004b, 2008b). In this chapter, I will focus on the educational features of Ross School from the perspective of mind-brain science and the similarities to my research and its applications for education.

The Concept of Spiral Curriculum at Ross School

One of the basic features of the Ross School is its educational system, which features a comprehensive spiral curriculum. Although a spiral is a trajectory of dots moving in 3-D space, the concept employed by the Ross School is not a simple spiral: the cross-section of conceptual dots that forms a spiral consists of flower petals (Gardner and Ross 2003), which represent the many educational subjects (academic, scientific, and artistic fields). The spiral trajectory ascends as human culture and civilization develop. The holistic integrated education provided at Ross progresses along this spiral. The integrated curriculum ensures the development of multidisciplinary understanding. With the integrated curriculum, student talent is nurtured over time to eventually achieve a balance of diverse or multiple intelligences (see Gardner, this volume). The buds of the cross-section at the beginning of the spiral gradually flower along with individual growth and development.

In Courtney Ross's new vision of education, the historical time axis is shortened to a learning time axis (a learning period) in which specific subjects of the curriculum are located in the order in which each discipline emerged in human history. To put it differently, this is an attempt to make human history and our learning process isomorphic. The history of the development of disciplines is essentially a natural growth. Education that follows such a natural flow is a more natural fit for humanity, thereby allowing students to learn without unnatural stress.

Part of the concept of the spiral curriculum was explained in Jerome S. Bruner's (1961) renowned book *The Process of Education*. The book is a summary of the outcome of the historic Woods Hall Conference held in the United States in 1959 and chaired by Bruner. Thirty-four great minds from different disciplines attended the conference and passionately discussed the future of education. Bruner's claim that "any subject can be taught at any time of development maintaining its essence" was the main hypothesis coming out of the discussions.

The academic, scientific, and artistic fields begin with experience (tacit knowledge), which over time moves to a stage of completion (explicit and formal knowledge). A completed structure has pros and cons: it can accelerate learning efficiency, but it tends to become boring, thereby depriving learners of their enthusiasm for or interest in learning. The Ross School is attempting to provide an appropriate balance of movement in both directions—from general to specific (or atypical) and from specific (or atypical) to general.

Mapping the Spiral on a Light Cone

I have been interested in the use of the concept of the spiral as a model of various kinds. The concepts of the spiral and the vortex are connected to the quintessence of physics in various ways. The Celts seemed to have sensed the depth of significance and mystery in a spiral. The Celtic spiral reminds us of cosmic space. I would like to take this opportunity to explain my tentative new concept of the spiral.

Hermann Minkowski's (1864–1909) concepts regarding the relationship of time and space (Minkowski 1908/1964) greatly influenced Albert Einstein (1879–1955)—who attended Minkowski's lectures at the Eidgenössische Polytechnische Schule (later Eidgenössische Technische Hochschule [ETH]) in Zurich, Switzerland (1896–1900)—in forming his initial ideas on the theory of relativity (Einstein 1905/1923, 1916/1997). Minkowski's diagram of a " light cone" makes it easier to intuitively understand the relationship between time and space in the theory of relativity (Penrose 1997). Figure 6.1 (left) shows our attempt to depict a spiral superimposed on the surface of a light cone. Infinitely narrowing the distance between one orbit and another depicted on the cone makes a 360-degree orbit become infinitely akin to a perfect circle. At the same time, the perfect circle is also a cross-section corresponding to one point on the time axis.

To apply the concept of the spiral to education, the contact point of the upper and lower cones—the origin—is set at a point in the past. However, in general, the origin is considered to be the present. Of the three dimensions, one dimension is set on the time axis (T) and the other two are set on a cross-sectional plane as X and Y. With light speed as C, the space axes are expressed as $X = CT$ and $Y = CT$.

For instance, when we view the beautiful starry sky while standing on the summit of a mountain, we are located at the origin of the time axis and the space axis, where the world we are viewing is all past existence. The stars we see in the distance are those that existed long ago—several hundred million years ago. We are also viewing below the summit the beautiful town lights of some microseconds ago, or a past that is very close to the present. If the origin is set at the present, the lower light cone is the past world that eventually converges with the present.

In contrast, the upper light cone designates a point in the future—a society that contains a future "us." Because no phenomenon goes faster than the speed of light, all phenomena exist within a space inside the light cone. Cause-and-effect relationships are also established along the time axis.

Viewed from somewhere on the time axis, the spiral in figure 6.1 converges on a plane. The cross-sections orthogonal with the time axis depict the world at each time "t" along the spiral. We can conceptually express all academic, scientific, and artistic fields on the cross-sectional plane. If we set the time axis around which the spiral trajectory revolves at a long time span, the circular plane formed by the spiral lines next to each other becomes infinitely close to a flat plane. The flower petals that emerged on the cross-section of the spiral in Ross School's concept of the curriculum can be expressed as flower petals spread around the central time axis of the spiral on the light cone.

Figure 6.1 (right) shows the academic and artistic fields existing at a specific time, depicted on the 2-D plane that allows the depiction of interdisciplinary connections. By drawing a straight line from the origin on the

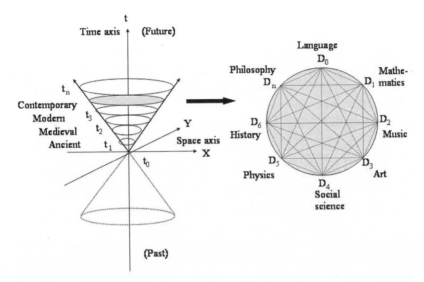

Figure 6.1. *Left:* When the time scale represents human history or an individual generation, a spiral cross-section corresponds to an era or a developmental stage, respectively.
These concepts are isomorphic even though their time scales are far different. The spiral
pathway, denoting education, progresses upward along the axis of historical development
in such a way that ontogeny quickly repeats phylogeny. *Right:* Top view of the cross-
section of the cone, showing various disciplines (D) at a given point in time and their
interconnections. The history of the development of each discipline would be represented
by a straight line extending from the origin of the cone at point t_0 and up the cone's side.

surface of the cone to each specific field, we can represent the history of the
development of each field, the progress of the educational curriculum, and
the improvement of learning results. For instance, the discipline of history,
or the content of historical knowledge to be taught or learned, as this has
developed through time and is continuing to develop, can be depicted as
a straight line from the origin of the cone and up the cone's surface. The
changing discipline or content of math can be depicted in the same way
(see also Abraham, this volume). Furthermore, the concept of "the spiral
on the light cone" can be used to introduce the perspective of "ontogenesis
recapitulating phylogenesis," which will be explained later, and to discuss
an optimal educational curriculum based on the development of a brain-
neurological system.

The Concepts of Phylogeny and Ontogeny

The Japanese kindergartens and child care facilities where I engage in collaborative research include nurseries run by Kimiko Saitō, a child care expert dedicated to the future of children. Her nurseries practice a unique child care method called *Saitō Hoiku* and have experimented with the hierarchical integrated care of disabled and nondisabled children. With phylogeny as a guiding principle, the development of a specific area of the human brain and the outcome of the integration of brain functions that have yet to be neurologically analyzed are gradually being systematized through many experiences (Koizumi 2007b; Saitō and Koizumi 2008).

Historically, Ernst Haeckel's (1834–1919) hypothesis that "ontogenesis repeats phylogenesis" (the embryo and fetus develop by quickly repeating the evolutionary process inside of the mother's womb: e.g., an embryo has a tail by the ape stage) has long created controversy (Gould 1977). Although this hypothesis was once denied, it has received renewed attention because of the recent rapid advancement of molecular biology. The Human Genome Project has revealed about three billion bases of human DNA and approximately twenty-two thousand human genes (initially believed to be over thirty thousand). Recent decoding of the genome of an amphioxus (a lancelet classified in cephalochordates that looks like a small fish but has no eyes and senses light by a small nerve nucleus) revealed approximately five hundred million DNA bases and about 21,600 genes. Whereas the number of bases of an amphioxus is one-sixth of that of a human, the number of genes of an amphioxus is almost the same as a human's. In addition, about half of the genes of an amphioxus are similar to a human's (Putnam et al. 2008).

In principle, physique-related genes that determine the positions of arms and legs as well as organs tend to be the same. A homeobox gene cluster (to code transcription factors that activate the cascading of the gene expression) forms various structures and functions as a subroutine that is preserved in the process of evolution. In fabricating evolutionarily established structural elements, it is the case with ontogenesis as well that forming a living organism as evolution has progressed is more natural than otherwise. This fact suggests a limitation of the spiral model of education based on Bruner's hypothesis. For humans, the fetal period through infancy involves much the same type of ontogenic development as that shown in the process of evolution. Evolution-like development in later periods, however, cannot be ignored. Moreover, any failure, caused by a brain development-related disability, to establish some foundational structures during babyhood and infancy can gravely hamper subsequent learning.

Mind-brain science and education research, including that which focuses on child care and child rearing, become important from this perspective as well. In Japan, the Japan Science and Technology Agency conducted a research and development program, which I directed, in the field of "Brain Science and Society." This program involved brain science-based cohort studies of human development (Japan Children's Study), including neurological studies on infants (led by Zentaro Yamagata, professor at the University of Yamanashi) (Koizumi 2006). In these cohort studies, the mental and physical development of many children born in a certain area is being closely observed over a long period. Such cohort studies, which are also called prospective tracking research of groups of individuals, have multiple precedents in research throughout the world, but ours are the first to be conducted by brain scientists, developmental cognitive neuroscientists, and child neurologists studying brain function. Pilot research is currently being completed on the observation of approximately four hundred children aged three months to three years and about 120 children aged five to eight years. From this, we have obtained a substantial amount of data. Also in progress is a cohort study of twins—the Tokyo Twin Cohort Project (directed by Jyukou Andou, professor of Keio University)—which is observing approximately two thousand pairs of twins (four thousand children) in cooperation with their nurseries (Koizumi 2006).

These studies of development have gradually been clarifying how learning is made possible by the existence of a set of basic brain functions, called "the bootstrap," that are akin to a basic command set read by a PC when it is booted up, and "the scaffold," a tentative foothold for a further structural development of brain functions. Primitive reflexes seen only during early infancy, such as the neonatal smile, the sucking reflex, the walking or stepping reflex, the palmar grasp reflex, the Moro reflex (if the infant's head suddenly shifts position, the arms jerk up, with the palms up and thumbs fanned out; it starts to disappear around two months), and the Babinski reflex (if a foot side is stroked, the toes are fanned out; it fades around the first year of birth), serve as primers for the next stage of functional development (Prechtl 1991). A primitive reflex and a following reflex serve as a bootstrap and/or scaffold. Experienced nurses and therapists have sometimes been able to wake up dormant functions in disabled babies and infants by using such reflexes as a trigger. The persistence, for a long time, of early reflexes that should disappear as children grow is regarded in neonatal medicine and child neurology as an indicator of possible brain disorder.

Our ongoing research reveals possible new methods of child rearing and child care during the fetal period, babyhood, and infancy through early childhood. Biological research on humans that develops in accordance with the process of biological evolution is gradually presenting us with the possibility that a new educational vision will be available for the period around birth. Pursuit of the aforementioned spiral model of education from the perspective of biological evolution will lead to new child care and educational methods.

Scientific Mind and Artistic Mind

Through mind-brain science and education research sponsored by the Japanese government, we have obtained various findings related to education, some of which have caused us to reconsider our thinking on the scientific mind and the artistic mind from the viewpoint of brain science. Our brain reflects the process of evolution. The brain stem—the center of the human brain—looks like the reptilian brain and is responsible for life-supporting systems such as breathing and blood circulation. It is surrounded by the old cortex, or the limbic cortex, in which the instincts and other sources of life reside. The old cortex is surrounded by the new cortex, which evolved rapidly when biological evolution reached primates. The new cortex is where intelligence resides. Sensibility (*Sinnlichkeit*) is considered to emerge by interaction of the old and new cortexes. The lateralization (e.g., right or left) of each cerebral cortex function has yet to be fully understood. For example, although most individuals apparently have left-hemisphere language specialization, some individuals have language function located in the right hemisphere. The dominant (language) hemisphere must be determined before surgical operation on the brain. The nondominant hemisphere, however, may also be involved: for example, in prosody production in speech. The left and right cerebral hemispheres are connected by nerve fiber clusters such as the corpus callosum and the anterior commissure.

My hypothesis on the difference between the right and left cerebral hemisphere functioning is as follows (see Koizumi 2008b). First, let us assume that the language areas (called Broca's area and Wernicke's area) are located in the left cerebral hemisphere. Actually, such is the case with more than 90 percent of us. In this case, the left hemisphere is for digital processing and the right hemisphere is for analog processing. In other words, the left hemisphere analyzes or decomposes the subject, whereas the right side synergizes or integrates the subject. The functional difference between the right and left sides of the new cortex in the surface cerebral layer is related to a kind of *intelligence*, whereas *sensibility*, which includes emotions, is closely connected to the deep part of the brain.

The scientific mind and the artistic mind are similar in that both are the product of the co-creation of intelligence and sensitivity. Intelligence alone does not result in creativity. The new cortex stores not only visual and other perceptions but also many other memories. However, regardless of how much knowledge or how many skills are crammed into the brain, without the enthusiasm or the aspiration to use that content, then, as the proverb goes, an "unused treasure is a wasted treasure." Enthusiasm and aspiration cannot exist without the functions of the limbic cortex. The cerebral structure that retains the process of evolution also shifts the origin of functions from the center to the surface.

From the viewpoint of brain science, the enthusiasm and drive to optimize intelligence for practical use are linked to a deep part of the brain. Assuming that ontogenesis follows the phylogenic process, a possibility arises that the young are better able to nurture the cerebral part of the brain related to enthusiasm and aspiration. Infancy or childhood is therefore a privileged time for learning.

The Scientific Mind

The development of the scientific mind in childhood was a topic discussed at a symposium held by the Sony Foundation for Education as part of the Sony Preschool Education Program for Children. As chairman of the Screening Committee, I supported planning and selection to bring together educators, child care workers, parents, grandparents, and students as participants. As table 6.1 shows, five characteristics are basic to the development of the scientific mind. The first three are qualities that are inherent to doing science. Although the second characteristic, "An open mind that accepts the truth without trying to bend the facts," and the third characteristic, "An honest mind that decides and acts without prejudice or bias," appear to be similar, the second concerns the input of information from the environment and the third concerns the output of information to the environment. The last two characteristics, "a mind that understands that all life within nature has value" and "a mind that respects diversity and is considerate of others," are concerned with the capacity to interact respectfully, empathetically, and cooperatively with others, including other forms of life, and can be described as the basis for a code of ecological sustainability. These two characteristics

TABLE 6.1. *Definitions of a Scientific Mind-Set Used in the Sony Preschool Programs*

(1)	A sensitive mind deeply moved by curiosity and the wonders of nature
(2)	An open mind that accepts truth and doesn't try to bend the facts
(3)	An honest mind that decides and acts without prejudice or bias
(4)	A mind that understands that all life within nature has value
(5)	A mind that respects diversity and is considerate of others

are intrinsic to the dignity of humanity and are increasingly being shown through science to be unique characteristics that make humans able and willing to exist above the law of nature: that is, to live in a higher state of harmonic symbiosis. Humans still retain the nature of an animal species but are able to overcome it through social norms based on ethics (Koizumi, Akita, and Yamada 2007).

This description of the scientific mind reveals the extended significance of science and the code of sustainability, itself not limited to the realm of science. We may expect this ethical foundation, which can be nurtured during infancy and early childhood, to bring forth the potential to shed light on the moral issues of our modern civilized societies. The Sony Preschool Education Program for Children accepts proposals for innovative educational models and programs for infants and small children. Through its Scientific Mind project, selected programs receive subsidies to be implemented in kindergartens and child care facilities nationwide. Many examples of facilities working to nurture "a sound scientific mind" in young children already exist.[2]

The Artistic Mind

I also recognize the significance of the artistic mind for education. As with the scientific mind, creativity is indispensable at its root. Both the artistic mind and the scientific mind require not only current forms of intellectual education that provide knowledge and skills but also an education that nurtures scientific and artistic enthusiasm and encourages interaction between the limbic cortex and the neocortex, thereby forming the foundation for aspiration and enthusiasm.

Let us take music as an example of an area that typically shows co-creation of sensibility and intelligence. Musical works that survive the test of time have a balance of sensibility and intelligence, with one or the other becoming more predominant in a given age. The balance of intelligence and sensibility in musical performance also varies across the ages, with one or the other becoming more predominant. Moreover, the balance may change even in the course of a single performance. Sensibility and intelligence are like substances that collide with each other, fight to dominate each other, and fuse at a high temperature. This characteristic may be common throughout all artistic fields (Koizumi 2008a). I must come back to the point that art education is not just for the sake of art. It can become a driving force to inspire creativity and enthusiasm in children who want to become scientists or engineers.

Toward a Hopeful Vision for Globalization

The biosphere is a thin layer of approximately ten to twenty kilometers (0.15–0.3 percent of the earth's radius of 6,400 kilometers). About half of the earth's atmosphere is contained in the first five kilometers above the earth's surface. Almost all living things reside in a band extending from five kilometers below to five kilometers above sea level. This thin layer, as the environment for all living things, is so fragile that human artifacts can easily damage it. For example, CFCs easily rupture the ozone layer that guards living things from harmful UV light. The pollution of the troposphere by greenhouse gases, a result of the rapid increase in human consumption of fossil fuels, has created the problem of global warming. This situation could have been predicted.

Awareness of environmental problems began with the discovery of so-called Minamata disease (mercury poisoning) around 1953 in Minamata, Japan. Just as Hiroshima and Nagasaki became ground zero for atomic bombing, Minamata became ground zero for environmental problems. Rachel Carson (1907–64) warned of environmental destruction due to pesticides and pollution in her book Silent Spring in 1962. Only much later, however, in the 1980s, did an awareness of global environmental problems and a concept of environmental assessment conspicuously emerge, and only after that did the concept of sustainable development arise.

To address current environmental conditions, children should receive a comprehensive environmental education from early on. Opulence has led us to discard leftovers in some countries, whereas children are starving in many other countries. To address such drastic inequalities in the world, education is necessary to raise our awareness. We will need to share a sense that we all inhabit the same fragile biosphere. In general, cutting-edge technologies and globalization tend to cause further inequalities, a basic problem that requires investigation of how we can realize a globalization that is based on the welfare of all human beings.

An excessive focus on ethnicity and ethnic history in education tends to prevent the nurturing of an understanding of cultural diversity. Where chain reactions of hatred persisted through international conflicts, science should conduct basic research to cut the chain of hatred. In psychology, neurology, and psychiatry, although research on *preference* and *dislike* exists, research on *hatred* or *abomination* is almost nonexistent. Many psychology dictionaries do not even include these terms. Love and hate exist in ambivalence, as two sides of the same coin. The saying, "Because of too much love, hatred grows a hundred times" describes the strong feeling that emerges when people are deprived of their loved ones. It is highly likely that this feeling is related not only to the limbic system but also to the prefrontal cortex. Strong hatred toward a person who has caused one to lose beloved family leads to revenge, which leads to further revenge, thereby expanding the chain of hatred. In mind-brain science research, we are preparing to tackle this critical issue (Koizumi 2007a).

Most of my time is spent at the Advanced Research Laboratory of Hitachi, Ltd., which is located on grounds that extend over approximately forty hectares in the Hiki Hills of Saitama Prefecture in Japan. Courtney Ross honored us with a visit in March 2005. In the gardens, there is a pond where swans—a gift from the imperial household—swim, and planted nearby is the peach-colored rose seedling that was sent to me as a gift by Courtney Ross. This species retains its tendrils and, if tended to properly, can be guided to form an arch that will be a symbol of the aforementioned spiral. I feel a strong attachment to this site, and it is a source of great joy to stroll by the pond, watch the rose grow, enjoy its fragrance, and hand-feed my friends the swans. Courtney Ross wrote that she would "visit the laboratory when the roses bloom," and every time I gaze at the blossoms, I look forward to our next meeting and hope that her educational activities dedicated to the future of children will develop into a magnificent blossom.

NOTES

1. In 2003, I was introduced to Courtney Ross by Antonio Battro of the Pontifical Academy of Sciences at the four hundredth anniversary of the academy's founding. We spent several days together in the Vatican's beautiful gardens. This encounter led to the next opportunity, initiated by Kurt Fischer, through which I participated in an educational workshop at the Ross School. This was immediately after the inaugural conference of the International Mind, Brain, and Education Society at the Harvard Graduate School of Education. In 2004, I, in turn, invited Courtney Ross to Japan when I planned and hosted the International Symposium on Brain Science and Education at the United Nations University

in Tokyo. The symposium was sponsored by the Japan Science and Technology Agency, an independently administered corporation. Courtney Ross visited us with her friends Antonio and Hanna Damasio, the eminent neuroscientists (see Damasio and Damasio this volume), and she gave a lecture that substantially contributed to the overall success of the conference. On the basis of the content of the symposium, a program for the public was produced (a series of four forty-five-minute TV shows) and aired on the Japanese Science Channel. The program is currently being viewed via the Internet and used in various schools in Japan and overseas as well as other educational institutions (Koizumi 2004a).

2. See the Web site of the Sony Foundation for Education on the Sony Preschool Education Program for Children, www.sony-ef.or.jp/english/preschool/.

REFERENCES

Bruner, J. S. 1961. *The process of education.* Cambridge, MA: Harvard University Press.
Einstein, A. 1905/1923. On the electrodynamics of moving bodies. In *The principle of relativity,* ed. A. Somerfeld, trans. W. Perrett and G. B. Jeffery. London: Methuen
———. 1916/1997. The foundation of the general theory of relativity. In *The collected papers of Albert Einstein,* vol. 6, *The Berlin years: Writings, 1914–1917 (English translation supplement),* trans. A. Engel. Princeton: Princeton University Press.
Gardner, H., and C. H. Ross. 2003. A compelling curriculum. In *Ross School,* 18–19. East Hampton, NY: Ross School.
Gould, S. J. 1977. *Ontogeny and phylogeny.* Cambridge, MA: Harvard University Press,
Koizumi, H., ed. 1995. *The Trans-disciplinary Symposium on the Frontier of Mind-Brain Science and Its Practical Applications.* Tokyo: Hitachi.
———. 1996a. The importance of considering the brain in environmental science. In *Environmental Measurement and Analysis,* ed. H. Koizumi. Tokyo: Japan Science and Technology Corporation.
———. 1996b. A trans-disciplinary approach through analytical science: Towards global sustainability and human well-being. In *Proceedings of the Trans-disciplinary Forum on Science and Technology for the Global Environment: Environmental Measurement and Analysis,* ed. H. Koizumi. Tokyo: Japan Science and Technology Corporation.
———. 1998. A practical approach to trans-disciplinary studies for the 21st century. *Journal of Seizon and Life Sciences* 9:5–24.
———, ed. 2000. *The Trans-disciplinary Forum towards the 21st Century: Developing the Brain: The Science of Learning and Education* [in Japanese]. Tokyo: Japan Science and Technology Agency.
———, ed. 2004a. Brain science and education [in Japanese]. Internet video. Science Channel. Produced by the Japan Science and Technology Agency. http://sc-smn.jst.go.jp/8/bangumi.asp?i_series_code=B043309&i_renban_code=004.
———. 2004b. The concept of "developing the brain": A new natural science for learning and education. *Brain and Development* 26:434–41.
———, ed. 2006. *The First International Symposium on Cohort Studies Based on Brain-Science.* Tokyo: Japan Science and Technology Agency.
———. 2007a. A new science of humanity: A trial for the integration of natural science and the humanities towards human security and well-being. In *What is our knowledge about the human being,* ed. M. S. Sorondo. Vatican City: Pontifical Academy of Sciences.

———. 2007b. Preface to *A method of child care during infancy and early childhood based on biological evolution*, ed. K. Saito [in Japanese]. Kyoto: Kamogawa.

———, ed. 2008a. *Brain science and the arts* [in Japanese]. Tokyo: Kousakusha.

———. 2008b. Developing the brain: A functional imaging approach to learning and educational sciences. In *The educated brain: Essays in neuroeducation*, ed. A. M. Battro, K. W. Fischer, and P. J. Lena. Cambridge: Cambridge University Press.

Koizumi, H., K. Akita, and T. Yamada. 2007. *Nurturing the scientific mind in early childhood* [in Japanese]. Tokyo: Shogakukan.

Minkowski, H. 1908/1964. Space and time. In *Problems of space and time*, ed. J. J. C. Smart, trans. W. Perrett and G. B. Jeffery. New York: Macmillan.

Penrose, R. 1997. *The large, the small and the human mind*. Cambridge: Cambridge University Press.

Prechtl, H. F. R., ed. 1991. *Continuity of neural functions from prenatal to postnatal life*. Cambridge: Cambridge University Press.

Putnam, N. H., et al. 2008. The amphioxus genome and the evolution of the chordate karyotype. *Nature* 453:1064–71.

Saitō, K., and H. Koizumi, eds. 2008. *Children are the future*. Kyoto: Freedom/Kamogawa Press.

Part III

Creativity and Integration

7

Multimedia Literacy

A Critical Component of
Twenty-first Century Education

ELIZABETH M. DALEY WITH HOLLY WILLIS

When I first met Courtney Ross in the early 1990s, it was clear that even then in her plans for the Ross School she was anticipating the dramatic changes that technology would bring to the generation then entering the world of formal education. She was also aware that traditional institutions were for the most part not thinking about addressing these changes unless it was to defend against them. Our early conversations centered on the critical issues of how technology and an ever-increasing visual media environment needed to be addressed at the earliest stages of education. While there are many innovations that Courtney has brought to her remarkable school and is now disseminating to others, this chapter focuses on those areas of audio/visual networked culture that the Ross School shares with the Institute for Multimedia Literacy (IML) at the University of Southern California's (USC's) School of Cinematic Arts.

The Ross School's Web site lists the embracing of new technologies as one of the three central principles of the school's vision. This is perhaps not an unusual goal to find on a school Web site today. What is significant about Courtney's approach is that from the beginning she understood that technology had to be integrated into the classroom not merely as computers and networks but also as means of enhancing a traditional curriculum. She recognized that the world our young people were entering required them to think in new ways that were enabled by technology and had foundations in the integration of sound and image in a networked environment, a world that did not privilege text as the only way to create meaning and understand information. This vision has consistently paralleled that of the IML. As we have struggled to broaden the definition of literacy, we have always found Courtney to be a fellow traveler.

It is clear that today's learners are part of a world that is increasingly wired. It is a world that has moved away from the static format of early Web sites, which simply delivered information, to a creative, dynamic community of users sharing similar interests and goals. It is a world characterized by mobility and on-the-go communication. Students will likely spend more than an hour a day online, and some will already be using the more than one hundred Web 2.0 applications available to students for note taking, tagging, mind mapping, and more.

Our students come to us with a strong online social network, using blogs, Facebook accounts, and Twitter to stay constantly connected with friends, sharing and shaping all kinds of media through YouTube and Jumpcut, and possessing a host of skills, including ease with collaboration, multitasking, and personal expression. However, while the statistics on technology usage are laughably out-of-date almost within days, two facts remain all too clear.

First, today's learners may be tech-savvy, but they're also critically naive: they do not know how to use these tools with sophistication or with a critical perspective. Recent tests gauging information and communication technology literacy showed that students lack many of the most basic skills needed for information literacy, including the ability to evaluate the information they find.

Second, students often enter institutions that are unable to keep pace with the technology and the cultural changes occurring around us. To date, most college and university initiatives related to technology move in a single direction: making it easier for faculty to deliver content to students or manage course information. They do not take into account the social transformations that have occurred, and many assume that the transformation has been solely technological. But it hasn't been; our culture is now one that enables and encourages participation through a rapidly expanding host of opportunities that young people are enthusiastically embracing and utilizing to their own ends.

To respond to the current technology explosion, we must consider how to transform the ways in which we think, we teach, and our students can learn. As John Thompson writes in an essay aptly titled "Is Education 1.0 Ready for Web 2.0 Students?" (2007) for the online education journal *Innovate*, "The generation weaned on television may have been happy to sit back and passively consume information fed to them from above, but those days are over."

This is one of the central questions that the IML has addressed since its inception in 1998. Through a series of experimental classes, labs, and faculty collaborations, the IML has focused on the creation of several cutting-edge programs that are as participatory, flexible, and dynamic as the world in which we live. While we began with an emphasis on visual literacy, we've evolved and now understand the central role that computational models play in thinking and expression.

But how did we get here? This chapter traces the evolution of the IML's core programs and key concepts. Several of its tenets echo or supplement those developed within the Ross School paradigm and show how the unique position of the institute within the School of Cinematic Arts, with its interdisciplinary blend of divisions (including Critical Studies, Production, Interactive Media, and Animation), has shaped a program that is uniquely attuned to the learners of the twenty-first century.

Evolution of the Institute for Multimedia Literacy

Generally, the acts of speaking, listening, reading, and writing, and their manifestation as oral and print media, are privileged in most university settings. Other media, which might include cinematic media and graphic media, tend to be marginalized or taught only in programs focused specifically on media and design. As Kristina Woolsey writes in her 2005 essay "New Media Literacies: A Language Revolution," "The prevalent judgment is that schools should focus on oral and print literacies, and that graphical, cinematic and multimedia literacies are interesting but not critical to preparation for general success and understanding." The IML's mandate from the beginning, however, has been to expand the definition of literacy so that "screen language" becomes as significant as the literacies related to reading and writing. This is not to say that the multimedia of the language of the screen *replaces* traditional literacies; instead, the modes complement, inform, and support each other in a dialogic relationship. Since 1998, when some of these ideas were initially formed in conversations with the film director George Lucas, this concept has been widely adopted, and colleges and universities across the country are developing programs that respond to the needs of twenty-first century students. And this is a necessary and appropriate response: we have not only a cultural responsibility but an ethical mandate to prepare our students properly, which means preparing them not only to read and write with the multimedia language of the screen but to engage the world with an understanding of the networked nature of contemporary life.

Institutions use a variety of models to implement new literacy education that emerge from disparate disciplines and points of view. For example, some programs are set in departments or divisions devoted to writing and rhetoric. Often, in this model, multimedia screen language is seen as "enhanced writing" or media-rich composition. Bringing multimedia skills to students "under the radar" as instructors employ new tools as a natural outgrowth of basic networked activity, this model has produced strong results. If we are all using course management systems such as Blackboard, it is not difficult to imagine how we might reconsider the writing and interactions that occur there and have our students consider these acts, too, as modes of composition. More often, however, this direction of media instruction begins to incorporate tools such as blogs and wikis or encourages the thoughtful deployment of images within the text. The model in this case, however, still starts with *writing* as the primary act and sees multimedia literacy as "enhanced writing."

Obviously, the institutional commitment to uphold reading and writing in a world amok with YouTube videos and poorly written MySpace pages prefers something called "enhanced writing" to multimedia literacy. Indeed, many university professors unfamiliar with the sophisticated research devoted to multimedia decry the "Disneyfication" of scholarship that utilizes the "bells and whistles" of sound, images, and video. However, a central tenet within multimedia literacy as we have conceived it at the IML is that what our students are doing is not only writing. We do not start with text and add images, nor do we compose on our desktops and then put that text online. Instead, we advocate a form of scholarly engagement that is not simply additive but integrated.

This integration occurs on multiple levels: it responds to different media platform offerings and the rhetorical needs of any given project. It also informs how we imagine the relationship between various courses and the corresponding media component. It explores the provocative capabilities of various tools in order to test new models of academic production.

An example will illustrate my point. The IML recently hosted a workshop in which twelve faculty members and graduate students from diverse disciplines and technical backgrounds came together for four days to create a project using the free open-source application Sophie, which was designed by the Institute for the Future of the Book and funded by USC's School of Cinematic Arts, with grants from the Andrew W. Mellon and John D. and Catherine T. MacArthur Foundations. We saw the workshop as a test—what would an anthropologist, a student of musicology, and a media activist create with this tool, which facilitates the easy melding of text, images, sound, and video?

In its simplest form, Sophie lets users make books; however, the pages of each Sophie book may also integrate an array of time-based actions, which makes Sophie also very cinematic. As one participant noted, Sophie insists that its users carefully consider how to choreograph the elements on any given page. While all participants came to the workshop with a finished text to use as a starting point, the majority of them said that simply importing that text was ill-advised. Sophie instead invites users to "layer" that text with annotations, additional information strata, and media. Once new elements have been added, the text often has to be rethought: it is now in a dialogic relation with the other elements, and the linear flow of information favored by the traditional essay gives way to the new tensions and possibilities of a very different form of authoring.

Questions continue to arise during the use of a tool such as Sophie, which includes the possibility for creating dense media "events" on its pages. At what point does authoring give way to "directing" or "producing"? Is it a form of media orchestration or choreography? We do not yet have names for these emerging modes, but the IML's dedication to an integrated model, one that listens and learns from the ground up rather than imposing from the top down, has allowed us to be agile in evolving tools, experimenting with them in the classroom or workshop settings, and responding in a relational mode that develops connections as needed.

Institute for Multimedia Literacy Honors Program

The IML's Honors Program was established in 2003 as a four-year undergraduate program in which students study the history and theory of scholarly multimedia production and complete their studies with a capstone multimedia project in their major. Thus far it has been a tremendous learning process, for students as well as for IML staff and faculty. While the curriculum outlines key principles based on more than fifty collaborative humanities courses and associated multimedia labs, it also remains fluid enough to shift as the emergence of Web 2.0 tools has radically transformed our pedagogical practices. As the first cohort of seniors completed their projects in the fall of 2007 and spring of 2008, we were able, perhaps for the first time, to craft a taxonomy of scholarly multimedia projects.

While the Honors Program was the IML's first fully formed program, we have always believed that success with multimedia literacy demands broad adoption; it cannot remain the luxury of a select few, nor can our attention be focused solely on students. Instead, multimedia literacy must span the curriculum, and its tenets must be adopted by faculty members who can expand and innovate with these tools in their own ways. It must advocate for change at the administrative level as well, championing variations in tenure and promotion assessment as faculty members engage in new forms of research and production.

Multimedia across the Core

To address the need for expansion across the curriculum, the IML joined USC's College of Letters, Arts, and Sciences to create and implement the Multimedia in the Core (MMC) program. The goal was to integrate general education courses with multimedia labs, thereby giving every student at USC the opportunity to work with these tools. While we had gathered extensive findings through prior experiments, we wanted to ensure that our goals were in sync with those of other experts in the field. In an effort to investigate this, we hosted the "Symposium on Multimedia across the Curriculum," in which invited speakers gave presentations on their own projects as a way of illuminating directions for the emerging MMC program at USC, followed by an intensive closing session in which the plans for the program were discussed.

The next step was to host a collaborative session with IML staff, college faculty designated to teach in the program, and teaching assistants. Designed as both a workshop to develop basic media skills with several Web 2.0 tools and a broader discussion of shifting pedagogical models, the event's main goal was to define the lab component of the course—MDA 140—and to delineate its relationship to the course to which it was attached. To facilitate this discussion and to enact the IML's objectives, the workshop incorporated a wiki open to the group; this became a space for all participants to contribute actively in the discussions.

Over the course of the workshop, agreement was reached on the following as a description of the course: "This course introduces multimedia as a critical and creative tool that functions to enhance traditional forms of academic work. Students will learn basic skills in multimedia authoring and complete the course having acquired proficiency in several core, media-based literacies described below. The precise nature of the multimedia work undertaken in this class will vary depending on the specific needs and content of the course to which it is linked."

Further discussion produced agreement on several "foundational literacies," namely those competencies that students understand and develop before finishing any variation of the course. These foundational literacies are distinct from the "recommended literacies," which are areas that may be adopted as needed depending on the focus of the correlate general education course. The foundational literacies determined were as follows:

1. Digital literacy
   - Proficiency in using basic tools of digital authoring
   - Understanding of storage, backup, compression, file types, naming conventions, etc.

2. Network literacy
   - Ability to use network-based software for sophisticated participation in online communities

3. Design literacy
   - Ability to use appropriate design principles in service of critical goals
   - Ability to control and articulate the relationship between form and content

4. Argumentation literacy
   - Ability to use multimedia to develop and express a persuasive thesis
   - Effective use of evidence and complex thinking in constructing an argument

5. Research literacy
   - Ability to perform effective, critical online research
   - Knowledge of academically appropriate protocols for selection, citation, and attribution of electronic source materials
   - Knowledge of fair use and copyright issues

The recommended literacies for the MDA 140 course were

1. Presentation literacy
   - Ability to deploy strategies for effective presentation using multimedia
   - Understanding and usage of appropriate tools for the publication or dissemination of multimedia materials

2. Visual literacy
   - Ability to convey information visually
   - Ability to understand and control systems of visual signification

3. Sonic literacy
   - Ability to communicate effectively with sound
   - Ability to understand and work with various components of sound

4. Interpretation literacy
   - Ability to use multimedia to enhance a critical interpretation
   - Ability to identify and articulate the cultural, historical, and ideological contexts of a media object

5. Annotation literacy
   - Knowledge of strategies for critical annotation of text, images, and media

6. Collaboration literacy
   - Ability to work effectively in a group authoring environment
   - Ability to design and lead a team project

7. Narrative literacy
   - Knowledge of basic components and genres of narrative
   - Ability to deploy elements of narrative in a critical context

8. Pedagogical literacy
   - Effective use of strategies for creating an effective tool for teaching

9. Interactivity literacy
   - Ability to communicate effectively in a nonlinear, interactive format
   - Ability to design an effective interactive interface or navigational structure

10. Code literacy
    - Ability to understand the basics of how code operates
    - Ability to write or use basic code

The discussion during this initial workshop was often heated, and the debate served to highlight some of the key tensions—conceptual, institutional, and pedagogical—while also showing that differences in perspective were not enough to deter the overarching desire to rethink teaching and learning. Faculty from outside the IML, for example, expressed an array of hopes for their upcoming courses: they hoped their students might begin to see their major or discipline in a new light; they hoped that the critical emphasis in the lab would contribute to the larger goals of inspiring a more engaged citizenry; they wanted to use the critical focus within the lab to have students think about the media practices in which they were already engaged; and they hoped to see how emerging tools and models might reinvigorate or redirect their own forms of research and scholarly practice.

Interest in using various forms of media, both in teaching and in student projects, led the IML to found the Multimedia across the College (MAC) program. This program invites all college faculty to propose a project or workshop that they would like to conduct with their students; selected proposals then receive use of the media labs, the support of a teaching assistant versed in multimedia authoring, and access to an array of workshops throughout the year designed to help build and support multimedia across the curriculum.

The Multimedia across the College program was founded to address two key issues. First, faculty members were often reticent to attach an entire two-unit lab to their courses, fearing that it would affect enrollment. Often students in general education–level courses were reluctant to extend additional effort. However, students in upper-division courses, or courses in their major, have greater incentive to work through ideas and research with more rigor and depth. Second, a program that offers support for a single assignment or project requires less initial commitment by often harried instructors. After only two semesters the program has tripled in size, and participants are enthusiastic about the impact it has had, both on their students and on their own teaching, research, and production methods.

Now that we are more than a decade into our project, we understand that institutional change takes time; as such, we see the Multimedia across the College program as a temporary one, a stepping stone to a fully integrated multimedia literacy standard that will affect every program and school within the university.

New Ventures

To make this dramatic change, support and venues for scholarly multimedia are needed for faculty. For this reason, we developed the online, peer-reviewed journal *Vectors: Journal of Culture and Technology in a Dynamic Vernacular*. Now in its third year, *Vectors* unites scholars with designers in an intensive collaborative process in which scholars rethink their work within the context of an interactive format. Using the journal's dynamic backend generator, scholars utilize a database structure and thus begin to see their work radically reconfigured. Previously undisclosed relations are revealed, and both the knowledge and form of the project are transformed.

The IML is also home to Critical Commons, a project that we intend to use to address copyright policies as they become increasingly problematic in educational contexts working with various forms of media. A recent study published by the Center for Social Media entitled "The Cost of Copyright Confusion for Media Literacy" (Hobbes, Jaszi, and Aufderheide 2007) showed the negative impact of unclear fair use guidelines. The authors noted that many teachers, especially in K–12 classrooms, are so nervous about violating copyright that they would prefer not to work with images at all, video included.

There are significant consequences of unclear fair use guidelines, and Critical Commons, a nonprofit advocacy coalition, is working to change this. Critical Commons will promote the fair use of media in educational contexts by providing resources, easy-to-understand information and tools for scholars, students, and educators, along with a participatory database of materials created by communities and shared within those communities. Like *Vectors*, Critical Commons will serve as a venue for exemplary models of academic work, in this case focusing on those that employ fair use or an open-education ethos in interesting ways. This project is the IML's way of tackling a central dilemma that inhibits the educational community from creating and engaging with the media culture of the twenty-first century. Copyright must be addressed in a reasonable way if we are to move forward.

Like many other institutions across the country, the IML is conducting research on mobile education, an open curriculum, and virtual worlds. In each case, however, our research moves beyond the "wow" factor that unfortunately drives many of these initiatives. With our space in the multiuser virtual environment Second Life, for example, we eschewed the idea that we should replicate the USC campus and instead focused on developing an educational space that takes advantage of a virtual world. We have immersive syllabi, inviting students to visit each week of the semester in spaces that house the lecture, readings, and media, as well as links to further material online. We are developing an immersive book, giving learners access to another experience of one of our key texts.

The space is also home to an array of student projects, including *Rivenscyr,* created by Honors Program senior Matt Lee. This project is a great example of what we call an "experiential argument." In this mode of scholarly multimedia, the author develops an argument but does so by creating an embodied experience such that users glean the maker's points only by becoming immersed within the space of that argument. In *Rivenscyr*, Lee argues that Sycorax, the mother of Caliban who dies prior to the play's beginning, nevertheless exerts enormous power within the play. He makes his argument, however, within Second Life, inviting visitors to move from room to room and level to level gathering information and snippets of the argument. The project includes a tremendous amount of text—entire versions of the play, for example, as well as background and supplemental information and the lexia that make up Lee's project. While *Rivenscyr* might have made a dazzling thesis paper, it is far richer as an immersive experience. Further, the conceptual, design, and technical skills that Lee developed and used on the project enabled him to understand his own argument more deeply by working through it in a nonlinear fashion.

As the digital world and the many platforms it offers us continue to evolve at breathtaking speed, the IML strives to expand on its initiatives, continuing to broaden the definition of multimedia literacy and increase its integration and acceptance at all levels of higher education, from freshman classes to PhD dissertations and scholarly publications. In spite of the successes we have had to date, we do not underestimate the obstacles and the level of resistance that exist within the academic community.

We are indeed fortunate to have a visionary partner like Courtney Sale Ross who has made a commitment to multimedia literacy in K–12 education at the Ross School. Ross is well aware that such literacy will not be achieved simply by providing laptops for the students and access to software; students must also receive the intellectual tools to disseminate, critique, and author media-based materials. Imagine how much further we could advance the concepts we are teaching our freshmen today if they had learned them in elementary school, hand in hand with the fundamentals of alphabetic literacy.

It is critical that projects such as those at the IML and the Ross School are understood and embraced as far more than clever academic experiments that make papers more "interesting" for a generation raised on the Internet. Rather, they must be seen as crucial contributions to ensuring that education at all levels is in sync with a world where modes of communication, as well as the methodologies for the creation and dissemination of knowledge, are changing exponentially with every passing year.

Multimedia are ubiquitous; in many ways they are the vernacular. Certainly they have become the dominant means of communication for the college-age students of today and will be even more so for those of tomorrow. If the educational establishment neglects to embrace multimedia as a fundamental way of both communicating and creating knowledge, it risks becoming marginalized, if not irrelevant, in many aspects of today's culture.

REFERENCES

Hobbs, R., P. Jaszi, and P. Aufderheide. 2007. The cost of copyright confusion for media literacy. Report for the Center for Social Media, September, http://www.centerforsocial-media.org/files/pdf/Final_CSM_copyright_report.pdf.
Thompson, J. 2007. Is Education 1.0 ready for Web 2.0 students? *Innovate* 3 (April–May), http://fseinnovate.fse.nova.edu/index.php?view=article&id=393.
Woolsey, K. 2005. New media literacies: A language revolution. Draft paper, New Media Literacies Project, May 22, http://archive.nmc.org/summit/Language_Revolution.pdf.

8

Object Lessons

SHERRY TURKLE

In the ongoing national conversation about science education in America, there is a new consensus that we have entered a time of crisis in our relationship to the international scientific and engineering community.[1] For generations we have led; now Americans wonder why our students are turning away from science and mathematics—at best content to be the world's brokers, broadcasters, and lawyers and at worst simply dropping out— while foreign students press forward on a playing field newly leveled by the resources of the World Wide Web (Friedman 2005). Leaders in science and technology express dismay. On this theme, Bill Gates (2005) stated flatly, "In the international competition to have the biggest and best supply of knowledge workers, America is falling behind." He went on: "In math and science, our fourth graders are among the top students in the world. By eighth grade, they're in the middle of the pack. By 12th grade, U.S. students are scoring near the bottom of all industrialized nations."

When the science committee of the House of Representatives asked the National Academies, the nation's leading scientific advisory group, for ten recommendations to strengthen America's scientific competitiveness, the academies offered twice that number. There were recommendations to support early-career scientists and those who plan to become science teachers. There were recommendations to create a new government agency to sponsor energy research and to use tax policy to encourage research and development in corporate settings.

As sensible as these recommendations may be, they deal largely with financial incentives and big institutions. Here I suggest a different tack, one resonant with the philosophy and practice of education I saw as a mentor at the Ross School. In this view, one approaches the teaching of science by looking to how objects, met early in children's lives, enter into the development of a love for science. The Ross philosophy respects the importance of the tactile, the sensuous, and the aesthetic in all aspects of the curriculum, with no exemption for science and technology. It values diversity in approaches to learning, including the learning of science. And it puts science in the closest possible relationship to art.

At the time of my first visit to the Ross School in fall 1997, its beautiful campus had not yet been built. My meetings with students and faculty—I was invited to speak about technology as an intimate partner in daily life—took place in a newly renovated school building that had very recently housed dental and real estate offices. The renovation was elegant, but what I remember most about those early years is how even modest spaces were transformed by art: beautiful reproductions of Asian art, classical and modern European paintings and sculpture, Oriental rugs. And there were computers all around, in every classroom, studio, and laboratory space. At the time of my early visits, it was still common practice for schools to isolate technology in "computer laboratories." At Ross, high technology was not isolated from Persian and Greek pottery. Art and science were considered together, within a curriculum envisaged as a spiral; from every point on the spiral one could see disparate elements of culture as one moved back and forward in time. From every point on the spiral, one could see that the disparate elements of the spiral formed a whole.

A curriculum that considers art and science together, a school environment rich in evocative objects—this is an idea that feels right to many people. Most often, the reason for their approval is intuitive: art and science together is a beautiful thing to believe in. Here I argue that the Ross School's art- and objects-infused scientific culture (and its technology-infused artistic culture) not only feels right but is right.

Objects

There are many paths into science. In one of them, imagination is sparked by an object. Some young people discover objects that can "make a mind," objects that become part of the fabric of their scientific selves. From my very first days at MIT in 1976, I found attachments to objects everywhere. I had students and colleagues who spoke about how they were drawn into science by the mesmerizing power of a crystal radio, by the physics of sand castles, by playing with marbles, by childhood explorations of air-conditioning units. And they spoke of new objects. I came to MIT in the early days of the computer culture. My students were beginning to talk about how they identified with their computers, how they experienced these machines as extensions of themselves. For some, computers were "objects-to-think-with" for thinking about larger questions, questions about determinism and free will, mind and mechanism (See Turkle 1984/2005).

Trained as a humanist and social scientist, I began to ask, What is the role of objects in the creative life of the scientist? What makes certain objects good-to-think-with? What part do objects take in the development of a young scientific mind? So, for over twenty-five years of teaching at MIT, I have taken a question as my first class assignment: "Was there an object you met during childhood or adolescence that had an influence on your path into science?" Over the years, assigning a paper on childhood objects has some-times provoked surprise, even anxiety. Students ask: "Why write about an object? Will I be able to find one?" I reassure these students that if they have trouble fixing on an early object, together we will find something appropriate for them to write about. No one will do poorly on this assignment. But then, once students begin to work, there are calls to parents to check their memo-ries. There are conversations with siblings. My students go home for vacation and return to MIT with an object in tow. I typically devote one or two class sessions for reports on the objects of childhood; students have trouble keep-ing to their allotted times, so we schedule extra meetings. Over the years, it has become clear that this assignment stirs something deep.

By the early 2000s, I had collected over 250 student essays, twenty-five years of student writing (see Turkle 2008b). I began to study them in detail, looking for patterns that might inform science education. Inspired by the essays, I asked several dozen working scientists (I refer to them as "mentors") to reflect on the same question I had asked my students: Was there an object that had led them into science, technology, and design? Predictably, many spoke of chemistry sets, crystal radios, and Lego blocks. But less predictably, and against prevalent stereotypes, they also spoke of cameras, colored cray-ons, lengths of straw. These objects, too, were described as integral to the development of scientific passions.

My use of the word *integral* is deliberate. In the stories I have collected, when students and working scientists speak about art or art materials, it is not to refer to such things as the beauty of cells or how the transcendent regularities of physics can be represented in aesthetically pleasing images. Instead, students and mentors focus on how the experiences of working with such things as clay, paints, and musical instruments (including tin whistles and music boxes) become woven into a scientific identity.

Art materials become "objects-to-think-with" for thinking about techni-cal ideas even as they are indissociably linked to emotionally charged nar-ratives of self-discovery. Recollections about the birth of scientific curiosity are romances. Young people fall for science, but science, in its turn, catches them, offers them something personally and intellectually sustaining. Putting children in a rich object world is not just a theoretically good idea. It is essential to giving science a chance. Giving science its best chance means guiding children to objects they can love, without prejudice that only an artist will attach to paint or only a sculptor will attach to clay. In rich object worlds, children make intimate connections that they need to construct on their own; what educators can provide are the conditions for their doing so.

Art and Science

As a child, the biomedical researcher Donald Ingber was drawn to visual arts: "Patterns and forms caught my attention and made my heart pulse more than sounds or music," he says (Ingber 2008). Ingber's interest in how things work (and his talent for disassembling and reassembling bicycles and broken televisions) caused family and friends to see him as a young scientist and shower him with what he calls "science toys." But Ingber ignored these. To him, chemistry sets and junior physics laboratories represented a side of science in which one just followed rules. Ingber was looking for something else. He turned to objects that gave him the feeling of "mak[ing] something my own." Above all, he turned to a Venus Paradise Pencil-by-Number Coloring Set: "It wasn't that science didn't interest me, but these kits all seemed to require that I follow rigid rules in order for their experiments to be successful. This was not as interesting as exploring what I could build without rules. I loved to see whether or not structures would hold their shapes when I released my hand, or what pictures I could draw by filling in numbered spaces with my vibrant colored pencils, often ignoring the pre-printed numbers" (255).

Ingber was colorblind, counted out of the game in art class. The Venus Paradise pencils taught him that "limitations can be circumvented. . . . The numbered pencils and the drawing templates allowed me (when I so wished) to circumvent the terror I experienced when a teacher asked me, for example, to paint something green, and I had no idea which paint cup to select" (255). The pencils provided more than a sense of competency; when Ingber ignored the preprinted numbers, they were a way to defy authority. And the pencils carried ideas. Ingber speaks appreciatively of "the school of Venus Paradise," where he learned "that there is structure to pattern and that function follows form, rather than the other way around. From Venus Paradise I learned that there can be simplicity in complexity, and that art and science are one and the same. . . . My Venus Paradise Coloring Set conveyed to me that everything has underlying structure, so even life can have architecture" (258–59).

Ingber identifies a moment with the pencils when a stroke on paper brought him to a "powerful idea" that organized experience and provoked new thought (see Papert 1980). For Ingber, this was the idea of the Gestalt: "After coloring in multiple scattered spaces, I was elated when I penciled in that key space that caused all the other colored tiles to merge into a single coherent image. The moment always came suddenly, a surprise I learned to anticipate with great expectation. It was in this way that I came to understand the power of the Gestalt, that the whole is greater than the sum of its parts, and that the overall arrangement of the parts can be as important as the properties of these components" (Ingber 2008, 255–56).

Ingber knew that the coloring set had its limitations; the drawings might provide material for thinking about the Gestalt, but his final products were not beautiful. He entered college as a science student and sought out "opportunities to better understand what was missing in those pencil drawings." This turned out not to be so easy. At Yale College, says Ingber,

> It was nearly impossible for a science major to take studio art. I nearly gave up after an unsuccessful midnight interview for entry into a painting course. But I became intrigued when I saw students walking around campus carrying polyhedral sculptures made of folded cardboard that were very similar in form to the viruses that I was studying in my science class on molecular biophysics. . . . I found a way to talk myself into this sculpture course and it was there that I had my first "Aha Moment," one that launched me on a path that I follow to this day. (256–57)

Ingber's "Aha Moment" opened him to thinking about sculpture and molecular biology at the same time. Ultimately, it was sculpture that brought him to "tensegrity," the idea that mechanical forces alter cell structure and have a determinative effect on cell functions. Tensegrity gave Ingber a lifetime of intellectual direction. Ingber notes that "the shape of cells turns out to be as important for biological relationships as are chemicals and hormones, an art-inspired insight with implications for cancer research, embryological development, and even understanding the sensation of gravity. [Tensegrity] has contributed to the development of anti-cancer therapies and nanotechnologies. Most amazing to me, it has led to a new way of thinking about the origins of life on this planet" (258).

Ingber's story is exemplary in many ways. What seemed a mismarriage of disciplines to Yale curricular planners was alchemy to Ingber. He was able to create a new kind of space in which the division between art and science was not relevant to creative practice. While it is a cliché to speak of beauty in the eye of the beholder, it is not cliché to think about what it takes to nurture a beholder able to bring the hues of art into his science. Ingber shows us a moment in which this happened: once invited to follow his instincts, once permitted to respect his intuition, he was able to see.

Ingber's experience with his pencils recalls how mathematician and science educator Seymour Papert (1980) describes the gears on a childhood toy car that awakened his interest in science and mathematics. Papert acknowledges the intellectual contribution of the gears: "I became adept at turning wheels in my head and at making chains of cause and effect. . . . I remember quite vividly my excitement at discovering that a system could be lawful and completely comprehensible without being rigidly deterministic" (vi–viii). But while the gears on the toy car brought Papert to mathematics, more than an intimation of mathematics brought Papert to the gears. They may have symbolized a connection to his entomologist father who gave him the car. Papert's father was a romantic but distant figure who spent much of his time doing fieldwork in the South African bush. Papert's facility with gears might have been the first thing his father took pride in, and once this connection was made, Papert's object choice was overdetermined. We cannot know. What is certain is that thinking with and about things is not a cold, intellectual enterprise but is charged with eros. Papert says: "I fell in love with the gears" (viii).

As in Papert's story, Ingber's objects brought him close to ideas and to emotions. Papert saw the differential in his gears and used them to identify with an absent father. Ingber saw the Gestalt in the Venus Paradise drawings and used the pencils for youthful rebellion against the conventionality of his suburban childhood. Growing up in Long Island, Ingber saw himself as destined for other things and other places. The pencils became a way to express his sense of difference as he deliberately used the wrong colors and painted outside the lines. Yet even as a child he knew that as a scientist he would have to temper rebellion with discipline. In Venus Paradise language, he would have to paint both within and outside the lines. The Venus Paradise Pencil-by-Number Coloring Set provided rich material for working through such issues.

Papert and Ingber's stories are unique, but the "overdetermination" of their object choices is not. Object choices are mobilized by the particularities of a life. So, for example, in my collection of MIT student narratives, the computer scientist Timothy Bickmore (2008) recalls a fascination with lasers that offered emotional support. Performing with the circus after his parents' divorce, Bickmore wanted to put a wall between himself and the audience.

He became an artist, using laser shows as his medium. The lasers provided a way to perform "in which the audience's attention was not focused on me but on an artifact of my construction. It felt safer" (145). As a young child, the media scientist Jennifer Beaudin (2008) developed a fear that she would have to leave her house as she grew up. Specifically, she had an anxiety of scale: she feared she would become too big for her house. She tried to master her fear by moving *closer* to her house as an object. Turning to pencils and drawing, she made detailed maps of the house, a child's version of architectural plans.

These examples make it clear how right the psychoanalyst Erik Erikson (1964) is when he says that play is children's work (222). Children use play to separate from adults and develop their own identities. Separation and individuation are the work of childhood, and children choose play objects that help them do this work. From this perspective, play, object work, is deeply motivated; the emotion that fuels the investigations of young scientists taps into this intensity.

What brought troubled midnight meetings at Yale would never happen at the Ross School. There, art is not adjunct but integral to the teaching of science. Children become comfortable with the idea that falling in love with technical objects, like falling in love with art, is something their teachers expect of them. Simple distinctions between art and science fall away, just as simple divisions between what is constraining and what is liberating fall away in the school of Venus Paradise. For Ingber, its constraining diagrams and rules helped him break out—from his town, from rigid disciplinary definitions, and from ways of thinking that divided art, science, and technology. What nurtures most are fertile confusions in thinking: we come to see colored pencils as doors to science; we find it natural to introduce the periodic table as a form of poetry and circuit boards as a form of art.

This perspective brings us to a very different place than we would get to with a question such as "What objects should children encounter to learn science?" The object that brings you to science doesn't have to be a "science toy." It has to be an object that speaks to a particular child. And it has to be an object that children are free to make their own in their own way.

Styles of Science/Styles of Art

At the Ross School, respect for individual styles is a deeply held value. The psychologist Howard Gardner is a longtime school mentor; his work on multiple intelligences informs how the school approaches individual children's paths to learning. Gardner's perspective looks for diversity where others have imposed uniformity (see, for example, Gardner 1983/1993). When you apply Gardner's ideas to science teaching, they challenge received wisdom about what constitutes a "scientific" style of work.

Stereotypes about scientific work would have scientists and engineers thinking through problems in a "planner's style," a top-down, "divide and conquer" approach that keeps objects at a distance. Of course, some scientists do use this style, and some use it most of the time. Others employ a hybrid style that moves back and forth from top-down planning to a more fluid, "artistic" method. I have described this second style as bricolage or "tinkering" (Turkle and Papert 1990).[2] Yet the "planner's" style has long been frozen in the public imagination (and to some degree, the science education community's as well) as *the* way one does things in science and, even more broadly, what it means to think like a scientist.

For the historian of science Evelyn Fox Keller (1983, 1985), a close look at scientists' practice calls into question the universality of this canonical style.[3] She insists that any description of scientific practice that puts scientists at a distance from their objects of study cannot stand alone. It needs to be complemented by descriptions that explore intimacy and presence. In other words, Keller describes a way of doing science that we associate with art.

The geneticist Barbara McClintock offers such a description of scientific practice when she writes of seeing herself "down there" among the chromosomes she studies. McClintock says: "I actually felt as if I were right down there and these things, they become part of you and you forget yourself" (quoted in Keller 1983, 117).[4] I hear echoes of McClintock's sentiments when the computer science student Austina De Bonte describes imagining herself as a piece of straw as she tried to build three-dimensional objects with structural integrity. These were *siaudinukas*, a Lithuanian folkcraft made by threading straw on pieces of knotted string.

Once De Bonte put herself in the place of the straw, she built her *siaudinukas* in an experimental, "painterly" style. She tried something, stood back, evaluated, tried something else, made small adjustments. A classic bricoleur, De Bonte (2008) played with her materials. "Sometimes I would just start stringing some straws together, looking for ideas; once something took shape, it was easy to find ways to extend or elaborate on it. Often I wouldn't be able to tell for sure whether a complicated structure would be solid until putting in the very last piece" (138). It was through this way of working that De Bonte looked for the rules behind what she calls "stable structure," structure that is, as she puts it, "rigid, reasonably strong, and structurally complete" (139). "I discovered, mostly by example and through trial and error, that I couldn't make a solid structure that wasn't based fundamentally on triangles. I also found that every 'link' in the *siaudinukas* was vitally important—the structure was often fully collapsible and foldable right up until the very last straw was secured. Furthermore, I discovered that this was actually the mark of a good structure" (139).

De Bonte had friends at camp who predesigned their straw structures. These classical planners did not do better work than she. They simply had a different style.

The year she wrote her essay on straws, I watched De Bonte run a small workshop on how to build *siaudinukas*. She brought straws and thread and Lithuanian snacks. One rapt five-year-old was always pleased when she could get an early-stage structure to stand on its own; this made it easier for her to thread the straws. De Bonte was gentle and firm in her rebuke that if it looked ready too soon, it wasn't ever going to stand on its own. The lesson needed to be repeated three times. Each time it seemed to have a wider meaning. In the end I was moved by what seemed its most general meaning: suppleness is the precursor to what is ultimately most secure.

The Physical and the Virtual

De Bonte's story, like any construction narrative, raises a question that was always present at the Ross School when teachers dealt with questions of design: When should materials be presented physically and when should they be presented on the computer? When should students be manipulating physical models and when should they be exploring powerful virtual realities?

Imagine an educational computer program to build virtual *siaudinukai*. A user manipulates physical dowels represented in collaboration with the machine. When a builder makes a simple structure, the computer transforms it into thousands of alternate configurations. The lesson of "seeming solidness" emerges from thousands of iterations of the program as robust structures pop up from the many configurations developed in collaboration with the computer. For some students, such multiple iterations of geometric possibilities would facilitate learning. And of course, thus programmed, building *siaudinukai* could take place on a vastly wider scale.

Contrast all of this power with how De Bonte learned the lessons of the *siaudinukai*—through her fingers and in community with her peers—as part of her contact with Lithuanian culture. For some people, when you take this away, what might have been magical about the straw shapes is lost in their digital variant. Otherwise put, in a digital world, children may get the point, but that may be all that they get. And for some people, it is the body-work of physical manipulation that makes all the difference in connecting to one's work. As one architect lamented when contemplating the movement of design pedagogy from pencil and paper to the world of computer-assisted design: "You love things that are your own marks. In some primitive way, marks are marks. . . . I can lose this piece of paper in the street and if [a day later] I walk on the street and see it, I'll know that I drew it. With a drawing that I do on the computer . . . I might not even know that it's mine. . . . People do analyses of their plan [on the computer] but they only fall in love with the marks they make themselves" (quoted in Turkle 2009, 15]). There are possibilities in digital media that should be pressed into the service of more effective education in science and design, and there are things we learn from the physical that are worth fighting for.

Awash as we are in new digital teaching materials, object play, distinctly old-fashioned, is not something to which today's teachers are particularly attuned. It is natural, in a time of crisis—and science educators do see their field as in crisis—to avidly pursue the next new thing. In contemporary educational circles, that thing has of course been the computer, seen for decades as a scarce and exotic commodity. The Ross School made a special contribution to this conversation about the physical and virtual. For at Ross, from the very start, computers were not a scarce resource. Teachers felt free to explore every subject using them, which meant they were also free to not use them. Ross was a testing ground for what pedagogical practice could be when computers were assumed as part of basic infrastructure. When computation is assumed, it loses its special privilege. To take poetic license, when it is everywhere, it can also be nowhere. In a fully resourced computational environment, teachers are free to put technology in its place.

In thinking about the pedagogical challenges of the virtual, a Ross School mentor, the physics Nobel laureate Georges Charpak, developed a science curriculum for French primary schools that takes the manipulation of physical objects as its centerpiece. Charpak's program is called *La main à la pâte* (Quéré 2006). In literal terms, the phrase refers to the hand as it kneads dough in the slow, artisanal exercise of making bread. Charpak's curricular mission is to have children "[discover] natural objects and phenomena, to bring them into contact with the latter in their reality (outside of virtual reconstructions), directly through observation and experimentation." My conversations with Charpak about *La main à la pâte* and science education centered on the question of speed.

Today, molecular models once built with balls and sticks give way to animated worlds that can be manipulated at a touch, rotated, and flipped; the architect's cardboard model becomes a photorealistic virtual reality that you can "fly through." These environments provide fertile thinking ground but are kinetic in nature. The metaphor of "flying through" is telling. Digital media rarely seem to want to be used slowly, least of all in the classroom.

Consider a Chicago high school junior's anxious description of the "SMART Board,"[5] an interactive digital tablet that her teacher uses in physics class. The teacher writes on the SMART Board before and/or during class and scrolls through it as class progresses. On SMART Board days, the teacher is simultaneously using an animated presentation tool, surfing the Web, and e-mailing pages of class notes to students. The student describes the frustration of trying to keep up with the pace of the machine: "It begins okay. But then we keep asking her to please, please go back; it keeps going forward and forward, there are a lot of variations, and we want her to scroll back. I wish she used the blackboard so it would all be up. And then she promises to e-mail it [the SMART Board pages] to us. But then she doesn't so it all is lost."[6]

In the hands of a master teacher, a technology such as the SMART Board might certainly be a plus. But like all digital technology, it makes it hard to resist velocity. Velocity tempts because it is so easily achieved. You can use the SMART Board at a measured pace, but to do so takes a control that few teachers seem to manage when the machinery is up and running. It is hard to slow down when you are tuned to a technological A.

The Resistance of the Real

When young scientists across generations write about what inspired them to go into science, they don't write about things that sped them up, they write about things that slowed them down. The computer scientist Gil Weinberg was slowed down when his childhood music box broke (Weinberg 2008). When it worked, each of its six colored buttons played a song. Weinberg enjoyed hitting buttons in rapid succession. In this way he could sample notes from different songs and use them to compose his own. But it was when the box broke that Weinberg's deeper involvement began. He conjured notes in his mind. He slowed down because "after each note I had to think really hard about where to go next. Should I go up or down? Should I take a small step or a wide one? I felt myself to be the melody trying to find its way. This was probably the first time I wrote original music" (Weinberg 2008, 118–

19). His relationship to the box taught Weinberg a new way to think about composition. He "became" each note and thought about where he (the note) "wanted" to go.

I think of the limitations of velocity—of Charpak, the SMART Board, and Weinberg's painstaking steps—as I study paths to science that exploit the pleasure of materials, of texture, of what one might call the resistance of the "real." In the early 1990s, the computer scientist Timothy Bickmore's experiments with lasers—"passing the laser through every substance I could think of (Vaseline on slowly rotating glass was one of the best)" (Bickmore 2008, 144)—recalls the physical exuberance of Selby Cull, whose path into science was through baking. For Cull, geology became real through her childhood work on chocolate meringues: "Basic ingredients heated, separated, and cooled equals planet. To add an atmospheric glaze, add gases from volcanoes and volatile liquids from comets and wait until they react. Then shock them all with bolts of lightning and stand back. Voilà. Organic compounds. How to bake a planet" (Cull 2008, 97–98). Cull's joyful comments describe the moment of scientific exultation, Ingber's "Aha Moment," the famed "Eureka" moment of raw delight.

And I see Charpak's focus on what is "at hand" in computer scientist Andrew Sempere's account of "falling for science" when he became involved with a Holga camera. His is a story of patience brought into the digital age. Sempere (2008) describes his Holga, a primitive plastic device, as having "all the mechanical accuracy and precision of a jar of peanut butter." The camera was literally pasted together: "The back leaked light. The film advance rarely worked. The flash shoe usually malfunctioned. The lens was plastic and distorted the image. On mine, the shutter often stuck. The whole thing obliged one to carry a roll of sturdy black tape, mostly to keep the back from falling off. The Holga was neither more nor less than it seemed—a chunk of plastic that let light onto a piece of paper" (Sempere 2008, 50).

As a high school student, Sempere was accustomed to working with digital photography. In that medium he worked quickly, took many photographs, manipulated them fluidly. Digital craft gave him the fantasy that he could capture and manage nature. In contrast, the modest Holga was humbling. It was not the strengths but the limitations of the Holga that "conspire[d]" to "lend even the most mundane subjects an air of analog beauty." In a digital photography studio, Sempere complained about all the materials he didn't have; the Holga taught resourcefulness. It slowed him down. "Working in technology, the lessons of the Holga have served me well. Among these is the notion that to be an artist or scientist implies a willingness to act as an observer, to keep a record that does not seek to eliminate the blurry edges, dark spikes, and imperfections, but rather celebrates them. This means learning to live with the messiness and disappointments of the real world and working through problems by making things that will in some way fail" (Sempere 2008, 51).

Nature encourages us to be messy because it is. When we deal with nature we have to get comfortable with the idea that we may break things that are not easily replaceable. We have to get comfortable with the idea that things may go unresolved for a while. In simulated science, there really doesn't have to be any waiting. Time can be sped up. And when something breaks, the simulation can always be run again; what was broken can be magically restored. Simulations encourage the idea that one can push forward to resolution—of the experiment, of the game, of the quest. One can push forward because possible resolutions are already there, in the program.

In practical terms, the Ross School balances the velocity of high technology with the more stately pace encouraged by art and a rich physical environment. Philosophically, the Ross School balances the temptations of velocity with the image of the spiral and its suggestion of continual return. The spiral is about reflection rather than speed. The spiral suggests that no matter what is being taught, immersion and multiple perspectives are valued, that it is important to take one's time, to live in the moment. Indeed, at Ross, meditation is practiced in the same rooms that are lined with computers.

The great and historically unique virtue of computation is that it is able to present an endless stream of "what-ifs"—thought experiments that try out possible branching structures of an argument or substitutions in an experimental procedure. Object passions, like meditation, bring us to the same enthusiasm for "what-is" that computation inspires for "what-ifs." We now live the tension between these two impulses; we need to cultivate the point at which they court and spark.

When children "fall for science" through art, the experience grounds them. They focus on the pop of colors as they create the Gestalt, on the "solidness" of straws when perfectly strung, on the textures of a grainy photograph. They share the concentration others experience when focusing on Lego bricks or a vacuum tube or on what kind of sand is best for building castles. The Ross School philosophy comprehends the complex ways all of these experiences can come together, how children use art to approach science and nature. Here the stakes for all of us are high because in doing so they may fall for the "what-is" of our planet and wonder at it, not only as a frontier of science, but as where we live.

1. This essay draws on (2008a, 2008c), my chapters "Falling for Science" (Turkle 2008a) and "What Inspires" (2008c) in my edited book *Falling for Science: Objects in Mind* (2008b). The "object stories" I quote here, from both students and senior scientists, are from that collection.

2. In a tinkering or bricolage style one gets close to, indeed intimate with, the objects of study. The idea of object intimacy is meant to evoke what the psychoanalyst D. W. Winnicott called the "transitional object," those objects that the child experiences both as part of his or her body and as part of the external world. See Winnicott (1989). As the child learns to separate self from its surroundings, the original transitional objects are abandoned; one gives up the prized blanket, the teddy bear, the bit of silk from the pillow in the nursery. What remains is a sense of a privileged space, a special way of experiencing objects that recalls this early experience of deep connection. Later in life, moments of creativity during which one feels at one with the universe will refer to the power of the transitional object.

3. Keller (1983, 1985) writes about scientists' resistance to acknowledging the intimacy of their connections to objects. She sees its roots in a male-dominated view of mastery that equates objectivity with distance from the object of study.

4. Keller (1983, 117) takes the exploration of the "close to the object" style as part of a feminist project in science but makes it clear that many male scientists work in this way. The scientific culture has made it hard for them to talk about it or even, perhaps, to recognize it for what it is. But once young male scientists are asked about their objects, they offer rich evidence of such intimacies. One of my students spoke to me about translating the tactile experience of playing with marbles to feeling the laws of "physics in his fingertips"; another spoke about diving deep within a prism for inspiration, shrinking himself, as did McClintock, to its scale in order to make his body feel at one with its structure: "Visualizing waves of light bouncing off nuclei, slithering through electron clouds, and singing across the vacuum between the stars became an obsession. I never tired of leaving the ordinary, everyday world, shrinking myself down to the size of an electron and diving headfirst into my prism where a front row seat for the spectacle of nature awaited" (Hermitt 2008, 46).

5. The SMART Board is marketed as a teaching tool that "energizes presentations and motivates learners." See www2.smarttech.com/st/en-US/Products/SMART+Boards/default.htm.

6. This citation is from an ongoing study of teens and digital technologies. All participants in this study have been granted anonymity.

REFERENCES

Beaudin, Jennifer. 2008. What we see: Walls. In *Falling for science: Objects in mind,* ed. Sherry Turkle. Cambridge, MA: MIT Press.

Bickmore, Timothy. 2008. What we build: Lasers. In *Falling for science: Objects in mind,* ed. Sherry Turkle. Cambridge, MA: MIT Press.

Cull, Selby. 2008. What we model: Chocolate meringue. In *Falling for science: Objects in mind,* ed. Sherry Turkle. Cambridge, MA: MIT Press.

De Bonte, Austina. 2008. What we build: Straws. In *Falling for science: Objects in mind,* ed. Sherry Turkle. Cambridge, MA: MIT Press.

Erikson, Erik. 1964. *Childhood and society.* New York: Norton.

Friedman, Thomas. 2005. *The world is flat: A brief history of the twenty-first century.* New York: Farrar, Straus, and Giroux.

Gardner, Howard. 1983/1993. *Frames of mind: The theory of multiple intelligences.* New York: Basic Books.

Gates, Bill. 2005. Speech presented at the National Education Summit on High Schools, Washington, DC, February 26, www.gatesfoundation.org/MediaCenter/Speeches/Co-chairSpeeches/BillgSpeeches/BGSpeechNGA-050226.htm.

Hermitt, Thomas P. 2008. What we see: Prisms. In *Falling for science: Objects in mind,* ed. Sherry Turkle. Cambridge, MA: MIT Press.

Ingber, Donald. 2008. What we sort: Venus Paradise Coloring Set. In *Falling for science: Objects in mind,* ed. Sherry Turkle. Cambridge, MA: MIT Press.

Keller, Evelyn Fox. 1983. *A feeling for the organism: The life and work of Barbara McClintock.* New York: W. H. Freeman.

———. 1985. *Gender and science.* New Haven: Yale University Press.

Papert, Seymour. 1980. *Mindstorm: Children, computers, and powerful ideas.* New York: Basic Books.

Quéré, Yves. 2006. Science education for children in France: The "La main à la pâte" program. In *First South-East European Summer School for Hands On Primary Science Education: Proceedings* [June 11–16, 2005, Zlatibor, Serbia]. http://rukautestu.vin.bg.ac.yu/handson1/pdf/quere.pdf.

Sempere, Andrew. 2008. What we see: Holga camera. In *Falling for science: Objects in mind,* ed. Sherry Turkle. Cambridge, MA: MIT Press.

Turkle, Sherry. 1984/2005. *The second self: Computers and the human spirit.* Cambridge, MA: MIT Press.

———. 2008a. Falling for science. In *Falling for science: Objects in mind,* ed. Sherry Turkle. Cambridge, MA: MIT Press.

———, ed. 2008b. *Falling for science: Objects in mind.* Cambridge, MA: MIT Press.

———. 2008c. What inspires. In *Falling for science: Objects in mind,* ed. Sherry Turkle. Cambridge, MA: MIT Press.

———. 2009. *Simulation and its discontents.* Cambridge, MA: MIT Press.

Turkle, Sherry, and Seymour Papert. 1990. Epistemological pluralism: Styles and voices within computer culture. *Signs: Journal of Women in Culture and Society* 1 (16): 128–57.

Weinberg, Gil. 2008. What we play: Music box. In *Falling for science: Objects in mind,* ed. Sherry Turkle. Cambridge, MA: MIT Press.

Winnicott, D. W. 1989. *Playing and reality.* London: Routledge.

9

The Trouble with Math

RALPH ABRAHAM

Since 1994, the Ross School on Long Island has evolved a curriculum based on a core of world cultural history using an outline I wrote and a long essay written by the historian William Irwin Thompson for the Ross School in 1995. Thompson has devoted considerable time to working with teams of teachers to develop specific course materials for this program, now known as the Ross spiral curriculum. Since each grade at the Ross School is devoted to an epoch of cultural history, and the epochs and grades follow in chronological sequence, it is possible to integrate all of the traditional subjects in the matrix of relationships from which they originally evolved. For example, when the sixth grade is devoted to the axial age, then ancient Greek math, science, art, philosophy, and so on may be taught together, evoking the cultural ambiance of the ancient world. This is the program that has evolved, although the historical sequence and integration of math is not yet complete. This chapter is devoted to describing a proposed program, based on my ideas as well as those of Rupert Sheldrake, William Irwin Thompson, and Courtney Sale Ross, that would integrate math more completely with the core of the spiral curriculum. Since mathematics is the universal language of space-time patterns and the common modeling strategy of all academic disciplines, math skills are highly advantageous for conceptually integrating historical data and understanding the gigantic complex system in which we live. We have therefore proposed that math skills and the concepts of chaos theory be given special emphasis throughout the spiral curriculum.

My ideas for math education have evolved over some fifty years of university teaching at the University of Michigan, University of California Berkeley, Columbia, Princeton, and University of California Santa Cruz. My research in dynamical systems and chaos theory was radically changed by the arrival in Santa Cruz of computer graphics technology in 1974. Early adoption of computer graphics in my research in chaos theory diffused into university teaching, with state-supported grants to introduce more visual representations in the introductory math courses, and the creation of the Visual Math Project at UC

Santa Cruz. A sizable National Science Foundation grant in 1980 was devoted to the validation of the visual approach for math education. We showed that more visuals resulted in less math anxiety. In the 1980s, the Visual Math Project grew into a master's degree program in applied and computational math, and then in the 1990s into a research program, the Visual Math Institute.

In 1987, a brief wave of popularity of chaos theory prompted me to begin writing *Chaos, Gaia, Eros* (1994). In that book I divided world cultural history into three epochs—static, periodic, and chaotic—each of which was tied to a particular development in mathematics. I had become friends with Thompson a few years earlier, and out of respect for his superior knowledge of history I sent him draft chapters for comment. He replied that he had himself devised a similar scheme, most recently published in 1986 in his book *Pacific Shift*. His own scheme, in which world history is outlined as having four major epochs, or *cultural ecologies,* each characterized by a different mathematical style or *mentality*—arithmetic, geometric, dynamic, and chaotic—is credited in *Chaos, Gaia, Eros*. Later I learned that he had been working on these ideas since 1961 in his undergraduate honors thesis influenced by Gregory Bateson, Vico, and Heinz Werner. When Courtney Sale Ross contacted me in 1995, after reading *Chaos, Gaia, Eros*, to request that I help her turn my book into a curriculum for the Ross School, we brought in Thompson as well and together began the ongoing project to create the Ross spiral curriculum, a new school program integrated by world cultural history.

This chapter discusses the problems and strategies of the math component of this history-based program for middle and high schools, as it has evolved in the context of my work with the Ross School over the past fourteen years, and then proposes a new program in outline form. This program has influenced the Ross spiral curriculum but has not yet been fully integrated, partly because of the pernicious influence of standardized tests, as discussed below.

Bifurcations of Cultural History

The word *bifurcation* is taken from the jargon of chaos theory, as explained in great detail in my book *Chaos, Gaia, Eros* (1994). But in our context, it means a major shift in history. My emphasis on historical transformation derives from my conviction that we are experiencing one on a massive scale, as argued by Ervin Laszlo in *The Age of Bifurcation* (1991). Through an understanding of earlier historical transformations, we may improve our chances of surviving this one and creating a viable future for humankind on planet Earth. This level of understanding is an important goal of our program.

The major transformations in world cultural history that Thompson and I, at first independently and then together, have outlined, are expressed in terms of shifts in mathematical thinking. This has enabled us to develop a program that integrates mathematics with cultural history and aims at creating an awareness and understanding of the special role of mathematics in the evolution of consciousness. With immersion in a given cultural ecology, the intertwined paths of math, science/technology, languages/writing/literature, and graphic arts/music become one knowledge. The development of this knowledge through time, with special emphasis on the major points of bifurcation, provides the strongest base for understanding the present and creating the future. Establishing this base is the main goal of our integrated program, of which the math thread is an integral part.

The Changing Nature of Mathematics

Mathematics may even be older than speech: indeed, speech may have evolved from it. Since our ancestors' development of language, math has evolved in giant steps. And since the computer revolution, a new image of the subject is gaining acceptance: the study of space-time patterns. Dynamic math is outpacing the static concepts established by the ancients.

Currently the main branches of mathematics are usually listed as arithmetic, geometry, algebra, and dynamics (a.k.a. analysis). Sometimes logic, topology, chaos theory, and other areas of mathematics are listed as well. We may refer to the branches by the code RGADX (for aRithmetic, Geometry, Algebra, Dynamics, and chaos [Xaos] theory).

Arithmetic is all about numbers, counting, and order. *Geometry* is the study of static spatial patterns such as triangles, circles, cubes, and pyramids. Both ancient branches of math are still evolving. *Algebra* is an extension of arithmetic dealing with the solution of equations, manipulation of polynomials, and so forth. *Geometric algebra* is an intermediate step in which geometrical constructions are used to solve equations (see Katz and Imhausen 2007 for more information). *Dynamics* deals with the analysis of motion in terms of distance, velocity, and acceleration. In its recent development there is an emphasis on so-called qualitative theory and long-term behavior: that is, where will this moving system end up? *Chaos theory* is a further development of dynamics, dealing with behavior that is chaotic—that is, neither fixed nor periodic.

All of the branches of math are useful in daily life as well as in scientific professions. R and G were established in the classical tradition as part of its curriculum, the quadrivium. A arrived in the Middle Ages and became part of the traditional school program in the Renaissance. D is relatively new; it was taught to college seniors in my parents' time and has now descended to high school in Europe and early college in the United States. X has just burst into popular consciousness in the past decade. It has yet to make a dent on most schools, but I am working on changing that. Computers have radically changed the way math is done and taught and the way new knowledge is found, especially in X.

Outline of Our Proposed Program

When Thompson and I began working together, I added an algebraic epoch to the arithmetic, geometric, dynamic, and chaotic epochs that he had proposed in his fourfold scheme of periodization. The sequence of world history that we employ, therefore, is:

1. Prehistoric cultures (arithmetic mentality)
2. Classical civilizations (geometric mentality)
3. Medieval civilizations (algebraic mentality)
4. Modern industrial civilization (Galilean dynamical mentality)
5. Contemporary planetary civilization (complex dynamical mentality)

And the major transformations are:

- R/G Shift, ancient Greece, 500 BCE
- G/A Shift, early Islam, 800 CE
- A/D Shift, Newton and Leibniz, 1660
- D/X Shift, atomic, computer, etc., 1945

To produce the curriculum, we mapped this scheme of history onto the grades. As noted above, each grade at the Ross School is devoted to an epoch of cultural history. The epochs and grades follow in chronological sequence, so that all of the traditional subjects, including mathematics, can be studied together and integrated into the matrix of relationships from which they originally evolved.

Regarding math education in the lower grades one may follow contemporary practice, emphasizing the meaning of numbers before the operations of arithmetic. Sharon Griffin's Number Worlds program is useful in this regard. We therefore begin here by considering the proposed math program for the middle school with the fifth grade.

GRADE 5

Core: The riverine cultural ecologies of ancient Egypt, Mesopotamia, and India, 3500 to 1450 BCE.

Math: In addition to the ongoing program of arithmetic, which includes fractions and decimal notations, begin ancient geometry and archeoastronomy.

GRADE 6

Core: Prophecy and cultural transformation, 1450 to 250 BCE. Moses, Pythagoras, Buddha, Confucius, Lao Tzu. Ancient Greece.

Math: In addition to the ongoing arithmetic program, which includes the elementary number theory of Euclid's *Elements*, begin the two-dimensional constructions of Euclid. There are forty-eight such constructions in books 1 through 6, and instructors should make specific selections. Ultimately, however, the goal is to eventually begin algebra with its roots in geometry. *The placement of* geometry *before algebra is historical.* So the constructions relating to *geometric algebra* should be included. See Katz (1993, 64–70). See also my *Visual Constructions of Euclid,* C#15 (Prop. II-11) and C#16 (Prop. II-14). Here I am beginning to deviate from the spiral curriculum as now taught. This alternative is similar to a proposal of Katz and Imhausen (2007).

GRADE 7

Core: Empires and religions, 350 BCE to 800 CE.

Math: More constructions of Euclid, building toward the five Platonic solids. Logic should be introduced from Euclid's theorems, which are intended to prove that the constructions are correct. Begin trigonometry applied to astronomy.

GRADE 8

Core: Climax of the Middle Ages, 800 to 1450.

Math: Introduce algebra as the recapitulation of geometric algebra using the rhetorical method of al-Khwarizmi, and progress to the symbolic method of Descartes.

GRADE 9

Core: Renaissance, Reformation, the New World, 1416 to 1688.

Math: Algebra with symbolic notation, polynomial functions, beginnings of calculus in Kepler and Galileo, anticipating Newton and Leibniz in grade 10.

GRADE 10

Core: Enlightenment and Romanticism, 1688 to 1865.
Math: Advanced algebra, calculus, and matrices.

GRADE 11

Core: Modern era, 1865 to 1948.
Math: Vector spaces, matrices, dynamical systems, modeling and simulation of complex dynamical systems, computational methods, statistics, logic and proofs.

GRADE 12

Core: Contemporary era, 1948 to the present.
Math: Electives, including fractal geometry, chaos theory, and complex systems.

The Sheldrake Principle (1981)

One of our main assumptions in drawing up this curriculum is that it is easiest for individuals to learn a subject in the sequence through which it has developed historically.

I call this the Sheldrake principle because Rupert Sheldrake, a contemporary English biologist and neovitalist, has proposed it as a corollary to his theory that a hypothetical field, the morphogenetic field, is the organizer of forms in nature (Sheldrake 1981, 180–81). Sheldrake and I met in 1982, and this idea emerged in conversation. He explained that I might learn to serve in tennis more easily because so many others had learned it before me. I tried out his idea in my math classes at the University of California Santa Cruz and became convinced it worked.

Such a historical approach to math education has actually been discussed previously in the math education literature, and there are international movements devoted to promoting it (see the International Congress on Mathematics Education, the International Commission on Mathematics Instruction, and the International Study Group on the Relations between History and Pedagogy in Mathematics). This is because the historical sequence of math's development—RGADX: arithmetic, geometry, algebra, dynamics, chaos theory— parallels the sequence of the development of cognitive modes in the individual and evolutionary, providing a natural progression from primitive counting (a skill of newborns; see Dehaene 1997) through visual (preverbal) modes of geometry and geometric algebra, to the rhetorical modes of early algebra and the abstract-symbolic modes of modern mathematics, including dynamics and chaos theory. Thus our curriculum also unfolds in tandem with the main developmental stages of the individual that are outlined by Piaget, in what we have called the rectified Sheldrake principle. Extensive support for this approach may be found in Furinghetti and Radford (2002).

The Importance of Euclid

After the R/G bifurcation around 500 BC, arithmetic, geometry, and geometric algebra were rapidly developed by the Pythagoreans. This rapid development culminated in the Academy of Plato around 350 BC. The results were collected in logical sequence in texts called *stocheia* (elements) by various editors. Euclid was one of these, and his text was so successful that it became the second most published book of all time, after the Bible, and the most influential math text of all time until very recently.

The *Elements of Euclid* develop these topics in thirteen books containing 645 propositions, concerning

- Plane geometry of triangles
- Plane geometry of circles
- Regular polygons in or around a circle
- Proportions (ratios)
- Number theory
- Solid geometry, especially of the regular solids

Of these 645 propositions, 60 are constructions and the others are used to prove that the constructions work reliably. The *kataskeuai* (pronounced *ka-tas-key*, meaning "constructions") may be regarded as the skeleton, the goal, and the most ancient part of the elements. Also known as *sacred geometry* and as *ancient geometry*, they are fundamental to the classical cultural ecology and were embedded in stone by the architects and builders of ancient times. The 48 fundamental constructions of plane geometry constitute the heart of the classical math curriculum.

The early study of Euclid is important in that it can give students a solid historical basis for understanding advanced mathematics. The constructions of Euclid span the history of mathematics from ancient Mesopotamia and Egypt up to the seventeenth century: that is, the time periods of grades 5 through 8 of our program, the epoch of the geometric mentality. They lead naturally into the introduction of the concepts of algebra, which emerged around 800 CE, and its symbolic notations, which came only around 1600, at the end of the geometric period. Given that this stage of the cultural evolution of mathematics was prerequisite to the creation of the dynamics and calculus of Kepler, Newton, and Leibniz, its study is prerequisite for a student learning these concepts, basic to the dynamic mentality. It is also an excellent preparation for understanding chaos theory.

It should be noted that Euclid himself, in editing the *Elements*, was meticulously faithful to the Sheldrake principle, the preservation of historical order. This is the reason that constructions of the golden section appear twice: in book 4, according to the Pythagoreans, and in book 6, after the theory of proportions, as Heath notes in his commentary. On a larger scale, the presentation first of geometry, then of geometric algebra, and finally of algebra is in accordance with the historical development of mathematics, unlike the standard curriculum today, in which the historic order of geometry and algebra is reversed.

How did this change occur? After the Enlightenment, circa 1800, the logic of Aristotle was blown up into a new paradigm for mathematics, called *formalism*. The months were renamed (e.g., *July* became *Brumaire* in French) to avoid the taint of history, and math was reorganized according to its logical as opposed to its historical order. The *Elements* of Euclid followed the traditional names of the months into the dustbin of history, and there began a disease of our current cultural ecology, of which widespread math anxiety, or damaged ability to do mathematics, was just one of the symptoms. As the *Elements* were abandoned and replaced by inferior works, the math crisis and math anxiety rapidly grew.

Math Anxiety

Math anxiety is a pathology produced in many individuals during their school years. It is a cognitive disability in which the natural human capacity for doing math is damaged. Even some people who succeed in technical and mathematical professions may be functioning at a fraction of their full potential because of the debilitating effects of this acquired disability. Its primary symptom is a flush of anxiety (math anxiety) or the urge to flee (math avoidance syndrome) when math comes up.

In her important book *Overcoming Math Anxiety* (1978/1993), Sheila Tobias points to word-solving problems as the crux of the problem of math anxiety. She describes the main flaws of the current school math program as:

- Domain disintegration (assuming knowledge from another discipline that has not actually been developed)
- Time disintegration, or anachronism (requiring concepts that are going to be, or should be, introduced later)
- Cultural disintegration (using metaphors foreign to the cultural context of the skills required)
- Mode disintegration (making use of too few, or inappropriate, cognitive modes)

Tobias's list highlights the very deficiencies that our own program counters through coordination of all disciplines, presentation of topics in their historical order, integration of mathematics with cultural history, and the use of multimedia technology. While Tobias's book is aimed at curing math anxiety, our program aims at preventing it.

The traditional math curriculum fosters math anxiety. My own theory is that math anxiety arises when a math topic is presented to students prematurely, at a time in their schooling (frequently around grade 7 or 8) before the prerequisite cognitive skills are well developed, so that they are unable to fully understand it, do not master it, and are left with the erroneous impression that they are at fault. More specifically, the concept of an unknown number (basic to algebra) is introduced too early, and geometric constructions, which build visual intelligence, are omitted or introduced very late when in fact they should be included from the early grades onward.

A curriculum that presented mathematics in historical rather than logical sequence, in particular restoring Euclid as a basic math text for the middle and high schools, would thus be a giant step toward the elimination of math anxiety. Further, it has long been known that math requires the coordinated modes of verbal, visual, and symbolic representation: the dynapic technique, for example, the method that mathematicians use to communicate among themselves, combines verbal description multiplexed with symbolic statements and a line-by-line drawing. But traditional math curricula underutilize some of these modes or do not use them at all; visual representations are particularly likely to be missing. Multimedia supplemental materials and the dynapic technique may be used to augment the traditional textbook-based program beginning no later than middle school. Howard Gardner's work on multiple intelligences has supported this view. We believe that correct math training encourages the coordination of the various cognitive modes and their balanced development in childhood. On a larger scale, such a revised program would require the creation of adequate new texts, the retraining of teachers to use graphics and to follow the sequence geometry, geometric algebra, algebra, and the abandonment of standardized tests that misrepresent math.

The tried and proven traditional program for school math is a tried and proven cause of math anxiety. It is unfortunate that so often the response to widespread math failure is merely to intensify the same efforts. For instance, a *San Jose Mercury News* article from July 27, 1999, entitled "Math: A Great Divide: Dismal Scores Reveal How Far California Schools Lag in Achieving Standards Called among the Toughest in U.S.," offers three suggestions for improving academic performance in math: train teachers in advanced math concepts; try out and buy new textbooks; and focus on preparing students to take algebra in eighth grade. School administrators in the San Jose Unified School District plan to begin upreparing students for algebra as early as fourth grade. According to the theories presented in this chapter, nothing could be worse than these suggestions, especially considering the fact that geometry is not presented until the ninth grade, if at all.

The Tyranny of Testing

As the *San Jose Mercury News* article suggests, low test scores in mathematics fuel renewed efforts to teach to the test, but such efforts only produce more math failure because standardized tests uphold traditional methods of teaching mathematics that are producing the low test scores in the first place. Standardized tests dominate the programs in schools, public or private, and cripple the evolutionary tendency of teachers, pupils, and parents to adapt the curriculum to individual skills and needs. This worldwide tendency is antievolutionary in that the standardized tests are very expensive and therefore slow to change. Perhaps more in math than in other subjects, the cognitive modes used in the tests are poorly adapted to the subject, and training for the test deviates from a balanced and coordinated development of modes. In particular, the visual mode is underutilized or uncoordinated with verbal and symbolic modes.

Math programs in schools worldwide—especially in the United States—are stuck in a loop. A faulty program presents the wrong material, out of sequence, without adequate cognitive modes, and set students up for failure. Young people of all levels of natural ability are convinced that they cannot learn math. These people become parents with math anxiety, and they pass this on to their children; it becomes a family disease. Then this anxiety manifests in the creation of standards and standardized tests. Standardized tests such as the SAT discourage curricular reform in that schools are under strong pressures to focus on aspects of a discipline that the test emphasizes and to give scant or no attention to aspects that the test omits. Regarding the math section of the SAT in particular, two problems might be instanced. First, under "Arithmetic" are included "word problems involving such concepts as: rate/time/distance, percents, averages." Yet dynamics is not an arithmetic concept. The difficulties students have with word problems may stem from this in part, while word problems on weights and measures (under "Geometry") may be easier. Problems on dynamics probably should be moved to the physics section of the test. Their mistaken inclusion under "Arithmetic" inclines school math programs to undertake these concepts too early. Second, "formal geometric proofs" are excluded from "Geometry." Of course these may be difficult to test with multiple-choice questions. But the explicit exclusion of this material from the SAT makes likely its exclusion from the entire high school program, which has unfortunately led school geometry programs to focus exclusively on the content, as opposed to the method, of geometry.

The Importance of Teaching Chaos Theory

Chaos theory was not known by this name until 1975 or so. For almost a century it was called dynamical systems theory, a topic of pure mathematics little known to the scientific community. After the computer revolution, chaotic motions became visible on computer graphic screens, and an awareness of their significance began to spread among scientists. In 1971 this awareness materialized as a technical report published in a journal of theoretical physics, and the chaos revolution was on. It took an additional fifteen years to sweep throughout the sciences and reach public awareness. All of this amounts to a major paradigm shift as chaotic behavior moved from mystery to familiarity (Abraham and Ueda 2000).

The most frequent application of dynamical systems theory is to the technology of modeling complex natural systems. The importance of chaos theory has been in this context. Because of the new wisdom of chaotic motions, many more complex systems now have useful models: the biosphere, the global economy, climate change, the human immune system, and so on. Different models for subsystems, created by scientists of disjoint specialties, may now be combined into a single complex supermodel, thanks to chaos theory. It provides a new technique for the unification of the sciences. Offhand it is not obvious that the chaotic motions of chaos theory have any direct bearing on the chaotic experiences of everyday life. However, as the applications of chaos theory to the social sciences evolve, more and more everyday chaos, including world cultural history, is brought into the embrace of chaos theory.

Since chaos theory is a new branch of math, it is relatively independent of the main topics of the traditional program. Therefore, it is quite accessible to people without an extensive math background. Calculus, for example, is not required. The plane geometry of Euclid is an excellent preparation. The applicability of chaos theory to the complex space-time patterns observed in nature and in human society make it an important subject for everyone to learn. And the paucity of background knowledge required makes it accessible to all. Math anxiety is usually triggered by high school algebra and its arcane symbolic notations, while most students feel comfortable with geometry. Since chaos theory builds upon geometry without requiring algebra, it provides a fresh start for those afflicted with math anxiety and may actually restore math confidence.

Our proposed program, then, relies on the synergistic operation of several features—integration of mathematics with other disciplines; adherence to a curricular sequence based on the historical order of the field's evolution and the developmental order of individual capacities; and recruitment of multiple modes of representation, particularly the visual. It prevents math anxiety; illuminates the cultural meanings of mathematics, thereby deepening students' knowledge and interest; and builds a strong foundation for understanding not only mathematics as it has evolved up to this point but mathematics as it is currently unfolding in chaos theory.

NOTE

Many thanks to my coworkers at the Ross School, especially Kurt Fischer, Victor Katz, Courtney Sale Ross, Bruce Stewart, and William Irwin Thompson. My proposed program outline incorporates several suggestions of Victor Katz for grades 8 through 11. A great number of teachers have given us useful feedback, and I thank them all.

REFERENCES

Abraham, Ralph H. 1994. *Chaos, Gaia, eros: A chaos pioneer uncovers the three great streams of history.* San Francisco: Harper San Francisco.
Abraham, Ralph H., and Yoshisuke Ueda, eds. 2000. *The chaos avant-garde: Memories of the early days of chaos theory.* Singapore: World Scientific.
Dehaene, Stanislas. 1997. *The number sense: How the mind creates mathematics.* New York: Oxford University Press.

Furinghetti, F., and L. Radford. 2002. Historical conceptual developments and the teaching of mathematics: from philogenesis and ontogenesis theory to classroom practice. In *Handbook of international research in mathematics education,* ed. L. English, 631–54. Mahwah, NJ: Lawrence Erlbaum.

Katz, V. J. 1993. *A history of mathematics: An introduction.* Reading, MA: Addison-Wesley.

Katz, V. J., and A. Imhausen. 2007. *The mathematics of Egypt, Mesopotamia, China, India and Islam: A sourcebook.* Princeton: Princeton University Press.

Laszlo, Ervin. 1991. *The age of bifurcation: Understanding the changing world.* Philadelphia: Gordon and Breach.

Sheldrake, Rupert. 1981. *A new science of life: The hypothesis of formative causation.* Los Angeles: J. P. Tarcher.

Thompson, William Irwin. 1971. *At the edge of history.* New York: Harper and Row.

———. 1986. *Pacific shift.* San Francisco: Sierra Club Books.

Tobias, Sheila. 1978/1993. *Overcoming math anxiety.* New York: Norton.

Part IV

Theories and Practices

Choreographing the Curriculum

*The Founder's Influence as Artist,
Visionary, and Humanitarian*

DEBRA MCCALL

Logic will get you from A to B. Imagination will take you everywhere.

Albert Einstein

Courtney Sale Ross envisioned a school that would prepare students for active engagement in the twenty-first century. As an artist, she brought a visual sensibility to this endeavor and often employed imagistic metaphors to convey her vision. In the early years a series of images of a caterpillar's metamorphosis into a butterfly was mounted in the faculty lounge. Every year or two she would ask where we, as a faculty, thought the school was in the process. This was an apt metaphor for the Ross School. A filmmaker, gallery owner, and curator, Courtney Ross thought in terms of preproduction, production, and postproduction. These phases guided the school's evolution. Imagination was the core of her inspiration. "Don't focus on the obstacles; imagine and dream the possibilities," she would advise her faculty. As a humanitarian, she frequently reminded us why we were involved in this innovative endeavor by quoting H. G. Wells: "Human history becomes more and more a race between education and catastrophe." Ross was to be a prototype of education, one that could be replicated, exported, and adapted to other schools, regions, countries, and populations. It was to serve the common good. Partially borrowing from the Temple at Delphi, "Know Thyself in Order to Serve" became the school's motto for action.

Underlying each of the emergent phases of the Ross School—development of its innovative integrated, global curriculum; creation of a middle school, a high school, and a K-12 program; implementation of senior projects; admissions to institutions of higher learning; the Ross Institute Academy; the Ross Global Academy Charter School in New York City; and Tensta Gymnasium in Stockholm—rests the vision of an artist and humanitarian who understood that the critical condition of education in the late twentieth century required urgent change. Courtney Ross was able to deliver this change because she generously catalyzed a creative, passionate, and willful community devoted to students' holistic growth, development, and engagement. This is what she refers to as "educating the whole child for the whole world." With an impeccably degreed and award-winning faculty that included an ethnomusicologist (Kenneth Sacks), painters (Jennifer Cross and Christina Schlesinger), a 3-D artist (Diane Gerardi), a Romanian spelunker and biologist (Serban Sarbu), a naturalist (Hugh McGuinness), a choreographer and dance historian (Debra McCall), a divinity professor and mathematician (Rick Faloon), an art historian/curator (Therese Lichtenstein), a museum educator (Martha Stotzky), a Shakespearean actor (Gerard Doyle), writers (Mark Foard and Geoff Gordon), historians (Matthew Aldredge and Carrie Clark), graphic designers (Julie Iden), a wildlife preservationist (Greg Drossel), photographers (Alexis Martino), media theorists (Reggie Woolery and Adele Madelo), an animator (Kerry Sharkey-Miller), a filmmaker (Marie Maciak), an anthropologist (Sally Booth), and an advanced chaos theorist (Gottfried Mayer-Kress), Courtney Ross oversaw the fashioning of a world-class curriculum that addressed how students could excel in the new global landscape.

The Ross School's earliest phase, prior to implementation of the spiral curriculum, was a home-schooling experiment of sorts. With Steven Ross working in Asia, Courtney, their daughter Nicole, and a friend of Nicole's, Nicky Haramut, traveled to Japan and China. The two girls learned Chinese calligraphy and Japanese dance and visited the great monuments. When Steven fell ill, the family returned to East Hampton, where a few more students joined a small group devoted to experiential study and on-site learning in Greece, London, the Galapagos, and Washington, D.C. From this one grade level emerged the desire and need for a middle school.

Caterpillar (Preproduction)

Study the past if you would define the future.

Confucius

Implementation of the spiral curriculum and growth into a middle school was marked by an exciting, dynamic new form in education. This would be a school with a curriculum fashioned by a poet and historian, William Irwin Thompson, and a chaos dynamics theorist, Ralph Abraham. It would be a curriculum rooted in developmental theory, consciousness study, and cultural philosophy. One strand of its architecture was literary and poetic, the other mathematical and operational; the two intertwined to form a double helix of cultural study and mathematical constructs that would cohesively serve as the school's philosophical DNA. With pedagogical scholars such as Howard Gardner, who shaped our best-practices approaches, Ross School moved from a utopian home-schooling experiment into a bona fide middle school in 1995–96.

The newly recruited faculty received two weeks of professional development with the architects of the curriculum and a variety of mentors. The teachers were tasked with inaugurating the new "evolution of consciousness" curriculum in the most dynamic, engaging form possible. Study of all disciplines was to be informed by cultural history, which lay at the core of the spiral curriculum and unfolded chronologically through the grades. Each grade level represented a historical period focused on comparative analysis of world cultures of the period. Each grade had a theme—fifth was "riverine culture"; sixth, "prophecy and cultural transformation"; seventh, "world empires and universalizing religions." Cultural history served as the nucleus around which all disciplines integrated. Integrated units and interdisciplinary projects enlivened the classroom with multiple perspectives. When students studied Mesopotamia in cultural history, they also constructed miniature floodplains in science. While learning of the emergence of writing and the alphabet, they made cuneiform clay tablets and cylindrical seals in art. When studying the world's first poet, Enheduanna, in English class, they wrote hymns to the Sumerian goddess of fertility, Inanna. As they pondered the Sumerian discovery of base 60 in mathematics, they threw pottery on a wheel. When examining the first code of law by Hammurabi, they sketched a replica of his stele in the school gallery, and as they planned a menu of the ancient Sumerian diet they visited a local organic farm and baked a variety of breads in wellness class. The focus was to teach art, literature, science, math, and technology in historical context. As students who come to Ross from other schools describe, "It makes sense to learn this way—all the classes relate to each other, and history advances as we move through the grades."

Integration across disciplines was beautifully depicted in Courtney's early "flower design" of the curriculum. As she spoke to faculty during our many brainstorming sessions, she would often sketch ideas to convey her vision. Since our filmmaker founder was a visual thinker, we soon learned that when we wanted to get our ideas across to her we too would best benefit by presenting a visual image, graph, or depiction—not unlike a storyboard. Many designs—even weavings of "thematic content threads" from team meetings—were created. An exhibition of the visual work generated in those early years would have served as an insightful portfolio for the curriculum's evolution.

Two memorable interdisciplinary and inter-grade projects marked the first year. The first ten days of rolling out the curriculum were to include all history up to the point of the fifth grade's study of river civilization. The faculty decided to begin each day with a storyteller, Diane Wolkstein, reading the myth of the Sumerian goddess Inanna to the group of all-female students. By the tenth day, it was complete, and the grades broke off into their respective historical periods. During those ten days, faculty designed a series of prehistory workshops: cave painting after that of Lascaux, sundial construction, astronomical observation, seed planting, fertility sculptures, nature walks, fire making, mask making, drumming. On day ten, the rollout culminated in a boisterous drumming and dancing circle with each student introducing her mythological masked figure through gesture, sound, and rhythm. The second project was a "J term" (January) in which all regularly scheduled classes ceased for three weeks while small inter-grade groups chose from a hat the name of a Caribbean island for in-depth study. From exploring the island's geography and natural habitat to its economy, writers, artists, musicians, history, cuisine, and local culture and contributions, students created a variety of "products" to demonstrate their understanding of their islands. At the final exhibition, each of the island groups displayed books filled with songs, short stories, poems, paintings, and photography. A group was then selected to visit the Bahamas and learn the culture firsthand while making a film and Web site about the experience to share with their fellow students in East Hampton.

End-of-year trips were thematically integrated with the curriculum. That first year, the fifth grade examined Boston as a "river civilization": they canoed down the Concord and compared the Declaration of Independence to Hammurabi's Code of Law, Bunker Hill to Sumerian monuments, and Boston's City Hall to an upside-down ziggurat. The sixth grade's trip to Washington related the history and architecture of the capital to their study of ancient Greece and "cultural transformation," while the seventh grade in Rome investigated the republic and imperial period as illustrative of "world empires and universalizing religions."

It is important to note that the parents of the early years were, themselves, a unique group. Some were educators looking for an innovative model; others had established alternative preschools in the East End of Long Island. There were artists, accountants, gallery owners, farmers, small business owners, and parents in service professions. Despite a small population in those years, our students represented all members of the local community—whites, African Americans, Native Americans from the local Shinnecock Nation reservation, Tibetan refugees, and Vietnamese immigrants. The parents were active participants. Hesitance gave way to trust as they witnessed their children's projects and excitement throughout the first months. They realized that when they asked, "What did you do in school today?" the answer, instead of being "Nothing," could be an explanation of how the Pharos at Alexandria was similar to the lighthouse at Montauk. They reported being relieved that their children awoke happy, wanting to go to school, and were happy upon arriving home, full of stories of the day. And on Valentine's Day of our first year, the entire community gathered for a potluck dinner and contra dancing in a local community house, cementing the bonds and celebrating the work accomplished.

What was fashioned in the first few years of the school was what Courtney Ross and the faculty often described as "choreography." The students' chronological "steps" through history and the interdisciplinary dance of the disciplines flowed to form a spiral pathway through the grades—one in which students revisited areas of the world and themes. They saw that understanding the past helped them to make sense of the present and to envision the future. The ever-evolving spiral comprised disciplinary depth, a sensitivity to global culture, and a plurality of intelligences manifested in engaging curricular lessons and colorful performance-based projects—all echoing the founder's artistic, humanistic vision.

Chrysalis (Production)

> The principal goal of education in the schools should be creating men and women who are capable of doing new things, not simply repeating what other generations have done.
>
> Jean Piaget

> Our mission is to change the way education meets the future; to foster interdisciplinary, integrated thinking and innovative leadership; to engage fully in the global community; and to facilitate lifelong learning.
>
> Ross School Mission

In the third year of the spiral curriculum boys were admitted, and the class grew to three times its original size to form the first ninth grade of the new Ross High School. Ross was in the midst of converting a medical building to accommodate the ninth grade, so classes were held at a local camp until shortly before Thanksgiving. Every Friday, the faculty would pack art, artifacts, curriculum, technology, and sports supplies into a large caisson, and every Monday they would unpack them. The "pioneering" metaphor was not lost on the group. The ninth-grade team was creating a curricular narrative for the early 1300s through 1688. It had two working teams, each comprising members from cultural history, English, math and science, languages, wellness, performing and visual arts, and media studies. The vertical scope and sequence of each discipline ("domain" in Ross-speak) served as the warp to the weft of the interdisciplinary grade-level teams. We called this dynamic interaction "the tapestry." Some of the most meaningful professional development took place that year. At the kickoff of every unit of study, the two teams would order in dinner. While each faculty member presented the important understandings of his or her content area for the unit, remaining team members noted opportunities for integration.

Courtney Ross had always been intimately involved with the design of the school environment, but her prominent design role in these formative years resulted in a characteristic style for Ross School. When the students arrived at the new high school in November, a soaring Nike graced the glass entrance. Wooden cubbyholes for the Chinese slippers required inside buildings stood upon masterfully crafted stone floors. As students made their way upstairs, they discovered a Brunelleschi-like Duomo, just in time for the start of the Renaissance unit. Inside this handsome structure with colored intarsia walls, students could simultaneously view two images of Renaissance art in the round. The Duomo became a favorite for classes, but the soaring art room next to it attracted students and faculty alike for drop-in classes. Each high school classroom was thoughtfully designed with paintings, statuary, and scientific mechanisms representing the grade level's historical era, allowing teachers quick access to art and artifacts. This was "classroom as educator," as Courtney described. Downstairs in the carpeted library, a series of painted lunchboxes rimmed the ceiling. A solarium with huge tanks for ecology experiments was adjacent to the library/screening room. Conscious thought had been given to the design, demonstrating the respect Courtney Ross holds for teachers, students, and their learning. The slippers, carpeted floors, soft lighting, tone bells, and wooden lockers made for a quiet environment. Since this was the first structure renovated for the school, it was a gift of possibility from Courtney Ross. It inspired in faculty and students an imagination for what might be possible and established a standard for performance; it catalyzed a commitment to experimentation and excellence.

For the first day of the Renaissance unit, each faculty member stood by an image of Raphael's painting *The School of Athens* to help students identify the illustrious personae. The tradition holds to this day. Students were encouraged to "think like Leonardo" as they dissected frogs in biology, undertook observations of nature, drew the world around them, and measured with Geometer's Sketchpad the accuracy of perspective of various Renaissance masters. During that initial year, a Tibetan monk was in residence. Serenely, day after day, he artfully constructed an immense sand painting. As it grew in complexity and color, his audience grew in size and volunteers assisted. It became a place for daily meditation but also provided the students an opportunity to ask about the meaning of the symbols, the tenets of Buddhism, and the monk's life and training in Tibet. A few weeks after its completion, the sand was dissembled and carried to the ocean to rejoin nature. The mutability of this Buddhist tradition fostered ongoing inquiry from the student body. Soon after, they implemented a variety of sustainability reforms.

A quantum leap in development occurred over the next two years as we approached the first Ross School senior year. The tenth grade began with a unit on absolutism in which students constructed a series of water pumps and fountains for their "Versailles gardens" on the high school green. In their Enlightenment salons, ancien regime cupcakes were served while students discussed the rights of man, and woman. In their study of the French Revolution, they enacted trials and built a makeshift guillotine in science class. Their reading of Mary Shelley's *Frankenstein* inspired experiments with electricity, while their immersion in Romanticism led them to paint and write with a passion appropriate to their age.

Eleventh grade heralded the appearance of another structure, the Media and Humanities Building, a glass twin to the ninth-tenth high school building. The eleventh grade at that time studied the period from post–Civil War through the present. The building reflected the design style of Josef Hoffman and the Wiener Werkstätte of Vienna in the early twentieth century. In the center of the building sat a two-story glass structure that became the home of Spiral Pictures. Led by film teacher Marie Maciak, a number of students produced work that would be honored at local and international film festivals. Understanding the role and impact of the moving image on young people long before YouTube, Courtney Ross envisioned the Media Center as a film/video production and Web broadcast center. Next to the broadcast studio was the music rehearsal room, with indigenous instruments and a large screening space. It not only hosted a jazz ensemble led by Hal McKusick, a jazz great, but gave rise to an international project for the millennium: Sonic

Convergence. Courtney Ross envisioned a global collaboration with students from China, Sweden, and Ross that would use technology to support a globally composed piece for the millennium. Students met three times in each country over a period of eighteen months, during which they composed and rehearsed. Between meetings, they e-mailed small movements of the piece. Finally, they reunited to perform a grand symphony conducted by Quincy Jones, a friend of Courtney Ross.

Because media emerge as a prominent phenomenon in the twentieth century, the eleventh grade spent a full trimester using film in conjunction with the curriculum. In their study of colonialism they filmed mock trials of charismatic leaders of anticolonial rebellions and, as a jury, debated the pros and cons of conviction. Moving on to modernity with study of Einstein, Freud, Poincaré, Picasso, and Berg, they performed their understanding of this paradigm shift with jazz compositions, modern dances, film in the style of *Metropolis,* modern literature, quantum theory drawings, psychological photo essays, and more.

As the first eleventh-grade class came to a close, two new buildings were about to change the landscape and community of the Ross School: the Senior Building and the Center for Well-Being. The twelfth-grade course of study was designed as a recapitulation of the K–12 curriculum, from the Big Bang to the present. Its new building, the Senior Building, housed a gallery/foyer on the main floor with art representing all periods in the curriculum. Lining the halls were replicas of paintings from the Renaissance through contemporary times. In the lecture hall, where a glass wall framed the outdoor forest, seniors attended college-style lectures in science, literature, and art history. They also staged performances, engaged in debates, and organized human rights film festivals.

With years of interdisciplinary learning behind them, and a unique course every year of high school—in which one trimester each was devoted to visual arts, performing arts, and media—students come to their senior year as intrinsically integrating thinkers and informed aesthetes. In the senior project, they explore their "passions" in depth. They bring raw material to finished product over the course of three phases—research and development, production, exhibition and presentation—and are evaluated on process folios, product, and presentation. After the exhibition, in which all students' work is displayed, the presentation consists of the student explaining the process of the project, the obstacles and solutions, the skills acquired, and his or her learning and production style to fellow students, local community mentors, administration, and faculty. The exhibition and presentation not only emphasize reflective and metacognitive components of learning but propel the student to cultivate both design and verbal presentational skills, reinforcing these as skill sets necessary for the future. Each year students stun the community with their senior project creations—a flying machine fashioned with the same tools used by Leonardo da Vinci, fundraising to rebuild an orphanage in Thailand, a Museum of the Chinese Language, a medicine wheel painting and Web site on Native American healing, films and photo essays about "The Other Hamptons" (the lives of such workers as farmers, landscapers, immigrant day laborers, and fishermen), to name a few. By the end of this process, students have developed both an expertise that allows them to act as mentors for the community and a confidence that propels them into their future.

As the soaring arched beams of the Center for Well-Being were slowly maneuvered into place, students, parents, and faculty tracked construction on the campus Webcam. Urban Reininger, our longtime technology faculty member, was the most popular man on campus, helping everyone connect to check on its completion. When the final beam settled and the interior was installed in concrete form, Courtney Ross convened the construction workers, architects, community planners, students, parents, and faculty for a barbecue, dance, and celebration with a country western band. It became apparent at that juncture that this majestic building would forge a new relationship between Ross and the local community. Up to that time there had been no large gathering place on campus for events, sports, or community gatherings. Now there was a Great Hall where the entire community could gather for morning yoga, basketball games, and fundraising evenings. There was the Court Theater for performance and screenings; a stunning mirrored movement room for yoga, dance wushu, and tai chi; a meditation room for contemplative retreat; a koi pond; a reception area with fireplace; and a café on the top floor that seemed to levitate in the treetops of the woods outdoors. The interior reflected the founder's acknowledgment of Eastern and Western forms of wellness: there were tatami mats, kimonos, Greek statuary in Olympian poses, African masks, and Native American weavings and medicine wheels. Suffolk County happens to be the largest agricultural producing county in New York State, so the café, with its wood-burning oven and its innovative chef, Ann Cooper, spawned the creation of R.O.S.S.—regional, organic, seasonal, sustainable—a culinary philosophy that engaged the students in visiting and working on local organic farms, planting gardens, and enrolling in culinary classes. These prescient programs were to be replicated nationwide.

In tandem with the Center for Well-Being's appearance, the school's motto, "Know Thyself in Order to Serve," actively flourished. Service had been an integral component of the school's mission from the beginning. Although students regularly committed themselves to service in conjunction with their curriculum, they now had the space to organize larger functions. Weekly assemblies featured heads of charitable organizations such as Hoops for Hope. Our ceramicist, Diane Giardi, started Empty Bowls, a project in which students sold bowls they had made in class to raise awareness of, and funds for, hunger relief. Barbara Raeder, a Ross School fifth-grade teacher, organized one of the more successful, lasting service ventures with her 2002–3 class. After 9/11, students discovered that children their age were not able to attend schools in Afghanistan because many had been destroyed or there was no pay for teachers. Having learned that a teacher's monthly salary was $35 a month, they set about raising money for Schools for Hope, an organization that supports schools in Afghanistan. They maintained that support for over three years, raising thousands of dollars to sustain schools in the war-torn region.

The advent of the Center for Well-Being also ushered in a new era of community engagement. Gratifying as it was to see the school's motto enacted, it was also exciting to welcome the community's participation in evening learning programs and lectures, in special visits to our café to dine with the students, and in fundraising and service events. That first year, upon Courtney Ross's suggestion, the school hosted a Valentine Ball for seniors in the community. They arrived dressed to the nines. Recently, a World War II veteran visiting for lunch on Veteran's Day remarked that the ball had been one of the most memorable events for local seniors in the last ten years. Another visit to our café resulted in a collaborative lunch program between a local public school and the Ross School. Currently, a well-attended adult evening program offers everything from belly dancing and forensic science to classes in Italian and Arabic.

In this stage of production, the school consolidated around its mission and core values—courage, cooperation, gratitude, integrity, mindfulness, responsibility, and respect—and developed graduation outcomes that established holistic expectations for a Ross School graduate. The saying goes that it takes three years to make a Ross teacher and three years to coalesce and refine a grade-level curriculum. Enough years had passed for this to occur. During these generative years, many exemplary integrated projects were created—in the "India project," as part of the fifth grade's study of river cultures, students performed a version of the Bhagavad Gita in Sanskrit and learned

Bharat Natyam to perform Shiva's Dance of Creation; in the seventh grade "Maya unit" students played Mayan football and drank thick cocoa from cups they had crafted and painted with Mayan hieroglyphs; in the eighth grade "medieval Islamic society unit," students researched, wrote, and performed historical memoirs about medieval Islamic figures and hosted a Middle Eastern banquet.

The culmination of the production phase was the school's accreditation by the Middle States Association of Colleges and Schools, a process guided by Michele Claeys, a longtime member of the Ross School administration. The accreditation team cited Ross for its exemplary fulfillment of its mission. And because of Ross's unique and successful global commitment, it was the first secondary school to be awarded the organization's international accreditation status.

Metamorphosis (Postproduction)

> The self is not something ready-made, but something in continuous formation through choice of action.
>
> John Dewey

Going Global

After we had graduated several classes our students established a record of college acceptances, and parents relaxed about the viability of the Ross model. Courtney Ross and the faculty were able to shift attention to a new challenge. She had always intended for the Ross School to serve as a prototype for export and adaptation to other schools. Synchronistically, a partner arrived in the form of Tensta Gymnasium, a public high school on the outer perimeter of Stockholm, Sweden, that served many immigrants. Students from the Middle East, eastern Europe, and Africa, many of whom have escaped extreme political and social conditions, constitute approximately 90 percent of the population at Tensta. To keep these students engaged, Tensta decided to offer a global curriculum and sought out Ross. Taking the adaptation to heart, Tensta systemically transformed its school. Over five years of teacher-student exchanges and professional development training, one of the more successful milestones of this adaptation has been their development of integrated units and projects. One new integrated project invites students to assume the personae of Enlightenment figures in order to debate the virtues of freedom. Witnessing an Iraqi girl, a Somali boy with little formal schooling, and others from very diverse cultures and backgrounds engage in this debate is deeply compelling. The school's learning environment has been redesigned; faculty sit in teams, not disciplines. Open spaces were created for each team section where students could comfortably gather and collaborate on projects. Each student has a laptop computer. Currently in the process of becoming accredited as a Ross School, Tensta has dramatically improved teacher and student retention, and one of its programs, the Social Economics and Business Administration Program, was cited as exemplary by the Swedish government.

During the period of Tensta's developing partnership, Ross was fortunate to host two Harvard scholars on sabbatical, Marcelo and Carola Suárez-Orozco—they are now at the Institute for Advanced Study in Princeton and at New York University. Their comprehensive work on contemporary global immigration and education sparked a reexamination by Ross faculty of the meaning of educating for the future. Not only did their presence catalyze thinking about teaching students from an array of cultures and educational backgrounds, but Carola's work on student engagement was a refreshing approach for considering the theory of multiple intelligences and differentiated learning. Marcelo has edited two volumes, *Globalization: Culture and Education in the New Millennium* (M. Suárez-Orozco and Qin-Hilliard 2004) and *Learning in the Global Era: International Perspectives on Globalization and Education* (M. Suárez-Orozco 2007), co-sponsored by the Ross Institute and the University of California Press, that have advanced research and discussion indispensable to Ross's mission of "educating the whole child for the whole world."

The school's "M-terms" constitute another phase in globalizing the curriculum. In inter-grade groups, students study a subject in depth for three weeks. Many M-terms take place through service learning travel. From raising funds and supporting awareness of HIV-AIDS in Kenya, to building houses in Brazil with Habitat for Humanity, to working to save endangered species in the Caribbean, to building a school in Mozambique, students have developed a sensitivity and understanding of other cultures while serving as international ambassadors for the Ross School and their country.

Courtney Ross sponsored three M-term trips in 2006, 2007, and 2010 on the preservation and transmission of knowledge from the ancient world through the Middle Ages to the Renaissance—what she coins the Golden Matrix. In the first trip, students traveled to southern Spain to study the culture of tolerance, *La convivencia*, which flourished among Muslims and Jews during medieval al-Andalus. While searching for evidence of cultural fusion, Courtney's keen eye led students to decipher evidence of Arabic calligraphy in synagogues, Visigoth crosses in mosques, and the delicate influences of Islamic architecture in Christian palaces. She encouraged students to digitally map the pathways of trade and ancient knowledge from Baghdad and Constantinople to al-Andalus and emphasized the unique complexity of the schools of translation in Cordoba, Seville, Toledo, and Granada. She arranged for scholars and experts to provide daily lectures and workshops on mathematics, architecture, theology, politics, dance, music, and irrigation technology, which elucidated the efflorescence of medieval Andalusian culture. In reflection, students wondered if the United States is the al-Andalus of our time. The fact that Cordoba's culture of tolerance was destroyed by an invasion of extreme religious ideology provided insight into the fragility of our own democracy. Likewise, the archeology of learning was excavated in the stones of Athens and Florence the following year when students continued their exploration of generative moments of civilization and the preservation and transmission of goods, culture, and knowledge from the ancient world to the Renaissance. A final trip to Istanbul and Egypt to study Byzantium and ancient and Alexandrian Egypt will complete study of the Golden Matrix.

Completing the Whole

Once collaboration with an international public school partner in Sweden was accomplished, the next initiative was to extend the Ross model to New York City. Ross Global Academy Charter School opened its doors in 2006–7 with admission by lottery. The first year entailed development of both a lower and a middle school at the Tweed Courthouse in lower Manhattan, home to the New York City Department of Education. Actualizing Ross in a public school environment has provided a new forum for public-private exchange and interaction, fostering relationships between teachers and students of the city school and the school on Long Island. Concurrent with the establishment of Ross Global Academy, Ross expanded downward, adding prenursery through fourth grade. Formerly the Hampton Day School and then the Morriss Center, the lower school has enthusiastically embraced the Ross model. Teachers have discovered that the Ross curriculum imbues a philosophical cohesion to its pedagogical, cognitive, and developmental program. It has been fascinating to observe the evolving K–4 aspect of the curriculum that had existed only in theory before the expansion. The response of teachers, students, and parents has been overwhelmingly positive.

Instrumental to the accomplishment of the exportation and adaptation of the Ross model has been the role of the Ross Institute Academy, formerly the Ross Teacher Academy. The academy provides professional development training/workshops/coaching and multi-media resources to public and private educational institutions. It accredits all Ross model schools such as Tensta, aligns the Ross model to New York State and New York City Department of Education standards, oversees the curriculum of Ross Schools, and represents the Ross model at conferences and symposia. Initiatives in progress include engaging partners in research on twenty-first-century skills, mind-brain education, and developing multimedia products that embody the Ross model.

The Whole Child for the Whole World

The object of education is to teach us to love beauty.

Plato

One memorable Ross student's college application explained, "At Ross, we don't just learn about other cultures and history through books. We dance to their music, cook their foods, compose to their rhythms, create art in their style, debate their politics, analyze their philosophy and attempt to understand them from multiple perspectives." Alumni explain that their integrated learning provides them a unique perspective in college. We hear from colleges that our students are synthetic thinkers, that they feel comfortable approaching their professors for conversations and ask the deeper questions. Venturing further into graduate school and the job market, they report thinking holistically and are often drawn to the artistic and service sectors.

Courtney Sale and Steven J. Ross shared a vision for the children of the future—to empower them to meet the twenty-first century with equal opportunity, meaningful knowledge, and cutting-edge skills by establishing an innovative school of research, culture, the arts, humanities, technology, and science. They achieved more than the creation of a transformative school. They created a thriving community and generated a philosophy of learning.

Courtney Ross often refers to the great centers and academies of learning—ancient Athens and Alexandria, medieval Baghdad and al-Andalus, Constantinople, Renaissance Florence—as models from which we can draw inspiration and to which we should aspire. When Pythagoras arrived at Croton in southern Italy, the site of his future school, his first piece of advice to its citizens was to build a shrine to the Muses at the center of the city in order to promote civic harmony and learning. Courtney Ross has been our muse through these years—inspiring poetry, song, art, history, theater, dance, math, and science. She has realized her dream of an academy for the new century. From one school we have grown into many. From a small group of faculty and staff we have developed into a family of educators devoted to bold reform. From a small group of stellar mentors we have forged partnerships with exemplary programs and institutions. Her courageous leadership and generosity have confidently led us into the new century, equipped to face the challenges ahead. Her unrelenting spirit and innovation, her aesthetic touch, and her love for children and learning have graced our community so that every student can indeed venture forth as a "whole child for the whole world."

REFERENCES

Suárez-Orozco, M. M., and D. Qin-Hilliard, ed. 2004. *Globalization: Culture and education in the new millennium.* Berkeley: University of California Press.

Suárez-Orozco, M. M. 2007. *Learning in the global era: International perspectives on globalization and education.* Berkeley: University of California Press.

11

Mathematics and Culture

WILLIAM IRWIN THOMPSON

The chaos mathematician Ralph Abraham is passionate about the disastrous impact of the plague of "math anxiety" on American culture (see Abraham, this volume). I am a living example of the educational damage that the conventional American approach to mathematical instruction can inflict. In spite of my interdisciplinary interests, and an Ivy League PhD in cultural history and literary studies, I am practically a functional illiterate in mathematics. What I remember of math instruction in parochial, private, and public schools is rote "drill and kill" commands in soulless operations completely disconnected from any larger meaning. The sort of person who flourished under this sort of care was the kind of person who loved puzzles, codes, and algorithms completely unconnected to the world of emotions, relationships, history, and culture in general—the sort of person who preferred to take something out of the context that gave it meaning, the sort of person who was good at making atom bombs, or is now good at engineering plants and animals, but not so good at asking about the unimagined side effects on people, birds, bees, and butterflies.

The only time that math made any sense to me was when, after flunking geometry three times, I ended up in a summer high school makeup class with an amateur teacher, an engineer who had not been trained in "education." He brought into class an overhead projector, and rather than demanding—as all my other teachers had—that we memorize theorems and axioms in a kind of Euclidean Baltimore Catechism, he asked that we think visually in a new culture of relations in which the rote material receded to become a ground against which a new figure emerged. It was as if this teacher had plucked on the chords of my corpus callosum and lit up the whole right hemisphere of my brain. For the first time in my life, math began to make sense as it became part of new kind of visual thinking. Not only did I pass the course, but I got my first B+ in math!

Now, mind you, at the time that I was this summer school dunce, I was studying Latin, Spanish, French, and Russian—all at the same time—and getting As in all of these courses. I was also reading Melville, Thomas Wolfe, and the *Tao Te Ching* on my own outside of classes, so it is fair to say that I was not stupid, but math was meaningless to me because it had never been invested with any meaning or culture at any time during my entire primary and secondary education. Math was something you needed in order to make atom bombs, and since at that time—in the 1940s and '50s—we were taught to jump under our desks and cover our heads in dread of a Russian atomic attack, the only relationship math had with anything in my life was with the mysteries of physics and the construction of atom bombs. But I didn't want to grow up to be an atomic scientist; I wanted to grow up to be a poet. In fact, my first experience of an epiphany of the muse came as an auditory experience of "channeling" a daimonic realm of poetry that came right in the middle of a high school geometry class taught by one of the worst teachers I have ever had.

Math instruction should be more mystical and shamanic, and certainly Ralph Abraham with his Visual Math Institute has worked hard his whole life to climb the shaman's ladder to the realm of the gods and celestial intelligences to bring back a healing balm to the afflicted. After a career in university teaching, he now sees that students are too damaged by the time they reach university level, so he has shifted his attention to curricular design for primary and secondary levels of instruction. As one might expect, the teachers who have been trained in professional schools of education do not like his approach and fear that students will not be able to perform well on the machine-scored tests that determine their schools' standing and their merit increases in salary. "Teaching to the test" has now become a social imperative so reinforced by politicians that it is not likely that the United States will improve in the near future. But even if one accepts the validity of testing, results show that American students' performance declines as they move from primary to secondary education. In other words, the more they are taught mathematics in the Good Old American Way, the worse they get.

Now I am enough of a historian to know that the United States will disguise its crisis by continuing to import math teachers from Europe and Asia, in much the same way that it backs up its militarily generated national deficit by importing foreign capital through the sale of Treasury bills. And I am also enough of a historian to know that the kind of history one constructs is generally the history of one's intellectual constructions. So if one lives in a world of idolatrous belief in the power of technology, then history will be simply a history of technology: who killed whom with what from the Stone Age to the Plutonium Age. Ralph Abraham and I believe that math should be more mystical and shamanic, and he has argued in his recent essays for a more mystical and shamanic prehistory of math.

Perception is a matter of selective attention. If you are a bee, then you can see stripes on flowers in the ultraviolet spectrum that humans cannot. If you are a bird or a goldfish, then you can see four dimensions of color vision— and whatever that can be like we humans with our mere three rods and cones can have no idea. And so when Abraham and I look at prehistory and history, we see things that others either overlook or claim cannot possibly be there. I looked at the statuette of the Venus of Lespugue that I bought in the Louvre Museum gift shop and said to myself that it just could not be simply a fat lady meant to symbolize fertility. Considering the unrealistic proportions, and remembering mention of the ratio of the length of the head to the length of the torso in the Canon of Praxiteles from my art history classes at Pomona College, I suggested to Abraham that perhaps something else was at work in the statue, that perhaps there was an embedded code of ratios in the segmenting of the anatomy. Abraham analyzed the figure with his computer, and when he added the culture of musical scales to the lengths of the sections, he found a key to the code of the icon (Abraham 2006).

The likely response of a scholar or prehistorian would be to say, "Nonsense! We all know that Stone Age humans are primitives and don't have a culture of music and mathematics until the Greeks created Western civilization." Denial is the traditional academic response to the perception of anomalies in a paradigm. When first confronted with meteorites, academics said, "Nonsense! Stones just don't drop out of the sky!" When confronted with fossils, they said they were relics of Noah's flood. When confronted with a Neanderthal skull, the German experts insisted that the grotesque skull was probably that of a French soldier from the time of Napoleon. As Max Planck said of these sorts of trained experts: they never change their minds, they simply die, and younger people come along for whom the new paradigm is not so disturbing. So let us leave the experts to their well-earned mortality but go on to ask the few of us who are open to the idea that Ice Age art is not as primitive as we thought and that music, chanting, dance, mythology, and mathematics were most likely at that time one integral cognitive system. And may they become so again in a once and future science.

The statuette of the Goddess of Lespugue presents us with a developmental model of human cognition that begins to be isomorphic to new models in cognitive science in which human emotions are recognized to be essential to the development of higher judgmental skills (see Damasio and Damasio, this volume; Damasio 1994, 1999). Music attunes emotion to attention, to pattern, and this sensitivity is probably earlier than verbal consciousness. In other words, in Dehaene's (1999) contention, Piaget got it wrong when he claimed that certain mathematical perceptions developed after children learned to talk. Perceptions of rhythm, pattern recognition in dance, and a subitizing awareness of quantity are anterior to linguistic expression and are expressed by birds as well as the higher primates.

Consider for a moment what it means to make an Acheulian fist-hatchet. You see a rock, and you select it out of one set to make it conform to membership in a new set. Through patterned activity, the rock moves from membership in the set of possible use as a fist-hatchet to full-fledged membership in the set of actual fist-hatchets. Here hand-brain coordination is also interacting with category formation, with the categories that can be later articulated in a grammar that specifies substantives or nouns. In other words, linear theories of causation are inadequate. We have to think in terms of complex dynamical systems, mutually interacting causal chains, and emergent domains. Vertical posture, encephelation, social formation, communication systems, category formation, and tool manufacture all interact with one another through time to generate the cascade of bifurcations that we call the hominization of the primates.

If math is prior to linguistic articulation, then math should be easier than poetry for most people, and it would be if it were embedded in the matrix of music, emotional values, and linguistic meaning that it once had. The Goddess of Lespugue is quite literally that matrix, that maternal, material body of resonating cosmic vibration in which the One becomes the many. So if we really understand the front and back of this little statue, it should have the impact that gazing on the archaic torso of Apollo had for the poet Rilke.

Fist-hatchets also teach us that some knowledge is haptic. If you map the amount of brain area that goes to administer the work of the hand and the good old opposable thumb, you will come up with a very great area indeed. Here again, there is a certain kind of skill that is right hemispheric and configurative. I learned this once again when I would play with Legos with my younger son. I could make the most amazing and complex spaceships and castles, and entire towns that would cover almost the whole of the floor of his room as my addiction to Legos grew—and all of these without a plan, simply by thinking hapticly with my fingers and following the implications of individual moves and connections. Like birds flying in a spherical swarm, I had no master plan; there was simply the signaling connection of agents next to one another in which single moves created new implications for pattern unfoldment. In fact, had the Legos company given me a plan, I might not have been able to invent forms and buildings that were much more original than the ones recommended in the box.

Something like this sort of haptic knowledge is, I think, what is going on with the megalithic stones, the Bethels of Scotland that Keith Critchlow (1979) has analyzed and considered to be early prehistoric examples of the Platonic solids. Just as the construction of an Acheulian fist-hatchet would affect category formation for a hominid, so the construction of a Platonic solid would stimulate the visual imagination of a megalithic human. Perhaps "pet rocks" became a craze in the seventies because the New Age movement was retrieving—in Marshall McLuhan's (McLuhan and McLuhan 1988, 7) terminology of the tetrad in which new media obsolesce present media but retrieve previously obsolesced media—rocks that had once served as "familiars," as portable temples for the incorporation of one's angel, djinn, daimon, or spiritual guide. Perhaps in another system of category formation and membership in sets, the possession of such totemic stones indicated membership in a particular mystery school—a sort of merit badge for initiates.

If one endeavors to put haptic with conceptual, musical with mathematical, emotional with factual, one comes up with a way of mystical knowing that we see expressed in medieval calligraphy and the cognitive bliss of the medieval Neoplatonists, whether they are in the Islamic, Judaic, or Christian traditions. Fra Angelico's Cortona *Annunciation* seems to be a cultural hinge for the swing from the medieval to the modern, for it is both advanced and archaic at the same time—with one aspect of the painting recovering sacred traditions and another looking forward prophetically toward contemporary appreciations of topology and multiple dimensionality. This balance was very transient, for certainly the transition from the Renaissance to the Baroque and the Rococo performs a move into a world of three dimensions in which the trompe l'oeil of theatrical scenery transformed Catholic rituals into Italian opera for the new wealthy class.

Secularization and desacralization have had their time in the sun, and modernism's disenchantment of the world has taken over the humanities in postmodernism's deconstruction of text and tableau. In reaction, the capitalists who serve as presidents and members of the board of trustees for universities have taken the postmodernists at their deconstructing word and are now deconstructing English as the foundation for the liberal arts, just as in the previous generation they eliminated classics as the foundation for a Western civilization curriculum. The fundamentalists of the Abrahamic religions are making their own contribution to the decline of science and the liberal arts by trying to deconstruct the Enlightenment to take us back into a violently simplified world in which women have no place outside the home. The remnant of the revelations of the second and more global Enlightenment of the sixties and seventies would prefer to move on into a spirituality that is more planetary and individual, as is expressed in the Dalai Lama's recent efforts at MIT to create a bridge between meditational practice and consciousness studies in Western cognitive science. In the visual math of Ralph Abraham, and my efforts to work with him in articulating a new kind of cultural history, as seen in the spiral curriculum of the Ross Schools, we are trying to build a bridge across C. P. Snow's "two cultures," one that can become a new kind of Golden Gate.

REFERENCES

Abraham, R. 2006. The Canon of Lespugue. *Epigraphic Society Occasional Papers* 24:169–74.
Critchlow, Keith. 1979. *Time stands still: New light on megalithic science.* London: Gordon Fraser.
Damasio, Antonio. 1994. *Descartes' error: Emotion and human reason.* New York: G. P. Putnam.
———. 1999. *The feeling of what happens: Body and emotion in the making of consciousness.* New York: Harcourt Brace.
Dehaene, Stanislas. 1999. *The number sense: How the mind creates mathematics.* London: Penguin Books.
McLuhan, Marshall, and Eric McLuhan. 1988. *Laws of media: The new science.* Toronto: University of Toronto Press.

12

The Butterflies of the Soul

ANTONIO M. BATTRO

As the entomologist chasing butterflies of bright colors, my
attention was seeking in the garden of gray matter, those cells
of delicate and elegant forms, the mysterious butterflies of the
soul, whose fluttering wings would someday—who knows?—
enlighten the secret of mental life.

Santiago Ramón y Cajal

The Unfolding of a Metaphor

Metaphors are the seed of many scientific models. At the Ross School we
were willing to explore how a metaphor can serve as a trigger for interdisciplinary work in a school. Santiago Ramón y Cajal (1923/1981, 99), one of the
founders of modern neuroanatomy, suggested that the neurons were those
"mysterious butterflies of the soul" that "would someday enlighten the secret
of mental life." At the Ross School several mentors, teachers, and high school
students organized a network of literature, visual art, music, sculpture,
dance, history, computers, communication, and neuroscience. The results
were amazing: a fifteen-year-old girl produced a video that is still presented
to many academic audiences around the world. The process took several
months of interaction at many levels. It reflected the remarkable potential
and flexibility of the educational model in place at the Ross School.

According to I. A. Richards (1936, ch. 5), metaphors cannot be reduced to
their literal meaning and are central to the practice of science as well as other
disciplines. They are a privileged path toward understanding; they are also a
common field to share new meanings from different perspectives. When we
decided at the Ross School that we wanted to explore this particular metaphor, many unexpected and interesting things occurred. First, we became
engaged in the search of the roots of the word *butterfly* in several languages:
borboleta, schmetterling, mariposa, papillon, farfalla . . . all were so different!
It was difficult to decide in which way we should orient our quest. At this
stage the help of the Latin teacher, Clement Kuehn, and the librarians, Elizabeth Angele and Dale Scott, was key. Finally we found that the French *papillon* is related to the Latin *papilium*, for butterfly. And *papilium* is related to

palpitare, to flutter. We started to associate words with actions such as "those fluttering wings." We consulted the famous text of George Lakoff and Mark Johnson, *Metaphors We Live By* (1980), and read their concept of a metaphor as a means to map structure from one domain of experience onto a different one. We discovered that the metaphor was a transfer of meaning *(metapherein, translatio, transferentia)*. In our case it was a transfer over two bridges: from "neuron" to "butterfly" and from "butterfly" to "soul."

We left the neurons aside for a moment and searched to know more about the butterflies in Maria Mandel's text *The Butterfly* (1991). Butterflies are Lepidoptera, from *lepis* (scale) and *pteron* (wing). Now we were a bit closer to the words of Cajal: those wings were pointing toward our mental life! We were reaching the realm of the mind, *mens* in Latin, *psyché* in Greek. We consulted Rowena and Rupert Shepherd's book *One Thousand Symbols: What Shapes Meaning in Art and Myth* (2002). We found that the Greek *silphe* also means "butterfly" and that the Sylphes are those invisible female spirits of the air whose voices are heard in the wind. Wind, wings, air, spirit, soul, mind, immortality. It was clear that the semantic fields did interact to produce a transference of meaning from one domain to the other. Female spirit? Psyche, the goddess of love? All of us knew the myth of Cupid (Eros) and Psyche. We searched for a famous Latin text, the *Metamorphoses* of Apuleius. It was fun to read *The Golden Ass,* and it wasn't too difficult to do it even in Latin with some help. It was the long, charming, and incredible story of the young girl Psyche, who became Cupid's lover and finally was made a goddess. Therefore, Psyche became our target and our icon. We identified many representations of Psyche in the Western world, in particular the famous sculpture of Canova, *The Kiss of Cupid and Psyche* (a plaster model is at the Metropolitan Museum of Art). We found that in most works of art the girl Psyche had—butterfly wings! Normally angels and gods are represented with bird wings (Cupid, for example). Why this exception? There was no easy answer to that. But butterfly wings were inspiring. Some suggested that the transformation of a caterpillar into a butterfly is a sign of resurrection, of immortality. The immortal soul! We formed a group of four high school students, Bronwyn, Dan, Marshall, and Zoe, and the film teacher, Maria Maziak. A teacher showed us a video of a ballet with charming movements of veils as wings. Following that example some students went to the beach to construct and play with big butterfly wings. We needed sound, and someone thought of recording the wind playing on the sailboats of the beautiful port of Sag Harbor near the school. Summertime was approaching. The Ross School provided the technology and the support of the media experts.

But we also needed some help from neurobiologists. We weren't satisfied collecting static views of the neurons under the microscope; we really wanted to have some live images. We were searching for neurons flying like butterflies! We consulted a colleague, and he gave us several links to remarkable online video images of living neurons. We asked for permission to use them. We studied the movements of the growth cone, spine motility, and some other basic functions of the neuron. Finally, fifteen-year-old Bronwyn, the girl in charge of the video project, spent a part of her summer vacation working at the school trying to make a bridge—a metaphor—between the beautiful butterflies and the marvelous neurons.

The Interdisciplinary Process

Our project was modest, a very small one in comparison with many more elaborate initiatives of the Ross School. However, the process that led to the video *Mysterious Butterflies of the Soul* had many interesting and hidden features that we can now explore in order to describe how the Ross School works. First, the title itself provides some glimpse of the spirit of the institution. In fact, the notion of "soul" is sometimes disqualified among scientists and in many places replaced by neutral terms like *mind* or *cognition*. In that sense, it was interesting to learn that Santiago Ramón y Cajal, the great pioneer of modern neuroanatomy, was agnostic but still used the term *soul* without any shame. It is important in education to keep the strength of concepts alive and not to be afraid of the implications that certain terms may have associated with them (Battro 2006). *Soul* is one of those key words in human history. In the same vein, Emily Dickinson, one of the rare poets who understood the sublime aspects of the human brain, wrote, "The brain is wider than the sky." Recently Gerald Edelman, Nobel Prize winner and founder of the theory of neuronal group selection, gave the poetic title *Wider Than the Sky* to a book with the subtitle *The Phenomenal Gift of Consciousness* (Edelman 2004). Students should learn from the masters how to blend poetry and science in their lives. We tried a similar approach when we introduced Cajal's metaphor, and I think we all, at some point, became aware of the nature of the words involved and their deep meaning. It wasn't difficult to speak about the soul at the Ross School, an institution open to the spiritual dimension of the human family. This essential commitment to the spiritual roots of humanity is key to understanding the school's mission. Students and teachers are permanently exposed to multiple expressions of spirituality from the West and the East. It was common for us to interact with visitors coming from different religious and spiritual traditions. Many works of art, gardens, books, paintings, and sculptures in the school are a permanent example of this open spirit. Also in some of their travels abroad students and teachers often visit relevant centers of spirituality. It can be said that the butterflies of the soul were already thriving already in the beautiful gardens of the Ross School well before we tried to capture them in our imagination, transformed in neurons of our brain.

Truth, Goodness, and Beauty

In the words of the old scholastic dictum, *Verum, bonum et pulchrum convertuntur* (Truth, goodness, and beauty are interchangeable). During my stay at the Ross School I had the good fortune to overlap with Howard Gardner and William Damon, who, with Michael Csikszentmihaly, had written the book *Good Work: When Excellence and Ethics Meet* (2001) and had come to the Ross School to work and write. Ramón y Cajal gave us a perfect example of "good work." He was discovering new truths of nature and providing new tools for understanding the nervous system. At the same time he helped to promote the highest scientific research in Spain and was adamant in the ethical values that such a mission implies. He was a good painter too, and his art became the best asset of his scientific findings. He himself produced all the figures in his texts—hundreds of them. They are so impressive that they are still reproduced in advanced neuroscience texts today. Ramón y Cajal was a model for generations of students. One of his disciples came to Argentina, and I was lucky enough to study neuroanatomy using his beautiful methods of staining with gold and silver. The "elegant forms" of the neurons were etched in my mind forever.

When we decided to follow Ramón y Cajal's metaphor we first wanted to bypass the way the brain is generally studied in laboratories (in standard microscopic preparations of dead neurons) and instead look at the living brain. So we used the powerful tools of the Web to search for images of living neurons, and with the help of some colleagues we finally found several good illustrations of the growing axons in search of synaptic contacts. As a matter of fact, our group studied the living neurons from the very start. I must say that this dynamic perspective is not very common even in medical schools. With this basic platform it was possible to instill life in our quest, to compare the delicate movements of the growth cone of the axon with those of the wings of a butterfly. The similitude was striking and so beautiful! This is the miracle of a good metaphor. Then we began taking pictures of living butterflies. Bronwyn spent a lot of time working at this. She visited the Bronx Zoo and took pictures and videos at the "Butterfly Zone."

The freedom to explore outside the classroom is a typical occurrence at the Ross School. Students are encouraged to explore. At one point during my fellowship at the school, Dava Sobel, the renowned author of *Galileo's Daughter* (1999), came to give a talk. She described her trip to Florence to see Galileo's manuscripts, her motivation to study the struggles of the great physicist in order to give a new foundation to our knowledge of the universe, and Galileo's great love for his daughter, who lived in a convent near his residence. Her talk about Galileo Galilei made an impact on the school. Santiago Ramón y Cajal was a scientist of similarly inspiring courage, and I was glad to have chosen such a great model. I was always impressed by the comparison between stars and neurons, and so were some of my students; they learned that a human brain has more neurons than our galaxy has stars. Incidentally, I remember the great physicist Minoru Oda at the Pontifical Academy of Sciences encouraging neuroscientists to explore the X-ray technology that astronomers use (Oda 2001). Once again the macrocosm and the microcosm, the stars and the neurons, appear: perhaps in the new metaphor we have the next project on neuroeducation at Ross.

A Spiral of Art and Science

Our video, in fact, was not about stars but about butterflies and neurons. It needed music. And instead of using the usual trick of downloading music we decided to produce new music. Sag Harbor near the Ross School was the chosen place for inspiration. Bronwyn went to the harbor to record the vibrations of the wind in the sails and cables of the boats. With the help of two musicians, Suzanne Farrin, composer in residence, and Sebastián Zubieta, director of musical technology, a sample of "concrete" original music was produced to accompany the dancing of the butterflies and the movements of the neurons. Bronwyn masterfully superimposed both kinds of "fluttering wings," those of the axonal growth cone and those of the flying butterfly, while playing with changes of scale, music, and colors. The macroscopic butterflies and the microscopic neurons were, finally, dancing together. I was privileged to see multiple versions of this amazing work, and I admired her effort to synthesize and eliminate uninteresting details. The time frame was very strict: no more than three minutes. She spent hours and hours editing the different pieces of the work. The art director Julie Iden made the DVD design, and the butterflies were then ready to fly around the world.[1]

I presented the video, *Mysterious Butterflies of the Soul,* at the opening session of a workshop entitled "Mind, Brain and Education" in November 2003 at the Pontifical Academy of Sciences, at the Vatican, during the celebration of the four hundredth anniversary of its founding. Galileo Galilei was a member of this academy founded by the young scientist Federico Cesi with the encouragement of Pope Clement VIII. Rita Levi-Montalcini, who won the Nobel Prize in medicine for her discovery of the nerve growth factor (NGF), was the honorary president of this workshop. We offered this modest but significant gift to the Pope John Paul II. His Holiness said to the academicians: "Scientists themselves perceive in the study of the human mind the mystery of a spiritual dimension which transcends cerebral physiology and appears to direct all our activities as free and autonomous beings, capable of responsibility and love, and marked with dignity. This is seen by the fact you have decided to expand your research to include aspects of learning and education, which are specifically human activities" (John Paul II 2003).

This humanistic approach was well received. At the meeting we launched the International Mind, Brain and Education Society, IMBES (www.imbes. org), and the journal *Mind, Brain and Education* (www.Blackwell-synergy. Com/loi/mbe). The quotation from Ramón y Cajal that opens this chapter also opens the introduction to the book that came out of this memorable meeting, *The Educated Brain: Essays in Neuroeducation* (Battro, Fischer, and Léna 2008). The dust cover of this edition, carefully produced by Cambridge University Press, is not a brain but a butterfly; the metaphor worked! With *Mysterious Butterflies of the Soul* we have generated, in a reduced format, a growing spiral of science and art. The spiral is also the deep core, the motor, of the Ross School curriculum.

NOTE

1. The DVD can be purchased at global@rossinstitute.org. See also Ross Institute (2004).

REFERENCES

Battro, A. M. 2006. Homo educabilis: A neurocognitive approach. In *What is our real knowledge about the human being?* Vatican City: Pontifical Academy of Sciences.

Battro, A. M., K. W. Fischer, and Pierre J. Léna. 2008. *The educated brain: Essays in neuroeducation.* Cambridge: Cambridge University Press.

Edelman, Gerald. 2004. *Wider than the sky: The phenomenal gift of consciousness.* New Haven: Yale University Press.

Gardner, Howard, William Damon, and Michael Csikszentmihaly. 2001. *Good work: When excellence and ethics meet.* New York: Basic Books.

John Paul II. 2003. Address of John Paul II to the members of the Pontifical Academy of Sciences. November 10. www.vatican.va/holy_father/john_paul_ii/speeches/2003/november/documents/hf_jp-ii_spe_20031110_academy-sciences_en.html.

Lakoff, George, and Mark Johnson. 1980. *Metaphors we live by.* Chicago: University of Chicago Press.

Mandel, Maria. 1991. *The butterfly.* New York: Stewart, Tabori and Chang.

Oda, Minoru. 2001. Why and how physicists are interested in the brain and the mind. In *Science and the future of mankind: Science for man and man for science.* Vatican City: Pontifical Academy of Sciences.

Ramón y Cajal, Santiago. 1923/1981. *Recuerdos de mi vida: Historia de mi labor científica.* Madrid: Alianza.

Richards, I. A. 1936. *The philosophy of rhetoric.* Oxford: Oxford University Press.

Ross Institute. 2004. Mysterious butterflies of the soul. www.rossinstitute.org/default.asp?nav=publications&content=butterfliesCD.

Shepherd, Rowena, and Rupert Shepherd. 2002. *One thousand symbols: What shapes meaning in art and myth.* London: Thames and Hudson.

Sobel, Dava. 1999. *Galileo's daughter.* New York: Penguin.

13

Educating the Whole
Child for the Whole World

The Ross Model in Sweden

SALLY BOOTH WITH MICHELE CLAEYS

Courtney Ross has left an indelible mark on contemporary conceptions of education. Her original vision of developing a model of education that nurtures curious, creative, and culturally and socially responsible students for the global era has blossomed into multiple schools, a growing support organization, and a vast network of like-minded educators, policy makers, scholars, and students. The Ross Institute is the umbrella organization that gives unity to the purpose and vision of the multiple projects—local, national, and international—developed by the Ross School and the Ross Institute Academy. All of these initiatives, which range from longitudinal research projects in partnership with universities, to mentorship and collaboration with scholars, artists, and community leaders, to professional development courses for schools interested in the Ross pedagogy and curricula, stem from Courtney Ross's goals of expanding a successful educational model to students in many different social and cultural contexts. The Ross Institute Academy works with schools, educational leaders, and faculty members to disseminate the research and pedagogical practices that have been so successful in Ross Network Schools. The groundbreaking work of sharing the Ross approach with teachers in the Swedish public school system has become a model for working with schools locally and abroad.

Postwar labor immigration followed by more recent admittance of large numbers of refugees and asylum seekers has transformed Sweden into one of Europe's most multicultural societies. At present about 12 percent of the country's nine million residents are foreign born (Caldwell 2005). In the capital city of Stockholm, more than 26 percent of the population is foreign born or the child of foreign-born residents, and in suburbs like Tensta, northwest of the central city, the figure is substantially higher. Considering these figures, how the second generation will be incorporated poses a great challenge—and opportunity—for Swedish society. In Sweden, as elsewhere, the prospects of the children of immigrants will be written especially in school. This chapter describes and assesses the introduction of innovative curriculum and pedagogical approaches from the Ross School into Tensta Gymnasium, a Swedish public high school (equivalent to grades 10 through 12 in the U.S. system) with a student population composed almost exclusively of children of immigrants, the vast majority of whom themselves are foreign born.[1]

The Context

Residential segregation and discrimination make for an unsettling incorporation of foreigners into Swedish society. In Stockholm and other Swedish cities, most immigrants reside in suburbs. "The areas that we call 'segregated' are actually very mixed. The segregated part of the country is the Swedish part" (Masoud Kamali, quoted in Caldwell 2005, 23). Suburbs in Sweden have much the same negative association and low status as ghettos in the United States; the inner cities have retained a high-status position. The inner city is associated with ethnic Swedes, expensive real estate, elite schools, and neighborhood safety. "A person stuck in central Stockholm would find none of the clues of heavy minority presence that a visitor to central Amsterdam or Paris or London gets" (Caldwell 2005, 22). Tensta neighborhood, northwest of Stockholm's city center, was about 40 percent Greek in the 1980s, although Kurdish Turks and Yugoslavians also lived there. By 2006, the population of the Tensta neighborhood was 85 percent immigrant. Many people now come from Iraq, Iran, Somalia, and Afghanistan. There are very few ethnically Swedish families with children living in the neighborhood. Many of the ethnic Swedes in the neighborhood are elderly and do not want to move. The isolation of immigrants influences the Swedish educational system. The scholar Mauricio Rojas explains: "In segregated areas schools are the key. Many Swedes think the areas are interesting to live in, and they're right. But they won't stay if they don't think their kids are getting a Swedish education" (quoted in Caldwell 2006, 57). Rojas argues that "white flight" from the suburbs occurs when immigrants compose 20 percent of the population and the schools become associated with immigrant students.

While Sweden's policy toward immigrants and refugees has been generous and open relative to other receiving countries, the long-term approach to integration of immigrants and refugees has become increasingly problematic. In the press and among ethnic Swedes there is a general recognition that the open-door policy toward immigrants and refugees is flawed. Many point to immigrant unemployment and crime to argue that the government policy must become more restrictive.

Some aspects of immigrant life are especially troublesome in Swedish mainstream public opinion. The language of immigrants—a patois of Swedish, Arabic, and youth slang—is looked down upon.[2] Honor killings among the Kurdish Turks are considered antithetical to modern life and unacceptable in the Swedish context. Arranged marriages set up in the Kurdish homelands present problems in terms of social expectations and immigrant entry numbers (Wikan 2008). The suggestion that Swedish courts adapt to *sharia* law—for instance, regarding marriage and divorce—in cases involving Swedish Muslims is objectionable to many. There is debate about wearing veils in schools. Alarm is expressed over the fact that birthrates are higher among foreign-born women than among ethnic Swedish women (Landes 2008). And there is a very low rate of marriage between immigrants and ethnic Swedes (Caldwell 2005).

From their point of view, immigrants feel excluded from mainstream society—their opportunities limited and their contributions overlooked.[3] Masoud Kamali, an Iranian-born professor of ethnic studies at University of Uppsala, writes: "Integration is a complete failure: no one can deny it" (quoted in Caldwell 2005, 22). Another scholar of immigrant origins in Sweden states that "many of us saw Sweden as the homeland of tolerance, solidarity, and democracy, based on the image of Sweden abroad. Yet the foreigners find that the longer they live in Sweden, the more foreign they feel" (quoted in Caldwell 2005, 22). "There can be few countries in Europe where natives know less about the ways of the Muslims who live among them than Sweden. The isolation of the apartments where immigrants mostly live has a lot to do with this" (Caldwell 2006, 55). Islamic radicalism is spurred by the alienation immigrants feel in Sweden: "One of the most important appeals to potential members is: 'Sweden will never accept you'" (Kassem Hamade, quoted in Caldwell 2006, 58).

The immigrants and refugees coming to Sweden today differ in significant ways from settled immigrant populations. They have fled terrible situations of warfare and crisis; their relocation is forced, rather than voluntary. Some have little or no educational background and limited facility with the Swedish language (Harrigan 2004). Teachers complain that it is difficult to teach new immigrant students Swedish because many of them lack basic reading and writing skills. Parents of immigrant students often do not learn Swedish and thus cannot help with schoolwork or interact with the teachers.

At Tensta Gymnasium, this situation is particularly problematic now.[4] Interviews conducted with teachers, students, parents, and administrators in 2008 and 2009 revealed the extent of the challenges. According to one teacher at Tensta, "Now the Somalis are the dominant population. Many Somali kids lack previous schooling and motivation. They are the hardest group to motivate." Another teacher explained, "We have huge difficulties with the Somalis. They are the group with no hope." Teachers recognize the enormous challenge posed by poor or nonexistent preparation for school. One said: "Teachers at Tensta have special challenges. The home situation is difficult, and the students don't have enough Swedish language to do well in school. So many of our students are really good at hiding their language problems! They can barely read or write or understand written text. But, you can't see this by talking with them."

Reaching out to the parents can also be fraught with difficulties. Parents may not attend school meetings even if mentors call to invite them. One teacher complained, "It's not part of their culture; we have to drag them in. They seem almost scared of the school!" Whether this is due to intimidation and humiliation regarding poor Swedish language skills or demanding work schedules, the administrators are trying many different approaches to get the parents to participate in school activities.

Administrators and teachers at Tensta receive little in the way of test scores or data on the students coming in from compulsory schools. In fact, most of the grades from compulsory schools are inflated unreasonably high; otherwise students in the ninth year are not promoted to the gymnasium. Thus when students arrive to Tensta Gymnasium they may fail the entry diagnostic tests; only in this way do teachers learn their students may not be prepared for gymnasium.

The 1995 policy of school choice, which uses a points system that factors in a student's grades and application (rather than residence), has also become a matter of serious concern. The previous system was based on residence, so Tensta Gymnasium was assured a student body with different levels of preparation and achievement. The new system also allows the highest-achieving students from the immigrant suburbs to attend the high-prestige city center schools. This new policy helps a select group of suburban students to better integrate with ethnic Swedes, but it can work to diminish the pool of high-achieving suburban students and thus lower the average outcomes at Tensta Gymnasium. Students want the high-prestige education associated with the inner-city schools, and they apply to enter these schools whenever their scores permit it. Since the implementation of the new criteria, Tensta Gymnasium has lost 30 percent of its students, mostly to inner-city schools. Further, the reputation of the Tensta area for crime and unemployment acts as a deterrent to ethnic Swedes who might otherwise consider attending the local school. In short, by the late 1990s suburban schools in general, and Tensta Gymnasium in particular, needed something innovative to succeed. The problems with effective integration of immigrant and refugee students (and their parents) into Swedish society and the division of students by achievement rather than residence gave policy makers and administrators the impetus to explore other alternatives and different educational models.

Adaptation of the Ross Model to the Swedish Context

The Ross presence at Tensta represents a confluence of many interests. The government wanted to improve the conditions of the school in the immigrant neighborhood as part of a general program to assist immigrant communities and improve the social services they received. The founder of the Ross School and Ross Institute, Courtney Ross, hoped that the Ross model would attract more students to Tensta Gymnasium and equip them with twenty-first-century skills and knowledge. The shared goal of the Ross Institute, the Stockholm educational ministry, and the administrators at Tensta Gymnasium was to adopt the Ross model to the Tensta Gymnasium. The Ross concept is grounded in the Ross curriculum, the spiral of cultural history, which is at once chronological, global in scope, integrated and holistic in composition, and thematic in organization (see Thompson 1996; McCall, this volume). The pedagogical approaches that allow teachers to engage students successfully in this curriculum are based on Howard Gardner's theory of multiple intelligences and project-based learning approaches.

Tensta Gymnasium is a school facing major structural difficulties. A number of students are academically unprepared and socially and economically disadvantaged. Students can apply to one of five programs in the disciplines of trade and administration, caregiving, natural sciences, social sciences, or introductory studies, a program designed to help students gain facility with the Swedish language and to improve their math and English skills. In the social science programs, for instance, some students entered with the lowest scores possible (the diagnostic screening features scores ranging from 1 to 9 on three different tests; some students earned only one point on each of the three tests). Furthermore, the school suffers from a strong bias against the neighborhood in which it is located. One teacher said that at the districtwide school fairs parents avoid the Tensta booth when they see the name; they fear having their children attend school in such a bad area. Another teacher said that if Tensta were in the center of Stockholm it would be one of the most prestigious schools.

National concerns regarding integration issues and problems with prejudice have great relevance for the administrators, teachers, and students at Tensta Gymnasium. Inger Nyrell, the principal of the school, says: "To challenge the prejudices is probably the hardest part of my work. There are so many preconceived notions about Tensta Gymnasium—that it is overcrowded, run down, and worn out—just because the school is in the suburb of Tensta. But in truth it is one of Stockholm's most beautiful schools. Concerning the teaching and learning environment, the quality is high, and we have more options for both students and teachers than most other schools" (quoted in Osgard 2008, 27). Teachers and students agree with Ms. Nyrell; one parent said: "The image of Tensta doesn't match the reality. The name is bad. The teachers know the school is good, the students know it, but the outside world thinks it's terrible."

Adapting the Ross concept to the school at Tensta required administrative and financial support from various levels. The supervisor of secondary schools for the city of Stockholm, Per Handhoff, sponsored this ambitious project. Thirty million crowns were set aside for the architectural renovation of the school; smaller classrooms were created to accommodate smaller classes. The areas for teachers were changed significantly. Instead of meeting in their domains organized by subject, they got new office spaces that allowed teams composed of teachers representing different domains to work and meet together on a regular basis. Glass doors and classroom windows were used to increase openness so that teachers could see students and vice versa (Malmstrom 2004).[5] There are open meeting areas in each wing of the building, designed to promote exchange of ideas between teachers and students.[6] Then Tensta received five million crowns extra for three years to carry out the Ross concept. Inger Nyrell, the principal at Tensta Gymnasium, said: "The support of Per Handhoff . . . was invaluable. He helped us to persuade teachers to participate in this project; those that did not want to participate, he helped them to move on. He realized that the Ross concept was our chance to survive. He wanted to develop something that was a real star in the city of Stockholm, and I think it is a star—*the* star in this city."[7] It is worth noting as well that all schools in predominantly immigrant neighborhoods receive 50 percent more financing per student, per year, to pay for smaller classes, extra tutoring, language classes, and other costs associated with new immigrant students.

Although Tensta Gymnasium administrators and faculty visited Ross School various times in 2002–4, the official launch of the Ross-Tensta project was in August 2004. In that year, the applications to Tensta increased dramatically. Tensta was considered "an exception in the suburbs" (Malmstrom

2004). The most important characteristics of the Ross project at Tensta are smaller class sizes (twenty students per class instead of the average of thirty-two), a wellness program that combines fitness and nutrition, and access to technology. But other, less tangible changes are also important—for instance, the formation of teams for teaching, the integration of different domains in teaching the curriculum, and the increased interaction and closer relationships between students and teachers and between teachers and administrators. All these features make Tensta Gymnasium an appealing educational choice for parents and students.

The Ross-Tensta partnership was conceptualized as a process by which Ross teachers and administrators would consolidate and then share the Ross curriculum and pedagogy with Tensta teachers and administrators in a series of professional development workshops and one-to-one mentoring over the course of five years. This has unfolded as a learning process for both the Swedish and American participants. Teams of Swedish teachers visit the East Hampton campus two times a year for a week to observe classes and team meetings, converse with their teaching counterparts, discuss larger structural questions, and address smaller practical issues associated with the curriculum. Visitors from Sweden have included teachers and administrators from Tensta Gymnasium as well as nearby schools interested in the Ross model—for example, teachers from Bussenhus and Hjulsta schools have accompanied the teachers from Tensta to seminars and presentations. Teams of teachers from the Ross School have gone to Tensta Gymnasium in October each year to present a series of professional development workshops that are essential to the Ross model. These workshops focus on descriptions of the spiral history curriculum and unique pedagogical approaches to show how to apply these effectively in the Swedish classrooms. They cover topics such as integrating technology in the classroom and using art and artifacts to enrich the teaching of history or science. In the spring of 2008, a visiting team of Ross teachers and administrators visited Tensta and investigated the various aspects of the Ross model as adapted to Tensta Gymnasium. At the end of the inquiry process, the visiting team unanimously recommended accreditation of Tensta Gymnasium as a Ross partner. In the winter of 2009, this accreditation became official. The Ross team agreed that Tensta Gymnasium had reached, or was in the process of reaching, full competence in applying the Ross model to the Swedish gymnasium, and the new name, Ross Tensta Gymnasium, indicates this important change in the school's status. This model includes the six elements essential to the Ross concept: ethos, spiral curriculum, pedagogical best practices, wellness and student services, technology, and learning environment.

Ethos

The ethos of the institution has to do with shared cultural expectations regarding morality and behavior toward fellow members of the institution. A new sense of collaboration evolved over the course of instituting the Ross model at Tensta. Teachers learned to work in multidisciplinary teams, and teachers worked closely with the administration to implement the Ross concepts effectively. When creating and changing an ethos of the school, Tensta was inspired by the Ross School to develop its own set of core values. The core values at the Ross School, as established by faculty and students, are cooperation, courage, gratitude, integrity, mindfulness, responsibility, and respect. The core values at Tensta Gymnasium are responsibility, consideration, cooperation, respect, and thoughtful language. These core values are printed and posted around the school. Teachers include them in discussions of time periods and episodes in history and ask students to identify the salience of these themes throughout their lessons.

Teachers feel that the core values have transformed students' behavior and expectations at the school. "We try to embody them as much as teach them. The behavior in study hall shows this; students are calmer, more engaged than they were before we had a set of core values." One teacher identified the most important part of the Ross model at Tensta Gymnasium as "changing relationship with the students! . . . It's come to the forefront as we go through the core values with them. We are always looking for better ways to engage students, to connect to parents, to call them and invite them to the school." Another teacher said: "We are seeing the results of these attempts. Students are fighting less, more involved in work." The next step in building upon the ethos of the school has to do with creating and establishing a mission statement that outlines the long-term goals of the students, the teachers, and the school.

Spiral Curriculum

The spiral curriculum of cultural history conceptualizes history as a series of shifts in consciousness and is presented both chronologically and thematically with a holistic and integrated approach by teachers in all domains. Tensta Gymnasium has done much to embrace the Ross curriculum, by elaborating upon concepts of cultural history within the Swedish national requirements, developing impressive integrated units, and creating a culture of integrated thinking.[8] Tensta has integrated the Ross spiral of cultural history with the national standards to create a coherent and effective "red thread" understood and adopted by a majority of the committed and impressive faculty.[9]

Pedagogy

Effective pedagogy is the key to successful education; the Ross spiral of cultural history inspires teachers to use engaging pedagogical approaches in the classroom. What strikes the observer is the passionate engagement of the administrators and teachers with the Ross project. In other Swedish schools, teachers are primarily subject-oriented; they do not plan curricular units with teachers from other disciplines. In the new Ross-Tensta model, teachers spend their free time in multidisciplinary office spaces, planning curriculum together, and talking about individual students. The teachers are committed and show great respect for the work of their colleagues and administrators in making the Ross-Tensta project come to life. They have understood well the ideas of the cultural history spiral and have shown enthusiasm and dedication in making sure the Ross spiral is linked in logical, coherent, and meaningful ways with the "red thread" of history as it is taught at Tensta. To combine the Swedish national standards with the Ross spiral of cultural history, students learn content *and* skills. And because the students are discussing the same periods in history in different classes from different disciplinary approaches, they have more time to discuss and understand complicated ideas. This makes it much easier and more effective for the students to grasp the important points and engage with the learning process. Tensta offers a different kind of history education than other Swedish schools. A student discussed a unit on medieval Islam: "You are more willing to learn when you know the thing you are studying has a background."

The Ross spiral curriculum is chronological in depth and global in scope. Students learn about more than Swedish kings and queens; they learn, through in-depth projects, about areas of the world from which their own relatives may have come. An Iraqi refugee claimed proudly: "I come from the Fertile Crescent!" Another ethnically Swedish student said: "I learned the real history of Islam, not just what we read in the papers about dangerous terrorists. I learned it's an important religious tradition." Furthermore, the links to other university programs give students whose families may not promote university expectations necessary exposure to higher educational ideals (Nilsson 2004).[10] Opportunities for foreign travel, facilitated by the Ross-Tensta partnership and other institutional support, have provided Tensta students with the cross-cultural perspectives so essential to twenty-first-century learning; students have visited China, the United States, Turkey, and Spain for trips oriented around business, education, and cultural exchange. This is an important and valued benefit for Tensta students; they often mention the global perspectives offered by their fellow students, the curriculum, and the opportunities to travel as unique to their experience at Tensta Gymnasium.[11]

The Ross-Tensta educational project directly broaches the pressing issue of segregation in Sweden. Principal Nyrell recognized early on the crucial role the schools play in the integration of immigrants. "We already have the global perspective here at Tensta with so many different nationalities of students. But we have to do something about these problems or we are a ticking time bomb!" Everyone involved with Tensta—policy makers, administrators, teachers, and students—has found that the Ross spiral curriculum is especially well suited to engage the predominantly immigrant student body. Further, both students and teachers value rather than disparage the great ethnic diversity of the student body. According to one Tensta student, "In my class there are students from Turkey, Finland, Greece, and Africa. Most are from Turkey, but everyone is friends with everyone" (quoted in Malmstrom 2004). In every classroom, at least ten nationalities are represented. A student applying to attend the school said: "It is good that people come from different places. Everyone has prejudices about how it is at Tensta. I had never gone so far on the blue subway line before I came here."

Whole Child: Wellness and Student Services

The first thing students at Ross School in East Hampton and students at Tensta Gymnasium bring up with pride about their schools is their wellness program. In the Ross philosophy, wellness is an integral part of learning—only a student who is well nourished and leads a physically active and balanced life can concentrate on academic studies. Since the start of the partnership with Ross, the food in the cafeteria at Tensta has improved markedly. A chef has been hired and tasked with creating healthy, hot breakfasts and lunches. In contrast to other public gymnasiums in Stockholm, at Tensta more physical education classes are offered, and students take a health education class every week for all three years at the school.

Tensta Gymnasium has also transformed its approach to the psychological and academic well-being of students since working with Ross. The administrators have created a successful support team composed of the assistant principal, the school nurse, a learning specialist, a counselor, and a study teacher; they meet weekly to identify and address student issues, remediate academic difficulties, and communicate with the relevant teachers and student mentors. The mentor program is also effective; each teacher mentor has approximately ten students assigned. The mentor keeps track of the student's attendance, personal situation, and academic standing and is the liaison between the student, the administration, and the parents. Often these relationships are close, and the mentors act as an alternative adult presence in the students' lives.

Technology

Being prepared as learners in the twenty-first century requires that teachers and students have easy access to technology and a competence in integrating technological skills with the educational process. Since aligning itself with Ross School, Tensta Gymnasium has adopted a one-laptop-per-student program, set up a wireless network in the school, and trained teachers to use technology in the classroom on a continual basis. Tensta has a technology integrator who works with teachers to encourage them to use new software and integration techniques in the classroom. Furthermore, teachers regularly communicate and store important information about the curriculum on the citywide collaborative online learning environment. Assignments, class presentations, and homework are shared between faculty and students in an organized, efficient way that facilitates record keeping and documentation. In the future this system will have individual development plans and attendance records to better focus attention on student goals.

Learning Environment

The space of learning—the halls that facilitate the flow of students and teachers, the walls that define the classrooms as spaces for learning, the external windows to the trees and public courtyards outside and the internal windows to the library, hallways, and teachers' offices—was totally renovated as the initial step in the adaptation of the Ross model at Tensta Gymnasium. The spaces where students and teachers learn and plan together are spacious, highly functional, comfortable, and beautifully furnished. There is natural light throughout and easy access to classrooms, teaching teams' offices, the library, the café, and the dining area. The classrooms are smaller than traditional Swedish classrooms to fit only twenty students. According to one Tensta teacher, "Much better teaching can happen in these smaller classes." Display spaces fit nicely into the architectural design of the school. Student art, reflecting the integrated curriculum, adorns the walls. One may see beautiful pencil drawings of canopic jars and models of Tutankhamen's funerary mask or paintings inspired by Islamic geometric designs of atomic structures of chemical compounds. The core values are posted throughout the school, in the halls, and on the walls of the classrooms. A recreation area in the center of the campus includes a (popular) ping-pong table and natural greenery. In a neighborhood with a reputation for unrest and danger, Tensta Gymnasium is a place of warmth, safety, and learning.

Assessing the Results of the Ross Model at Tensta

There is considerable evidence to demonstrate that the Ross-Tensta project has unfolded fully and has improved the educational experience of students and teachers at Tensta Gymnasium in numerous ways. In the course of these five years many people have worked cooperatively across the barriers of language, culture, and distance to effectively create a culture of integration at the school. This has been the culmination of Courtney Ross's long-term objective—to consolidate and share an educational concept that embodies lifelong learning and cross-cultural perspectives. The model has been strengthened through adaptation and refinement in the Swedish context of Tensta Gymnasium.

The impact of the Ross concept on the teaching and learning at the Tensta Gymnasium has been recognized by all participants—students, parents, teachers, administrators, and policy makers. Students have many positive things to say about their experience at Tensta. A conversation with six senior girls in 2009 is representative of their points of view. One explained, "We have more opportunities than students in other schools." Students felt that the multicultural student body and the global curriculum gave them a unique perspective. One said: "Sweden is a small country, and the world itself is much larger! Sooner or later you will have to go out of the bubble and actually meet other people!" Another continued, "Tensta prepared me. We know how to talk to all kinds of different people. I will have it easier in the future doing business or studying abroad."

These students deeply appreciated the curriculum and were able to articulate how effective it had been in changing their points of view. "We can connect things to each other and see this line, this connection with everything. Instead of separating science and history, we can actually see how the world developed and why it did in that way." Another student in the group we conversed with pointed out: "You need the bigger picture to know what's going on. You can't just take parts of history and parts of science; you need the bigger picture to understand the future, and you can't understand the future without understanding history!" The multidisciplinary approach to history was recognized as valuable. As one of the six girls put it, "You can use art to explain things. You can analyze something and think outside the box. This is very important; it allows you to create something, understand something outside of yourself." Individual projects also made a strong impression on these students. As part of an integrated project associated with the Ross concept called "Power and Change," students developed a project to promote the construction of a bigger prayer room in the school. They created a petition, wrote newspaper articles, and succeeded in persuading the school to increase the size of this multidenominational prayer room. "We made a difference in our school." Another integrated project about sustainable development and the food crisis allowed students to get a global perspective on starvation and abundance as linked phenomena tied to history, nutrition, politics, and climate change. Tensta students appreciated the pedagogical approaches of the Ross concept at Tensta. "Our teachers really put their soul into everything they do so you get really interested." The projects themselves were engaging and gave the students the confidence to go into the world. "There are a lot of Muslims in Sweden, but before coming to Tensta I didn't know anything about them. But after the medieval Islam unit, I have a better understanding of how important Islam is in the whole world. This is important because of all the xenophobia in our world today." One student we conversed with lavished the highest praise on the school: "Going to Tensta was the best decision I've ever made in my life!"

Parents of Tensta students also feel the Ross-Tensta project has been very successful. They are pleased with the multicultural perspectives offered by the curriculum and found in the student body itself. They feel that the students are prepared to work and live in a world characterized by globalization and rapid change. One parent observed: "Students need a global point of view, a broader cultural experience. Segregated society becomes a dead end for students today. A global perspective opens up doors of opportunity. If students are going to make it today, they cannot live in small circles. If they are going to make a difference, they need to broaden their skills, widen their perspectives. This school, with its culturally mixed population and its Ross curriculum and Ross method, is perfect preparation for the future modern world."

Teachers say that the planning of integrated units motivates them to think about the material in new ways; it is clear that the Ross project has inspired them to work more collaboratively in terms of incorporating new perspectives, teaching materials, and pedagogical techniques. They are unequivocal in their praise for the Ross curriculum and how it has influenced their students. A chemistry teacher claims the Ross model has engaged students who would have been overwhelmed and bored by the traditional Swedish education. A math teacher agrees, asserting that math is difficult to teach in any circumstance but that with the Ross model students get engaged without realizing it. An arts teacher says that the smaller class size and the unity of teaching teams have given students a feeling they are being cared for by a responsible, cohesive group of adults. A Swedish teacher thinks the integrated projects make the educational experience rich and engaging and put students on the path to lifelong learning. A science teacher says the students who have been taught with the Ross concept have a wider perspective on world history and current events; he claims they have more success in college than other students. And all the teachers agree that the project of adapting the Ross concept to the Swedish education has made Tensta Gymnasium an exciting place to work. A history teacher put it this way: "I like the buzz that goes around; we are much more engaged with each other and with the students. We are all talking about the projects!"

Principal Nyrell's statement sums up what many of those involved with teaching at Tensta feel: "The Ross model of integration and cultural history provides a more effective and informative education to the students. While we have the global perspective already here, due to the great number of immigrants from many world areas, this approach to education, and, history more specifically, will help us at this crucial point." At another time, Nyrell said, "The best thing we can do is to integrate these students into Swedish society." Tensta administrators believe the school is the institution most effective at promoting integration, and they readily acknowledge that the Ross spiral of cultural history is especially well suited to reach the immigrant student population. The Ross concept—the wellness program, the spiral curriculum based on cultural history, and pedagogy—has attracted students to enroll in Tensta Gymnasium.

Policy makers also recognize the success of the Ross-Tensta, and the school has attracted attention from educators from other schools and other countries. The long-term commitment and dedication of the Ross School founder, Courtney Ross, the principal, Inger Nyrell, and the assistant principal, Kerstin Friborg, have given this challenging project the foundational basis for success. The innovative teaching methods and organization of teaching teams at Tensta Gymnasium have been applauded as a successful model for education. In fact, more than fifty teachers are being trained at Tensta right now, and the university program for teachers, LHS (LärarHögSkolan), is considering formalizing teacher training at the school. An alderman for schools and culture in Stockholm said: "Students work on larger projects that are interdisciplinary and combine the subjects. In this way students develop a holistic approach and better understanding for development in a historical perspective. The installation of wireless network and laptops to every student means that communication with the rest of the world is easily achieved" (Nilsson 2004, 1). Thomas Persson, minister of education in Stockholm, has congratulated the administration of Tensta Gymnasium for earning the Ross accreditation after a long process of implementation and assessment. He also supports efforts of the Ross Institute to help other schools learn about the Ross concept and Ross methods of teaching. In the autumn of 2009, Tensta Gymnasium changed its name officially to Ross Tensta Gymnasium as a mark of attainment of this important stage of educational transformation.

Courtney Ross started a school to educate her daughter nearly twenty years ago. Her goal has been to share this innovative model for education with as many students as possible in order to best prepare young adults for the challenges facing them in this rapidly changing world. She has been instrumental in the collaborative project between the United States and Sweden to create a remarkable school that serves as a model and to help policy makers conceptualize new and more effective educational approaches.

NOTES

There are many to thank for helping me understand the Ross-Tensta partnership and write this chapter. First, I would like to thank Courtney Ross for her visionary approach to education—combining the best of multicultural, interdisciplinary, and historical perspectives in an effort to improve education. I would also like to thank the administration and faculty at Tensta Gymnasium—their warmth and dedication to the students and to educational innovation have been inspiring. Inger Nyrell and Kerstin Friborg have worked hard to improve the lives of their students. They have always been generous with their time and expert knowledge to help me gather information. The students of Tensta Gymnasium have made this study a pleasure; they have shared their ideas, insights, and challenges in an open dialogue worthy of world leaders and diplomats. Michele Claeys has been involved with the Ross-Tensta partnership from the very start and has been a great source of inspiration for the writing of this chapter. I am grateful that Marcelo Suárez-Orozco invited me to contribute to this volume. Finally, I would like to thank Jeffrey Cole, a continual source of intellectual companionship and insight on issues regarding immigration in Europe.

1. Since July 2009, Tensta Gymnasium has been renamed Ross Tensta Gymnasium.

2. These linguistic variants—e.g., Rosengard Swedish, Tensta Swedish, and Rinkeby Swedish—take their names from suburbs where immigrants predominate (Caldwell 2006).

3. A teacher explained that students understand well that "if your name is Ahmed, you won't get a good professional job in Sweden." A wry commentary about future possibilities is embedded in a joke told commonly at Tensta: "What's the difference between the Iranian and the Turkish immigrant in Sweden? The Turkish guy gets here and opens up a kabab stand. The Iranian guy gets here, goes to school, earns his degree, and then opens up a kabab stand!"

4. Tensta Gymnasium is a school of about 650 to 700 students, comprising three grade levels between year 10 and year 12; students enter at approximately sixteen years old. The school offers programs in the social sciences, the natural sciences (one, more difficult to enter, is a research-based program, renowned throughout Stockholm for rigor), business and administration, health care (this is vocational), and the so-called independent program for students needing remedial help in the Swedish language prior to enrolling in a regular theoretical or vocational program. See Tensta Gymnasium (2009).

5. Other schools in Sweden lock the doors of classrooms at all times, even when school is in session and lock offices even when teachers are inside them working. But Tensta has no such lockdown feeling; its doors are mostly open.

6. Jorgen Pudeck, architect from CederVall Arkitekter, pers. comm., 2008.

7. Inger Nyrell, interview by author, 2008.

8. Integrated projects developed within the Ross-Tensta curriculum include projects about sustainable development (involving natural science, social science, Swedish, and history domains), *Antigone* (involving history, social science, Swedish, English, and media and fine arts domains), and cell structure (involving natural science, history, and fine arts domains).

9. In the Swedish school system, *red thread (röda tråden)* means a main theme or governing idea.

10. Tensta has an arrangement with the Karolinska Institute, a university science program; classes meet at the Tensta campus, and Tensta students can take courses through this program. Another program, the KTH of the Royal Institute of Technology's School of Architecture, operates an annex at Tensta Gymnasium; this opens up opportunities of university-level work and partnerships for Tensta students. Students work in collaboration with university students of the KTH program to plan neighborhood projects and create community tours of the Tensta area (Tensta Connection 2009a, 2009b).

11. For the last student exchange trip to New York, nearly 20 percent of the school applied to fill the six coveted spots; they wrote essays and underwent an intense screening process.

REFERENCES

Caldwell, Christopher. 2005. A Swedish dilemma: Immigration and the welfare state. *Weekly Standard,* February 28, 19–23.
———. 2006. Islam on the outskirts of the welfare state. *New York Times Magazine,* February 5, 54–59.
Harrigan, S. 2004. Swedes reach Muslim breaking point. Fox News, November 26.
Landes, David. 2008. Higher birth rates among Sweden's foreign born. *Diversity Officer Magazine,* November 3, www.thelocal.se/15408/20081103/.
Malmstrom, B. 2004. Estetiska program lockar allt fler elever [Art programs attract more students]. *Svenska Dagbladet,* April 17.
Nilsson, E. 2004. Individualisation the best prerequisite for education. Stockholm City Council Project. *Globalisering och Larande* [Globalization and Education Newsletter], February 2004.
Osgard, I. 2008. Hon raddade skilan med Ross [She saved the school with Ross]. *Lara Stockholm* [Teach Stockholm] 3:26–29.

Tensta Connection. 2009a. About the project. http://newmediafix.net/daily/?p=2399. http://tenstaconnection.se/index.php?/project/about-the-project/.

———. 2009b. Tensta Konsthall presents: 16304/Architecture and production of architecture: Cities are made of this. May 14.

Tensta Gymnasium. 2009. Tensta Gymnasium. Retrieved May 1, 2009, from http://translate.google.com/translate?hl=en&sl=sv&u=http://www.tea.edu.stockholm.se/&ei=0GgdSvq4IpKoNYKUmeoF&sa=X&oi=translate&resnum=1&ct=result&prev=/search%3Fq%3Dtensta%2Bgymnasium%26hl%3Den%26client%3Dsafari%26rls%3Den-us.

Thompson, William Irwin. 1996. *Coming into being: Artifacts and texts in the evolution of consciousness*. New York: St. Martin's Griffin.

Wikan, U. 2008. *In honor of Fadime: Murder and shame*. Chicago: University of Chicago Press.

Epilogue:
We Are Waiting for You

PEDRO NOGUERA

In our country, graduations are very important. They serve as a rite of passage, one of the few ceremonies we use to mark the end of one phase of life and the beginning of another. Graduations are important not just because they provide students with the opportunity to be recognized for what they have done but also because they allow parents, relatives, and friends a chance to reflect on the students' journey, a journey that they all played major roles in seeing you through.

Yet even such occasions are not entirely joyous. Many commentators are issuing scary, ominous prognoses about the future to our graduates. At what should be a moment of happiness and relief when families normally revel in the accomplishments of their children who not only are becoming full-fledged young adults—many with driver's licenses and voter registration cards—but also are about to embark on a journey to college and independence (we hope), their well-earned joy is being snatched away by those who prefer to admonish our graduates about the formidable challenges in their future, prodding them not to get too carried away with their celebrations or to become too self-satisfied just because they have crossed this hurdle on life's journey.

While there may be a tendency to exaggerate the severity of the problems we face, we should recognize that these warnings are being issued because it is clear that hard times are coming in the years ahead. This is especially true for those of us who live in the United States, the only remaining superpower, who have known unparalleled wealth and opportunity for many years. The doomsday soothsayers are rightly pointing out that the future may be worse than the past: as our country becomes engulfed in a sea of debt and is forced to confront problems that have been neglected for too long, current and subsequent generations may not have it is as good as their parents. The problems are too formidable, too complex, and too severe to lend themselves to easy or quick solutions.

189

The recession of 2008–9 was just the tip of the iceberg. The futurists of doom and gloom point out that at this historical moment we are confronted by a broad array of ominous indicators and perilous trends:

- Our planet is in danger. As we sit here today, oceans are rising and polar icecaps are melting. In a matter of years, islands and coastal areas will be submerged and whole species of plants and animals will be rendered extinct.
- Water shortages, deforestation, and unpredictable and hazardous weather patterns are becoming major challenges to sustaining life as we know it. New and more deadly strains of infectious disease are spreading, including AIDS, cholera, malaria, swine flu, and others as yet unknown.
- Wars—conventional, chemical, nuclear, and unconventional—will become more frequent, and pirates, dirty bombers, religious zealots, and terrorists both foreign and domestic seem determined to wreak havoc, disrupt our sense of security, and bring a greater degree of fear and anxiety into our lives.

The list goes on: drug wars; uncontrolled immigration; the disappearance of honeybees, non-"reality" TV shows, and the American-made automobile; and the collapse of the Republican party (some might say that not all these changes are bad) are just some of the developments we have been warned about for the future. Even trends that we previously welcomed as positive signs, like the lengthening of human life, no longer seem beneficial when we consider that Social Security funds are rapidly being depleted and memory loss may well prevent us from even remembering who we are as we enter our so-called "golden years."

Current graduates could just dismiss these warnings as too much bad news and focus on their graduation parties instead. Or they could become depressed and withdrawn as they dwell upon the overwhelming problems we face.

Yet I would like to stress the good news to counter the gloom and doom. There is a third option—not because these predictions are wrong but because they don't provide us with the whole story. Not long ago I was listening to an interview with folksinger Pete Seeger—the American legend who had been nominated for the Nobel Peace Prize and had been a civil rights activist, an antiwar activist, environmentalist, and advocate for just about every important, but most often losing, cause to come along since the Great Depression. On the occasion of his ninetieth birthday, he had the nerve to say that he felt more optimistic now than ever before in his life. When I heard this I wondered, Had old age made Pete delusional? Had he stopped following the news, or had his mind finally given out on him so that he was no longer really in touch with reality?

But Seeger went on. His reason for optimism, he explained, was that more people in the world, and especially the United States, were aware and supportive of the need for change now than ever before. He said that today more people understood that our way of life, our way of interacting with the environment, of consuming and totally disregarding nature, was wrong and unsustainable; that justice had to be available for all, not just for those who looked and spoke and lived like us but, more importantly, for those who didn't; that war couldn't be the answer to conflicts; and that an affront to justice anywhere must elicit a response everywhere.

He was asked if his optimism had to do with the 2008 election of Barack Obama, and he responded by saying yes, but only in part. He pointed out the obvious: Obama was a politician confronted by a broad array of constraints and competing interests. He said that powerful, vested interests would make *the change we needed* hard to deliver. However, he said he was even more encouraged and optimistic about the fact that the majority of people had chosen Obama in 2008 and had done so despite the fear-mongering and lies directed against him, and despite his obvious differences from past leaders who had held the office of president.

I thought about his reflections on where we are, and I decided that I agree with Pete Seeger: these are times that are ripe for change. Unlike those who predict doom and gloom, I say nothing is guaranteed. Yes, global warming is a serious threat to the world, and war and disease are wreaking havoc on millions across the globe. But I truly believe that people equipped with intelligence, creativity, and a strong moral compass can find ways to overcome even these obstacles.

I know this from my own experience. As a college student, I was actively involved in the movement to end apartheid in South Africa. I participated in sit-ins and protests. I marched, organized boycotts against large corporations that supported the apartheid regime, and was arrested on several occasions. Despite my passion and commitment, it was hard for me to believe that one day apartheid would end and that Nelson Mandela would be released from prison and become president of the country that had imprisoned him. But it happened, and while change in South Africa is at best incremental, the ideological infrastructure that justified apartheid has been totally repudiated and will never again be able to return in that old form.

Change is real, but it is not guaranteed. We must work and plan for it. We must organize and insist upon it, and we must be willing to sacrifice.

Some of our students are better equipped than others to become leaders of change. Students who have been provided with an education that encourages them to think autonomously and critically, to question why things are as they are, to be creative, to solve problems, to learn about different cultures, and to overcome prejudices and fears will have an edge tomorrow. I am thinking of the education I have witnessed at the Ross School in Long Island as an embodiment of what is possible to achieve in educating the whole child for the whole world.

Today's students with their education can accomplish great and important things, and some of them will. Among current graduates in these times of trouble will be a leading researcher on clean, renewable sources of energy; a diplomat who will solve intractable global conflicts; a doctor who will travel to impoverished lands and develop solutions to nagging health problems; a business leader who will find ways to regenerate the economies of depressed Rust Belt cities; and a politician who will lead with intelligence, integrity, and moral conviction.

Even if some do not achieve greatness in their future vocation, they can still be great parents, neighbors, citizens, and friends. Greatness is defined not simply by the awards and recognition we receive but by our ability to use the talents we have been endowed with to help others, and thus each of us can be great in some way. As the Persian poet Rumi (1995, 68) wrote:

> There are two kinds of intelligence: one acquired,
> as a child in school memorizes facts and concepts
> from books and from what the teacher says,
> collecting information from the traditional sciences
> as well as from the new sciences.
>
> With such intelligence you rise in the world.
> You get ranked ahead or behind others
> in regard to your competence in retaining
> information. You stroll with this intelligence
> in and out of fields of knowledge, getting always more
> marks on your preserving tablets.
>
> There is another kind of intelligence,
> one already completed and preserved inside you.

A spring overflowing its springbox. A freshness
in the center of the chest. This other intelligence
does not turn yellow or stagnate. It's fluid,
and it doesn't move from outside to inside
through the conduits of plumbing-learning.

This second knowing is a fountainhead
from within you, moving out.

All of us must know that change is never easy. There are powerful interests who will resist efforts to make the world more peaceful, livable, and just, but you must also know that they are on the losing side of history. The motion of history is toward greater freedom, more tolerance and understanding, and, hopefully, less suffering. We will eventually get a national health plan that will provide affordable health care to all Americans. We will see legalized gay marriage in a few years, and I believe that we will see peace in the Middle East in our lifetime. Nothing is guaranteed, but with your talent, energy, and imagination you have the ability to help chart a different direction for our country and the world.

This is an exciting time to be alive and an important time to begin working to create a better world. The challenges we face may be great, but so are current students. They must be encouraged to rise to the challenge, think big, aim high, and not allow fear and doubt to keep them from doing great things.

I will close this book with the following words from the Hopi elders of Oraibi, Arizona (Elders Oraibi 2000):

> You have been telling the people that this is the Eleventh Hour.
> Now you must go back and tell the people that this is The Hour.
> There are things to be considered:
> Where are you living?
> What are you doing?
> What are your relationships?
> Are you in right relation?
> Where is your water?
> Know your garden.
> It is time to speak your Truth.
> Create your community. Be good to each other. And do not look
> outside yourself for the leader.

This could be a good time!

There is a river flowing now very fast. It is so great and swift that there
are those who will be afraid. They will try to hold on to the shore.
They will feel they are being torn apart, and they will suffer greatly.

Know the river has its destination. The elders say we must let go of
the shore, push off into the middle of the river, keep our eyes open,
and our heads above the water. See who is in there with you and
celebrate.

At this time in history, we are to take nothing personally. Least of all,
ourselves. For the moment that we do, our spiritual growth and
journey comes to a halt.

The time of the lone wolf is over. Gather yourselves!

Banish the word struggle from your attitude and vocabulary.
All that we do now must be done in a sacred manner and in
celebration.
We are the ones we've been waiting for.

Current and future students, we are waiting for you!

REFERENCES

Hopi Elders of Oraibi, Arizona. 2000. The Hopi elders speak: We are the ones we've been
waiting for. www.spiritofmaat.com/messages/oct28/hopi.htm.
Rumi. 1995. *The essential Rumi*. Coleman Barks and John Moyne, trans. San Francisco:
Harper.

Conclusion

MARCELO M. SUÁREZ-OROZCO AND
——— CAROLYN SATTIN-BAJAJ ———

Education systems around the world are facing unprecedented challenges and opportunities: they must educate ever more diverse cohorts of students to greater levels of competency at a time when societies, and their economies, have become increasingly interconnected and vulnerable to global upheavals. The forces shaping the lives of children growing up today are a complex network of interlinked micro, meso, and macro variables. The local realm—family, neighborhood, school—and the national realm are now thoroughly enmeshed in global processes. The basic paradigm of education and schooling, traditionally wedded to the cultural, historical, and ideological DNA of the autonomous, sovereign, nation-state, is anachronistic and out of touch with many of the most powerful forces that are shaping the world today. And while the old adage that "all education is local" endures, daily events remind us that in the real world much of what matters most is global or "glocal"—local isomorphs of larger, global phenomena.

We live in a world where a disaster in Afghanistan echoes instantaneously around the globe. A once local crisis now immediately can become an international catastrophe. Thus the H1N1 virus, which probably originated in a remote village in rural Mexico, spread to the rest of the world in a matter of days; and the World Bank estimates that after the collapse of Lehman Brothers in September 2008, in a matter of weeks an additional 90 million people were added to the approximately 1.5 billion people in low-income countries already living on less than 1.5 dollars a day (World Bank 2009).

The idea that the goal of education should be to prepare children for global competition is another vestige of twentieth-century thinking. It is a reality of the twenty-first century that the fortunes of children growing up in Helsinki and Kansas are tied in direct and powerful ways to the fortunes of children growing up in Helmand and Kandahar. The integration and disintegration of economies and societies call for a new agenda for education and the schooling of all children. Unless we work together to navigate the rough waters of the global era, we will continue to hit the multiplying icebergs threatening to drown us all: deep poverty, environmental degradation, devastating climactic changes, and growing inequalities.

The case for education has been made before, and we need not reiterate it here. Suffice it to say that a cottage industry of sociological, economic, demographic, and other research has tirelessly mapped the effects of education—measured most often by years of schooling—on individual socioeconomic mobility (human capital), social cohesion (social capital), health, and well-being.[1] The preponderance of evidence is hardly surprising: more schooling tends to generate powerful virtuous cycles. Perhaps the most exciting of these findings is the general nexus between schooling, literacy, and health outcomes throughout the world (see LeVine 2007; Bloom 2004). As Gene Sperling has noted, "While education has long been considered essential to raising lifetime earnings in both developed and developing nations, one of the most significant insights of the last two decades has been the power of education to improve health outcomes. In particular, improved education for girls tends to result in smaller and healthier families, as well as in lower infant and maternal mortality rates" (2006, xi).

Understanding the practical effects of education, while critical, is only the start of the conversation. The real challenge facing policy makers and educators today is articulating a theory of education for the twenty-first century that meaningfully relates individual citizens to the larger societies in which they live. What ought to be the purpose of a formal education? How can it be put to the service of human freedom, dignity, solidarity, and lifelong interpersonal engagement? While these essential questions have been part of the philosophy of education in many traditions, Western and other alike, finding real, actionable answers has never been more important. Globalization subverts the fatally parochial tendency to limit the conversation to local realities in bounded nation-states. New visions, new collaborations, and new innovation are thus required. What will it take to get there?

The case that has yet to be made is for globally minded and globally engaged systems of education. The question, then, is, How do we construct models of education that are more responsive to the demands, challenges, and opportunities afforded by the era of global interdependence and rapid change? In this book we review many of the lessons that one such model offers as a modest first step toward demonstrating that we can, and in fact must, create schools, and ultimately school systems, that prepare students for participation in a global society. Skeptics will surely point out the high costs associated with developing and sustaining innovative models like Ross, the forceful and charismatic personalities and leadership that made it possible, and the Sisyphean difficulties in taking it to scale. These are all obvious limitations, but the equally pressing concern remains: What are the core principles from successful models that can be studied, critiqued, modified, and then implemented by policy makers, teachers, and school administrators across diverse contexts?

We return to the idea of the architectures of care at Ross as a starting point from which to examine many of the basic elements of a successful education system for the global era. The concept of community is fundamental to how students, teachers, and school personnel understand and experience living, teaching, and learning at Ross. This architecture is built out of the multiple microcommunities that systemically develop among students, between students and teachers, among teachers, and between students and mentors. Interpersonal connections are the elemental structures creating a network of engagement that supports student growth and development and creates an enriching and stimulating learning environment for all community members. What is more, Ross paradigmatically engages neighbors, mentors, and individuals from near and far to participate in its expanding community. It does so by establishing formal mentoring roles, organizing activities and events at the school sites, and sharing the practices, values, and lessons of Ross with policy makers, teachers, principals, researchers, and other leaders via formal trainings and informal exchanges both local and global.

The deep sense of community that permeates Ross emerges organically out of a series of thoughtful decisions and structures. It is these structures and the values they embody that other schools can examine and adapt to their individual cultures and contexts. Another significant architecture at Ross, its engaging curriculum, offers a blueprint for creating and understanding the foundation of the school's vibrant community. In-depth disciplinary and interdisciplinary lessons, logically sequenced units, and autonomous learning contribute to students' sustained interest in school and investment in their academic community. The curriculum promotes this by placing relationships at the center of students' learning experience.

Students at Ross come to understand implicitly that their teachers respect them as budding young scholars. Countless assignments in which to pursue an independently chosen topic provide students the opportunity to showcase their own interests and talents to teachers, peers, and mentors, who, in turn, collectively support each individual's development. This serves to create powerful bonds among students and between students and teachers on personal and intellectual levels. Furthermore, students witness their teachers' own contagious excitement about the subject at hand; the widespread phenomenon of school boredom is replaced by curiosity, playfulness, and awe at the beauty of learning.

Ross Schools, by design, foster supportive relationships both inside and outside the confines of the classroom. In this way, three architectures align to produce a comprehensive educational experience for students. The final architecture, the actual physical space of the school, thoroughly reflects the spirit of community. At Ross, private meeting spots and larger common rooms are scattered across the campus, offering students and teachers myriad places to continue conversations or connect for the first time. The splendor of the Ross campus may fall on the extreme end of the spectrum; however, all schools can find ways to humanize existing spaces to strategically promote a sense of community, whether by creating a "café corner" in a classroom where young writers can meet and discuss their work, filling hallways and entryways with student artwork or reproductions of important artifacts, or opening the building up to the public for activities and classes in the afternoons—the possibilities are endless.

Conceptualizing the school as an engaging community of scholars is an important foundation for developing an educational environment for the twenty-first century. It then takes a strong mission, commitment, and coordination among all essential elements—from the physical building to the students and teachers who are teaching and learning inside the classrooms—to achieve this vision. Ross offers some critical insights into how to get there.

Abraham Flexner, a legendary teacher of Greek and Latin at the Louisville Male High School and the founding director of the Institute for Advanced Study at Princeton, once wrote, "Institutions of learning should be devoted to the cultivation of curiosity and the less they are deflected by considerations of immediacy of application, the more likely they are to contribute not only to human welfare but to the equally important satisfaction of intellectual interest which may indeed be said to have become the ruling passion of intellectual life in modern times" (Institute for Advanced Study 2009, 4). A paradigm of education privileging disciplined curiosity, the beauty of discovery, a ludic engagement with the world, and an ethic of care and solidarity will be less a luxury and a rarity than an essential requirement for the next generation of children to thrive. We must continue to cultivate, replicate, modify, and improve models of education that are built on these powerful and indispensable architectures.

1. The measure "years of schooling" is, unfortunately, a gross reductionism without reference to what matters most in education: *quality, mentorships,* and *relationships* ("relational engagement"), *intellectual curiosity, playfulness,* and *wonder* ("cognitive engagement"), and the quotidian *work of schooling* ("behavioral engagement"; for these three types of engagement, see M. Suárez-Orozco, Sattin-Bajaj, and Suárez-Orozco, this volume).

REFERENCES

Bloom, D. E. 2004. Globalization and education: An economic perspective. In *Globalization: Culture and education in the new millennium,* ed. M. M. Suárez-Orozco and D. Qin-Hilliard. Berkeley: University of California Press.

Institute for Advanced Study. 2009. *Institute for Advanced Study: An introduction.* Princeton, NJ: Institute for Advanced Study.

LeVine, R. A. 2007. The global spread of women's schooling: Effects on learning, literacy, health and children. In *Learning in the global era: International perspectives on globalization and education,* ed. M. M. Suárez-Orozco. Berkeley: University of California Press.

Sperling, G. 2006. The way forward for universal education. In *Educating all children: A global agenda,* ed. J. E. Cohen, D. E. Bloom, and M. B. Malin. Cambridge, MA: MIT Press.

World Bank. 2009. Overview: Understanding, measuring and overcoming poverty. http://web.worldbank.org/WBSITE/EXTERNAL/TOPICS/EXTPOVERTY/0,,contentMDK:20153855~menuPK:373757~pagePK:148956~piPK:216618~theSitePK:336992,00.html.

About the Contributors

RALPH ABRAHAM is Professor Emeritus of Mathematics at the University of California, Santa Cruz.

NICK APPELBAUM, a graduate of Oxford University and the Harvard Graduate School of Education, is a Ross School alumnus.

ANTONIO M. BATTRO is Senior Scientist for One Laptop per Child, Cambridge, MA.

SALLY BOOTH is the Associate Director of Research, Curriculum, and Professional Development at the Ross Institute Academy.

MICHELE CLAEYS is the Head of Ross School, East Hampton.

ELIZABETH M. DALEY is Dean of the School of Cinematic Arts and Executive Director of the Institute for Multimedia Literacy, University of Southern California.

ANTONIO DAMASIO is the David Dornsife Professor of Neuroscience and Co-Director of the Brain and Creativity Institute, University of Southern California.

HANNA DAMASIO is Chair of Neuroscience, Professor of Psychology and Neurology, Co-Director of the Brain and Creativity Institute, and Director of the Dana and David Dornsife Cognitive Neuroscience Imaging Center at the University of Southern California.

KURT W. FISCHER is the Charles Bigelow Professor of Education and the Director of the Mind, Brain, and Education Program at the Harvard Graduate School of Education.

HOWARD GARDNER is the Hobbs Professor of Cognition and Education at the Harvard Graduate School of Education.

VARTAN GREGORIAN is President of the Carnegie Corporation of New York.

CHRISTINA HINTON is a Doctoral Candidate at the Harvard Graduate School of Education.

HIDEAKI KOIZUMI is a Hitachi Fellow at Hitachi Ltd., Director of the R&D Division "Brain Science and Society" at the Japan Science and Technology Agency, and Visiting Professor at the Research Center for Advanced Science and Technology, University of Tokyo.

DEBRA MCCALL is the Associate Director of the Ross Institute Academy.

PEDRO NOGUERA is the Peter L. Agnew Professor of Education and Executive Director at the Metropolitan Center for Urban Education, New York University.

CAROLYN SATTIN-BAJAJ is a doctoral candidate in international education at New York University.

JOHN SEXTON is President of New York University.

CAROLA SUÁREZ-OROZCO is Professor of Applied Psychology at New York University, Co-Director of Immigration Studies at New York University, and a Member of the Institute for Advanced Study, Princeton.

MARCELO M. SUÁREZ-OROZCO is a University Professor at New York University, Co-Director of the Institute for Globalization and Education in Metropolitan Settings at New York University, and the Richard Fisher Membership Fellow at the Institute for Advanced Study, Princeton.

WILLIAM IRWIN THOMPSON is an independent scholar.

SHERRY TURKLE is the Abby Rockefeller Mauze Professor of the Social Studies of Science and Technology and Director of the Initiative on Technology and Self, Massachusetts Institute of Technology.

HOLLY WILLIS is a Research Assistant Professor in the University of Southern California's School of Cinematic Arts and Director of Academic Programs at USC's Institute for Multimedia Literacy.

Index

"Cost of Copyright Confusion for Media Literacy, The" (Center for Social Media), 106
creating mind, 53, 56
creativity: image manipulation and, 62; intelligence and, 89; multitasking and, 68; objects and, 111
Critchlow, Keith, 161
Critical Commons project, 105–106
Csikszentmihaly, Michael, 166
Cull, Selby, 120
cultural history: bifurcations of, 126–127; integration with math, 125, 128–130, 133, 142–143, 162; in Ross School curriculum, 125, 128–130, 143
culture: defined, 4; homogenization of, 46–47; mathematics and, 157–162
culture of engagement, 8–14

Dalai Lama, 162
Damon, William, 166
Darkness at Noon (Koestler), 34
De Bonte, Austina, 116–117
Dehaene, Stanislas, 160
Democracy and Education (Dewey), 74
Descartes, René, 64–65
Dewey, John, 73–76, 76, 151
Dickinson, Emily, 165
digital data, growth in, 27
disciplined mind, 53, 55
Dostoevsky, Fyodor, 29
dualism, 64–65
dynamics, 127, 128
dyslexia, 71

Edelman, Gerald, 165
Educated Brain, The (Battro, Fischer, and Léna), 168
education: analysis and synthesis *vs.* memorization in, 33; attention in, 66; brain science and, 61; brain's plasticity and, 65; for citizenship, 47; collaboration between researchers and practitioners, 69–70, 72 (*see also* research schools); concepts in, ways of presenting, 52; disengagement from, 9; effects, 196; emo-

tion in, 67; engagement and, 8, 9–14, 66–67; environmental education, 91; focused curriculum, need for, 31; global education, case for, 43–47, 195–196; globalization's challenges to, 1–2; goal, 145; individualization of, 52; Internet and, 45; left-brain, right-brain functioning, 50–51, 88–89; of mathematicians, 109 (*see also* math education); mind, brain and education research, 71, 74; moral behavior, 68; multiple intelligences (MI) theory, 51–52; neuroscience, 68, 72; physical health, 66; psychometric intelligence, 50–51, 52; scientific legitimacy, 50; of scientists, 109, 111 (*see also* science education); specialized knowledge, 27–28; in United States, 2; values and, 50; "Wikipedia-zation" of, 28. *See also* laboratory schools; learning; research schools; schools; universities
educational research, 58, 87
Einstein, Albert, 83
Elements of Euclid, 131–132
Eliot, T. S., 28–29, 30
emotion: in education, 67; in human behavior, 66–68; judgmental skills and, 159–160
Empty Bowls project, 150
engagement: behavioral engagement, 9; cognitive engagement, 10–11; education and, 8, 66–67; relational engagement, 11–14
engagement, culture of, 8–14
Enlightenment, the, 161–162
environmental education, 91
Erikson, Erik, 32, 115
ethical codes, 67
ethical mind, 53, 56–57
Euclid, 131–132, 136
experts, 159
Explorama at Danfoss Universe, 55

Farrin, Suzanne, 167
fire hatchets, 160–161
Five Minds for the Future (Gardner), 53–57
Flexner, Abraham, 198

Johnson, Mark, 164
Jones, Quincy, 148

Kamali, Masoud, 173
Keller, Evelyn Fox, 116, 122n3, 122n4
Kluckhohn, C., 4
knowledge: fragmentation of, 29–30; generalists, need for, 38; "half-life" of, 33; haptic knowledge, 160–161; historical context of, 38–39; limitations of, 36; nihilism about, 45; "self-inflicted amnesia," 39; "Wikipedia-zation" of, 28. *See also* information; learning; specialization
Koestler, Arthur, 34
Kohn, Alfie, 69
Kroeber, A., 4
Kuehn, Clement, 163

La main à la pâte, 118
laboratory schools: developmental psychology and, 73; Ross and, Courtney, 46; Ross Institute, 76, 152, 171; teaching hospitals compared to, 73; University of Chicago lab school, 73–75. *See also* research schools
Lakoff, George, 164
lasers in scientific education, 115, 120
Laszlo, Ervin, 126
learning: biology and cognitive science in research on, 70, 71–72; brains and, 65–66, 87; infancy or childhood as privileged time for, 89; isomorphic nature of history and individual, 83; learning time axis, 83; lifelong learning, 32–33; Sheldrake Principle, 130–131; "the bootstrap" in, 87; "the scaffold" in, 87. *See also* education; knowledge
Learning in the Global Era (Suárez-Orozco), 152
Lee, Matt, 106–107
Lemann, Nicholas, 35–36
Lesko, P. D., 31
Levi-Montalcini, Rita, 168
LHS (LärarHögSkolan), 184–185

literacy: fragmentation of, 32; information literacy, 98; multimedia literacy, 100, 106, 107. *See also* Institute for Multimedia Literacy
Lucas, George, 99

Maciak, Marie, 147
Managerial Literacy (Shaw and Weber), 32
Mandela, Nelson, 191
Martian interrogation of last person on Earth, a, 36–38
"Math: A Great Divide" *(San Jose Mercury News)*, 134
math anxiety, 132–134, 136, 157
math avoidance syndrome, 132
math education, 125–137; algebra in, 127, 128; arithmetic in, 127, 128; chaos theory in, 125–126, 127, 135–136; cultural history, integration with, 125, 128–130, 133, 142–143, 162; dynamics in, 127, 128; Euclid, importance of, 131–132, 136; formalism in, 132; geometric algebra in, 127; geometry, 127, 128; historical approach to, 126–131; multiple intelligences (MI) theory and, 133; spiral curriculum, integration into, 125–137, 143; standardized testing and, 134–135, 158; traditional curriculum, 133; visual approach to, 126, 133, 157; word-solving problems, 132, 135
mathematicians, education of, 109
mathematics: culture and, 157–162; linguistic articulation and, 159–160
McClintock, Barbara, 116, 122n4
McKusick, Hal, 147–148
McLuhan, Marshall, 161
Metamorphoses (Apuleius), 164
Metaphors We Live By (Lakoff and Johnson), 164
microexchanges, 6–7
Milosz, Czeslaw, 39
Minamata disease, 91
Mind, Brain, and Education (journal), 77, 168
mind, brain, and education research (the discipline), 71, 74

Rosovsky, Henry, 40

Ross, Courtney: brain science, 61; curriculum's "flower design," 143; design of school's environment, 146; education for citizenship, 47; educational research, 58; educational vision, 141, 148; International Symposium on Brain Science and Education (2004), 92n1; in Japan, 92, 92n1; learning time axis, 83; legacy, viii, 154–155, 171; long-term objectives, 182; math education, 125, 126; multimedia literacy, 107; schools as laboratories, 46; spiral curriculum, 18; technology in education, 97; Tensta Gymnasium, 175, 184; wellness to, 3

Ross, Nicole, 22n2, 142

Ross, Steven, 6, 142, 154

Ross Global Academy (RGA) Charter School: admission system, 153; class size, 21n1; enrollment, 21n1; free/reduced-price lunch program, 21n1; location, 3; minority students, 21n1; NYC Department of Education grade, 21n1

Ross Institute, 76, 152, 171

Ross Institute Academy, 153–154, 171

Ross Network Schools, 171

Ross School in East Hampton, 141–155; accreditation, 151; architecture of care at, 4–8, 197–198; class size, 13, 21n1; cofounders, 6; contributions to educational community, viii, 58; core values, 178; culture of engagement at, 8–14; educational principles, 2–3, 81; habitus at, 7; history of, 141–155, 185; interpersonal relations at, 6–7; location, 3; microexchanges at, 6–7; mission, 7, 145, 151, 165; as a model, 3–4, 27, 141, 151, 153–154, 196–197; motto, 7, 150; as a research school, 3, 76; vision, 97; Web site, 97
— class trips: Athens, 153; Bahamas, 144; Boston, 144; Egypt, 153; Florence, 153; Galapagos Islands, 142; Greece, 142; Istanbul, 153; London, 142; Spain, 152–153; Washington, D.C., 142, 144
— culinary philosophy, 149
— curriculum: adult evening program, 150; art in teaching of science, 115; brain, curriculum on, 77; cultural history, grades devoted to epochs of, 125, 128–130, 143; "flower design" of, 143; focus, viii; Golden Matrix, 152; intellectual foundations, 2–3, 143; interdisciplinary collaboration, 3, 143, 163–165; M-terms (March term), 7, 152; oversight of, 154; pace of, 121; process portfolios, viii; science of mind, brain, and education, 2; senior projects, viii, 7, 10–11, 148–149; spiral curriculum (see spiral curriculum); spirituality, Western and Eastern, 165–166; themes, grades devoted to, 143; theory of multiple intelligences, 2, 115–116; unit on absolutism, 147; unit on butterflies and neurons, 163–167; unit on colonialism, 148; unit on Maya, 151; unit on medieval Islamic society, 151; unit on modernity, 148; unit on Renaissance, 147
— early childhood program: enrollment, 21n1; origins, 153
— facilities: advanced technologies, 6; beauty of, 5–6; broadcast studio, 147; café, 149; Center for Well-Being, 6, 148, 149–150; computers, 118; Court Theater, 149; the Duomo, 146; Great Hall, 149; koi pond, 149; library, 146; meals, organic, 6; Media and Humanities Building, 147; meditation room, 149; movement room, 149; music rehearsal room, 147–148; reproductions of world's great art, vii, 6, 110, 146, 148; Senior Building, 148; silk slippers, 6; slippers, Chinese silk, 146; SMART Boards, 6, 119, 120, 122n5; solarium, 146
— faculty: chef, 149; composer in residence, 167; effort expended by, 11–12; enthusiasm, 12; experience level, 11; flexibility, 12–13; interdisciplinary grade-level teams, 146; listening by, 13; mastery of subject matter, 10, 11, 13; members, individual, 142, 149, 167; mentors, 118; professional development workshops, 77; scholars-in-residence, 76–77, 152, 166; Tibetan monk, 147